Book Two

**Alan Boyle
Christine Ditchfield
Maggie Hannon**

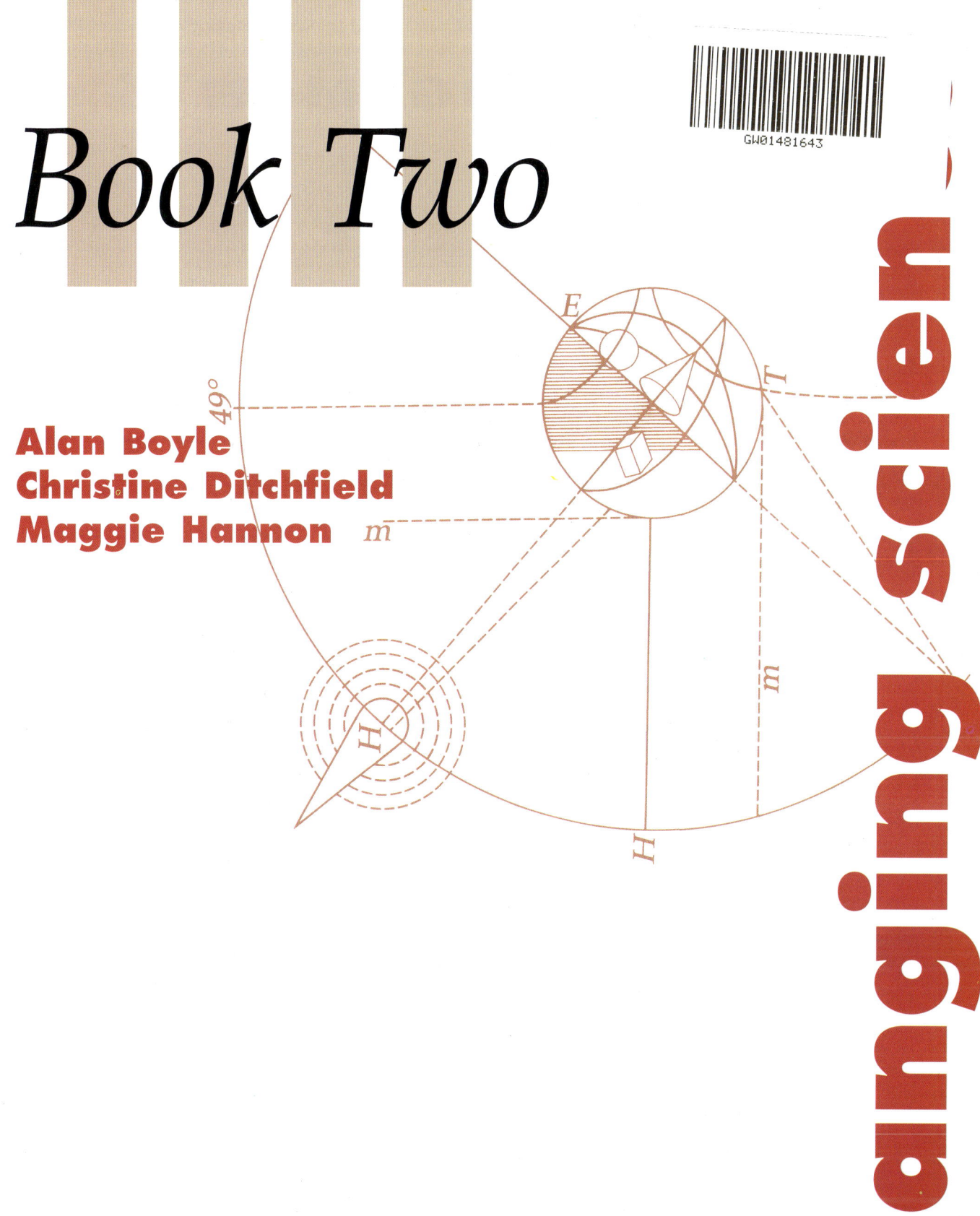

changing scien

Hodder & Stoughton
A MEMBER OF THE HODDER HEADLINE GROUP

ACKNOWLEDGEMENTS

The publishers would like to thank the following artists who drew the illustrations: Chartwell Illustrators; Mike Feeney of Red Herring Design and Illustration; Hardlines Illustration and Design; Hemesh Alles, Tim Beer and Mike Dodd of The Maggie Mundy agency; Kenneth Ovington of Precision Art; Oxford Illustrators; Peters & Zabransky; Liz Rowe; Andrew Warrington.

We are grateful to the following companies, institutions and individuals who have given permission to reproduce photographs in this book. Every effort has been made to trace and acknowledge ownership of copyright. The publishers will be glad to make arrangements with any copyright holders whom it has not been possible to contact

A. B. Dowsett/SPL 2 (bacteria); Alex Bartel/SPL 113 (both), 139; Alfred Pasieka/SPL 178; Andrew Henley/Biofotos 2 (kangaroo), 27 (left); Andrew Syred/SPL 151; Anthony Luke 167 (middle, 167 (bottom); Barbara Wace/Hutchinson Library 38 (lower top left); Ben Johnson/SPL 83; Biophoto Associates 7, 33 (top left); Brian Kenny/OSF 6 (top left); Bruce Coleman/Jean and Des Bartlett 32 (top); Bruce Coleman/Adrian Davies 6 (top right); Bruce Coleman/Hans Reinhard 112, 182; C. T. R. Wilson/PL 133 (right); Chemical Design Ltd/SPL 93 (middle); Chris Davies 2 (seaweed), 4 (right), 5 (top left, bottom left, bottom right), 10, 12 (second), 13 (right), 22 (middle left, centre left, right), 77 (bottom left), 96 (left), 106 (bottom), 118 (top), 136, 146, 148 (bottom), 152 (top left), 152 (right), 153 (top left), 163; Christer Fredriksson/Bruce Coleman 23 (right); Claudia Andujar/SPL 77 (bottom right); Colin Taylor Productions 31 (top left, bottom), 72 (top), 85, 93 (top right), 94 (top, right), 95 (bottom), 101 (top, bottom), 102 (bottom), 106 (top), 117 (bottom), 124, 132, 148 (top, middle), 152 (bottom left), 156 (top), 158; Crispin Hughes/Oxfam/Hutchinson Library 73 middle; David Hosking/FLPA 96 (right); David Parker/SPL 112, 121 (bottom); David Reed/Panos Pictures 78 (top); David Woodfall/NHPA 6 (bottom left); Dr Adrian Bell 77 (right); Dr B. Booth/GSF Pictures 82; Dr Jeremy Burgess/SPL 4 (middle left), 20 (top, bottom); Dr Stephen Coyne/Bruce Coleman 22 (bottom left); Dr B. Booth/GSF 96 (middle), 120, 173; Dr R. Stephenson 55; Eric Chrichton/Bruce Coleman 75; Eric Grave/SPL 33 (right); Erwin & Peggy Bauer/Bruce Coleman 25; European Space Agency/SPL 113 (right); Francis Leroy/SPL 182 (right); Frank Spooner Pictures 61; Fred Mercay/NHPA 5 (bottom right); Fritz Prenzel/Bruce Coleman 81; George Macarthy/Bruce Coleman 22 (centre right); Greenpeace/Dorreboom 70 (bottom); Griffen and George 73 (top); Hank Morgan/SPL 182 (left); Heather Angel 2 (azalea, cheetahs, cuttle fish, crocodile, lichen, horsetails, moss) 4 (bottom left), 13 (left), 40 (bottom); Hodder & Stoughton 8, 16; Holt Studios (Nigel Cattlin) 23 (bottom), 31 (middle left); Holt Studios (Miss P. Peacock) 43; Hutchinson Library 38 (top middle); I. Curie & F. Joliet/SPL 133 (middle); Image courtesy of the Chaos Laboratory, Scarborough, tel: 01753 500555 115; Institut Pasteur/CNRI/SPL 2 (virus); International Potato Institute/Cornell University 23 (left); J Bernholc et al, North Carolina State University/SPL 93 (bottom); J-L Charmet/SPL 127; J Allan Cash 5 (top right), 22 (top left), 27 (right), 37, 38 (middle left), 58, 58 (top), 140, 161, 170, 171 (top); J. C. Revy/SPL 9; Jane Burton/Bruce Coleman 31 (right); Jeff Foot Productions/Bruce Coleman 26 (right); John Canalosi/Bruce Coleman 40 (top); John Howard/SPL 107; John Matt/Hutchinson Library 12 (top); Jon Burbank 78 (right); Kermani-Liaison/Frank Spooner 93 (top left); L. R. Dawson/Bruce Coleman 3 (bottom); Leslie Garland 99, 104 (top); M. J. Adams/OSF 5 (middle); M. R. Phicton/Bruce Coleman 34 (top); Malcolm Fielding. The BOC Group/SPL 38 (bottom left); Mark Moffett/Minden Pictures 69, 76, 77 (top left); Martin Bond/SPL 104 (bottom), 112, 185; Martin Dohrn/SPL 137; Mike Holmes/Tony Stone Worldwide 70 (top); Mr Jens Rydell/Bruce Coleman 3 (top); Mr Johnny Johnson/Bruce Coleman 171 (bottom); N. Feather/SPL 133 (left); NASA 60 (right, top left), 62 (left, right), 176; NASA/SPL 38 (upper top left), 135, 174; New Scientist 177, 172 (right); NRPB 130; Ocean Drilling Programme 172 (top left, bottom left); Oscar Burriel/Latin Stock/SPL 178; P. Page/GSF Pictures 65; Pekka Parva/SPL 184; Peter Menzel/SPL 162; Phil Jude/SPL 113; Planet Earth Pictures 26 (left); Renee Lynn/SPL 112; Renner/BSIP/SPL 117 (top); Richard W. Beales/Planet Earth Pictures 42 (bottom left); Roddy Paine, Photographer 67, 84 (left), 84 (bottom), 95 (top), 97, 112 (middle 2), 153 (bottom), 155, 156 (bottom), 178 (centre and right); Roger Ressmeyer, Starlight/SPL 125 (right); Ronald Sheridan/Ancient Art and Architecture 142; Ronald Toms/OSF 121 (top); RONDI/TANI/SPL 38 (top right); Royal Greenwich Observatory/SPL 125 (left); Sarah Errington/Hutchinson Library 166; Shone/Frank Spooner 12 (bottom); Simon Fraser/RVI, Newcastle-upon-Tyne/SPL 12 (third); Simon Fraser/SPL 184; Sinclair Stammers/SPL 38 (bottom right); Soames Summerhays/Biofotos 2 (fish); Spectrum Colour library 84 (right); SPL 52/53, 181; Swan Photographic/Colin Page 2 (dragonfly); Swan Photographic/John Buckingham 2 (frog); Swan Photographic/Colin Page 2 (dragonfly); Swan Photographic/John Buckingham 2 (frog); Swan Photographic/T. G. Coleman 2 (middle); Telegraph Colour Library 42 (bottom), 73 (bottom), 113 (bottom right), 180; The Ancient Art and Architecture Collection 38 (bottom right); The Crown 72 (bottom); TRIP/B. Gibbs 178 (bottom right); TRIP/G. Horner 113 (middle left); TRIP/W. Jacobs 185 (top right); TRIP/A. Lambert 90; TRIP/Lee 185 (top left); TRIP/H. Rogers 103; Tom van Sant/Geosphere Project, Santa Monica/SPL 184; Tony Deane/Bruce Coleman 167 (top); Wayne Lankinen/Bruce Coleman 4 (top left); Weiss/Jerrican/SPL 23 (middle); Wings 42 (top); Xinhua/Gamma 79.

A catalogue for this title is available from the British Library

ISBN 0 340 55528 9

First published 1996
Impression number   10 9 8 7 6 5 4 3 2 1
Year   2000 1999 1998 1997 1996

Copyright © 1996 Alan Boyle, Christine Ditchfield, Maggie Hannon

All rights reserved. No part of this publication may be reproduced or transmitted in any form or by any means, electronic or mechanical, including photocopy, recording, or any information storage and retrieval system, without permission in writing from the publisher or under licence from the Copyright Licensing Agency Limited. Further details of such licences (for reprographic reproduction) may be obtained from the Copyright Licensing Agency Limited, of 90 Tottenham Court Road, London W1P 9HE.

Typeset by Litho Link Ltd, Welshpool, Powys SY21 7BE
Printed in Great Britain for Hodder & Stoughton Educational, a division of Hodder Headline PLC, 338 Euston Road, London NW1 3BH by Times Offset, Malaysia.

We would also like to thank the following examination boards for permission to reproduce questions:

Northern Examinations and Assessment Board: Chap. 1 Q1; Chap. 3 Q1; Chap. 4 Q8; Chap. 5 Q11; Chap. 6 Q8; Chap. 7 Q12, Q13 adapted; Chap. 8 Q3; Chap. 9 Q2.

Southern Examinations Group: Chap. 1 Q3; Chap. 1 Q4; Chap. 5 Q9; UE intro. Q1, Q3; Chap. 8 Q2; Chap. 9 Q1; Chap. 11 Q1.

University of Cambridges Local Examinations Board/Midland Examining Group Chap. 1 Q2; Chap. 2 Q1, 2, 3; Chap. 4 Q6; Chap. 5 Q10; Chap. 6 Q9, 10; Chap. 9 Q3; Chap. 10 Q1; Chap. 10 Q2, Q3; Chap. 11 Q3.

University of London Examinations and Assessment Council: Chap. 3 Q2, Q3; Chap. 4 Q7; Chap. 8 Q1.

Welsh Joint Examinations Council: UE intro. Q2; Chap. 11 Q2.

CONTENTS

Acknowledgements	ii
Preface	iv

STAYING ALIVE — 1

Variety: the spice of life — 2

1 From one generation to another — 7
- We're all different — 8
- From parents to child — 10
- When things go wrong — 12
- Like Mother . . . or Father — 14
- DNA: the life molecule — 18
- Explaining evolution — 20
- Interfering with evolution — 22
- Questions — 24

2 Behaving to survive — 25
- Sensing the environment — 26
- Light detection — 28
- Plant responses — 30
- The movement response — 32
- Finding the way home — 34
- Questions — 36

3 What future for life? — 37
- Evolution via technology — 38
- What future for elephants? — 40
- The sea: a healthy future? — 42
- Enough food for everyone? — 44
- How long will you live? — 46
- A question of research? — 48
- Questions — 50

MAKING MATTER — 51

Important matters — 52

4 Take one planet — 55
- Heavy weather — 56
- Predictable planets — 58
- Adventures in space — 60
- Space: the final frontier? — 62
- Planet Earth unmasked — 64
- In the melting pot — 66
- Questions — 68

5 Making up is hard to do — 69
- Riches beyond price — 70
- Changing patterns of weather — 72
- The one per cent key — 74
- If you go up in the woods today . . . — 76
- Where the mountains meet the sea — 78
- Questions — 80

6 Elements incorporated — 81
- Planet Earth – the factory — 82
- Metals or not? — 84
- Elementary patterns — 86
- Getting to know you — 88
- Periodic patterns — 90
- Building matter — 92
- Reacting speeds matter — 94
- The path to success — 96
- Questions — 98

7 Pure Magic — 99
- Reactions? No problem! — 100
- Electrifying reactions — 102
- Industry makes matter — 104
- Oiling the wheels of living — 106
- You can't always get what you want — 108
- Questions — 110

USING ENERGY — 111

Energy transfers — 112

8 Electromagnetic radiation — 115
- Bouncing and bending — 116
- Forming images — 118
- Colour — 120
- Electromagnetic spectrum — 122
- Bigger images — 124
- Questions — 126

9 Radioactivity — 127
- Breaking up — 128
- Serendipity — 130
- Detective work — 132
- Absorbing activities — 134
- Hazards and benefits — 136
- Questions — 138

10 Electromagnetism	139	**CHANGES**	161
Turning around	140	Spare parts for worn out limbs	162
Shaking and making	142	All about Eve	164
Stepping up and down	144	Deserts on the march	166
Power to the people	146	Nature's polymer industry revealed	168
Paying for power	148	Spots of bother?	170
Questions	150	Current pictures over the mantle	172
		Mercury the mystery planet	174
11 Electronic control	151	Big bang and the time detectives	176
Switches and sensors	152	Controlling changes	178
In control	154	Getting the message	180
Logically speaking	156	Cold storage	182
Flip-flop	158	Climatic change	184
Questions	160	Index	186

PREFACE — TO THE STUDENT

Welcome to **Changing Science Book 2**. We hope that the two books in this series will help you to improve your skills and understanding for Science GCSE Courses, and that you enjoy yourself while working through them.

In Book 2 you will continue to develop and practice the skills of a good scientist. That is:

- good communication skills
- the ability to weigh evidence and make judgements
- problem solving skills
- be a good team worker

Investigations still play a large part of this book. You will have many chances to do lots of exciting activities as you work through it. You will also have the chance to practise exam questions at the end of each chapter to test what you have learnt.

In this book you will find the *Changes* on pages 161–185, which will help to explain many scientific changes happening in the world today. It will also help you to apply your ideas about science and to assist your understanding. We hope you find this book exciting, informative and enjoyable.

Alan Boyle, Christine Ditchfield and Maggie Hannon

SECTION I

STAYING ALIVE

VARIETY: THE SPICE OF LIFE

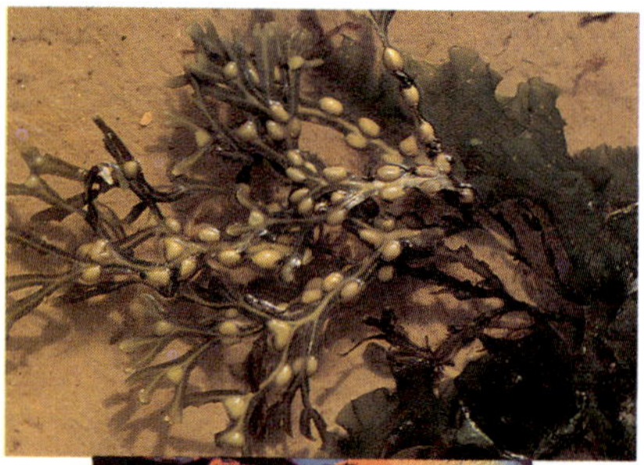

seaweed

You know that the variety of life on Earth is enormous. The estimate of the number of different species alive today varies from 5–50 million. Yet this is only a small fraction of the *billions* of species which have at some time lived on Earth but are now extinct. In this section we will take a closer look at the history of life on Earth from its beginnings millions of years ago. We will explore what causes life's variety and look at how human influence can change the course of evolution.

The next four pages remind you of the variety of life on Earth and introduce the main themes in the *Staying Alive* section of this book.

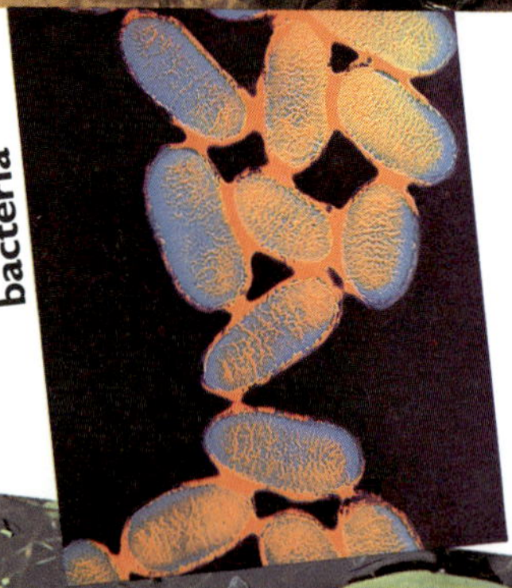

bacteria

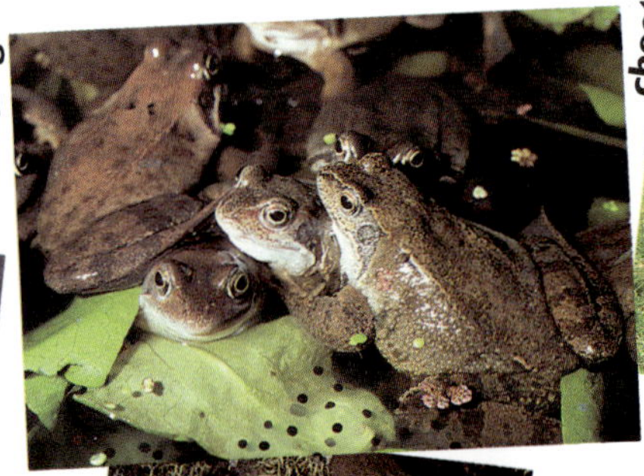

frog

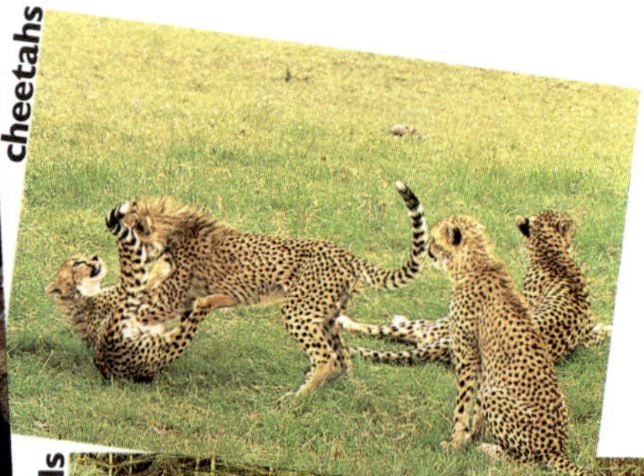

cheetahs

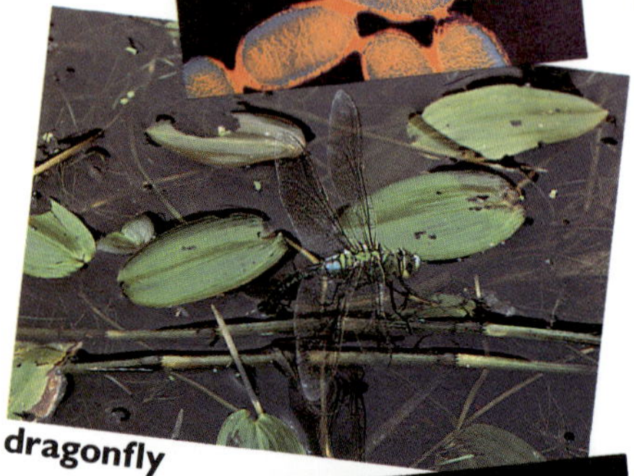

dragonfly

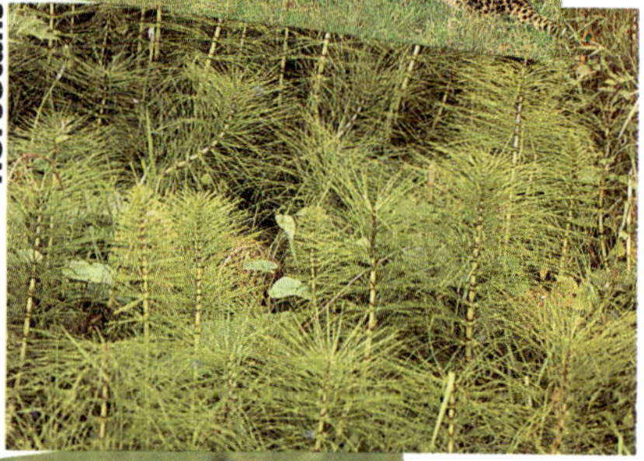

horsetails

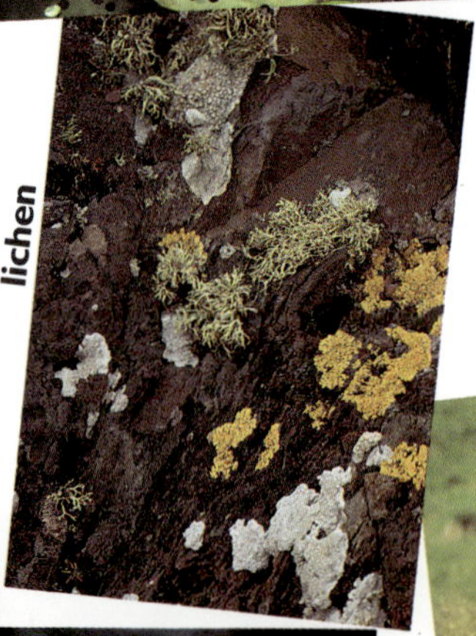

lichen

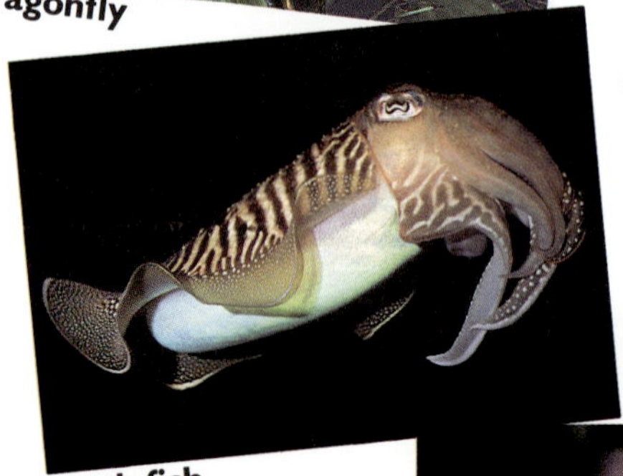

cuttlefish

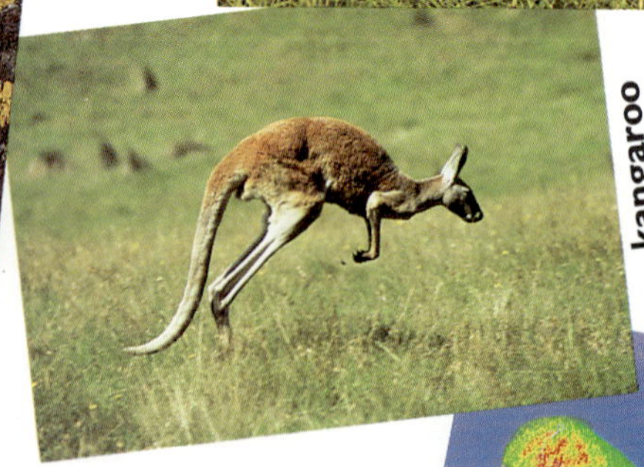

kangaroo

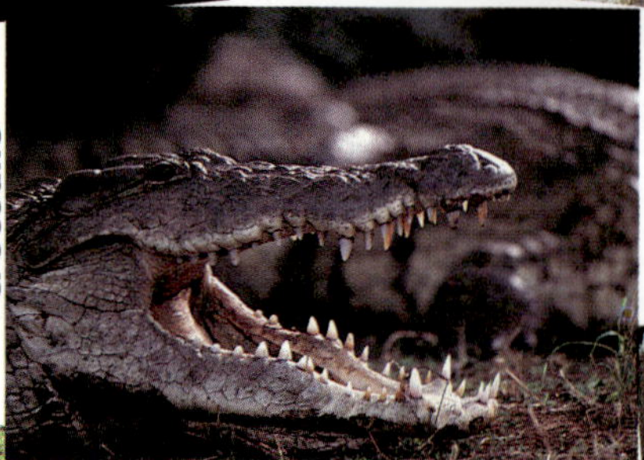

crocodile

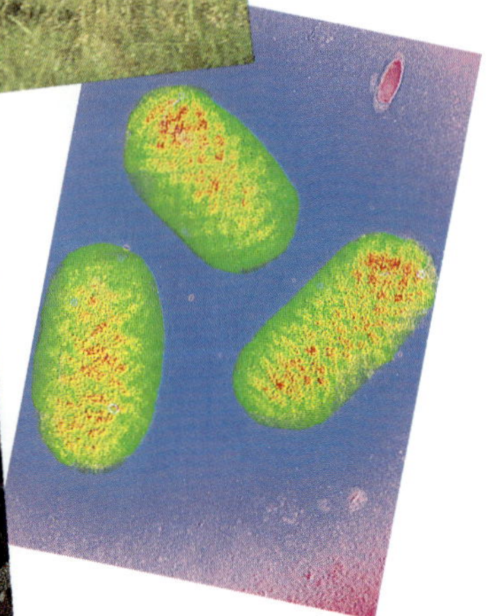

virus

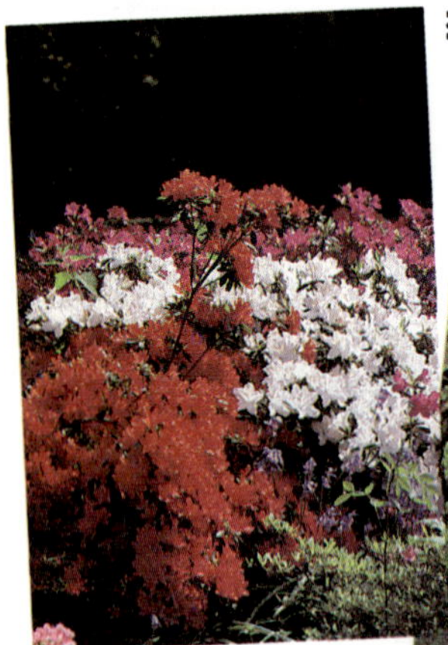

azaleas

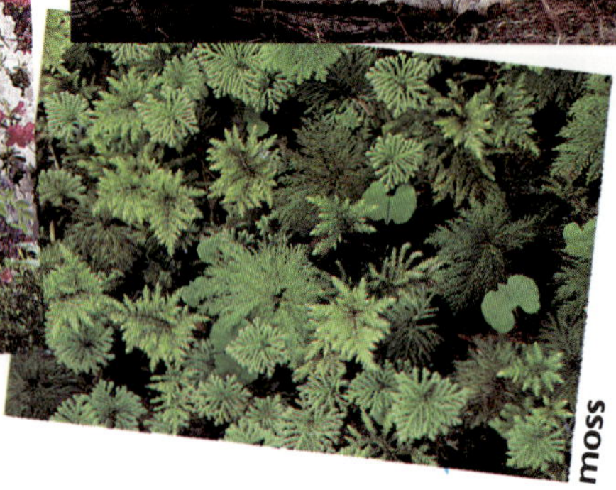

moss

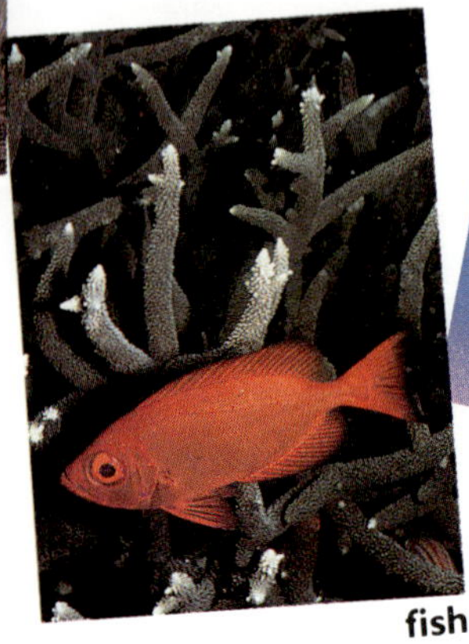

fish

STAYING ALIVE

BATS, BIRDS AND BEES

In ancient times these animals were probably classified into the same animal group: those that had wings. These animals don't have much in common apart from the fact that they can fly. Their body structures and behaviours which enable them to feel, feed, breathe, move, excrete, reproduce and grow are all quite different.

As people started to study living things in more detail, so they discovered the flaws in the original groupings. They continued to improve their classification systems and by the 1750s the Swedish scientist Carl von Linné [Linneaus] (1707–78) had developed the **Linnaean classification system** which is still used today. This system begins by sorting organisms into very large groups called kingdoms. Each kingdom is divided into smaller and smaller groups down to the smallest group which is the single species as shown in Figure 1.

It isn't surprising that over a hundred years later this classification system was used to support the theory of evolution. The closer that two living things are in the classification system, the closer they are related in evolutionary terms. Figure 2 shows some of the groupings arranged in a possible evolutionary sequence.

Figure 1

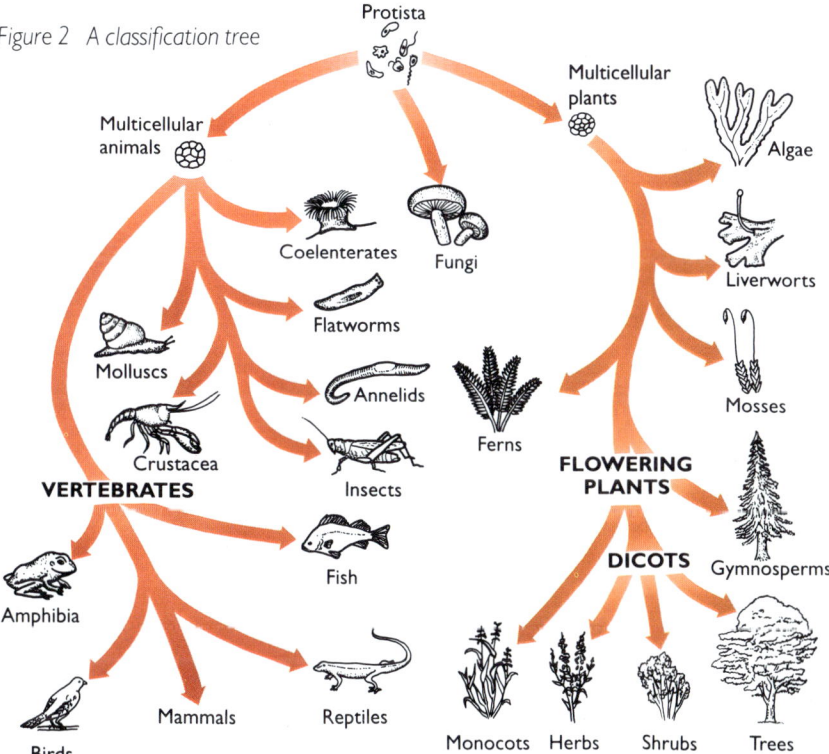

Figure 2 A classification tree

Of course, classification and evolutionary development aren't as tidy as this, as you will find when you work through Chapter 1 of this book. However, the Linnaean system does help us to identify different species and it is the basis of the identification keys that you have used.

STAYING ALIVE

1 Produce a table which lists some of the differences in structure and behaviour between the three animals in the photos on page 3. The following headings may help:
support, outer covering, movement, reproduction, breathing, feeding.
2 The photos (below) show animals from different species to those on page 3 but each could be grouped with one animal in the photos by the Linnaean system. Pair animals from the two sets of photos and try to give each pair a group name.
3 Use the photos on pages 2–4 and try to attach them to a group identified in Figure 2.

CAUSES OF VARIATION

The answer to all these questions lies in the genes. The more genes that two living things share in common, the closer they are likely to be in the Linnaean classification tree. Thus two organisms from the same species will usually have most of their genes in common. However, there is still much variety within the same species. Take *Homo sapiens* for example. Differences between humans are very superficial. For example, skin colour is affected by only 10 of the 50 000 or so human genes.

STAYING ALIVE

Scientists group two organisms in the same species if the organisms can reproduce together and produce fertile offspring. Generally, different species don't mate, and therefore don't produce any offspring. But variation isn't only caused by genes. Environmental factors can have a strong influence on variation.

A horse and a donkey can reproduce but their offspring, the mule, (shown above right) is infertile. So the horse and the donkey belong to different species.

4 Draw a diagram of a cell to show where the genes can be found.
5 Name groups of animals which will have many genes in common with the following:
   a humans
   b domestic cats
   c houseflies.
6 The plants on the right have been grown from cuttings of the same parent plant and so have the same genes. They have grown quite differently though. Make a list of possible reasons. You'll discover more about how a combination of genes and environmental factors create the enormous variety of life on Earth in Chapter 1.

STAYING ALIVE

BEHAVING TO SURVIVE

The behaviour of living things has both genetic and environmental causes. Much of the sheepdog's behaviour is built into its genes but with training it can develop new behaviours.

In the wild, different types of behaviour have evolved over millions of years to help the creature survive.

One characteristic of living things is that they are sensitive to changes in their environment. They react to protect, feed and reproduce themselves. In Chapter 2 there's a chance to find out more about animal and plant behaviour and how it is co-ordinated.

Human behaviour affects your everyday life but it can also have enormous consequences for life on Earth. Chapter 3 in particular uses the theme of the 'What future for life?' to explore the consequences of human behaviour on the future of the different species and the planet as a whole.

7 Make a list of the senses used by animals to pick up information about their environment.

8 You met the pattern used by scientists to describe the different elements of behaviour in Chapter 3 of Book 1 (The body in and out of balance).
  a Give an example of a reflex action.
  b Use these words to show how the reflex is brought about: stimulus, response, receptor, co-ordination, effector.

9 Explain how the behaviour shown in the photos below assists survival.

1 FROM ONE GENERATION TO ANOTHER

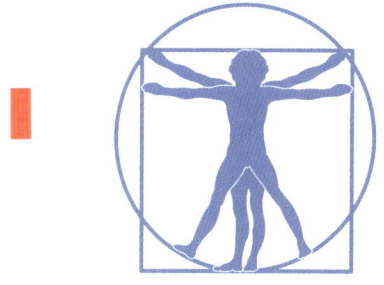

These human chromosomes shown below carry all the data necessary to create a new human being. This chapter explains how this is possible. We look at some of the consequences when things go wrong with this process. We also look at how such mistakes have led to the evolution of living things on Earth.

Contents
We're all different
From parents to child
When things go wrong
Like Mother . . .
. . . or Father
DNA: the life molecule
Explaining evolution
Interfering with evolution
Questions

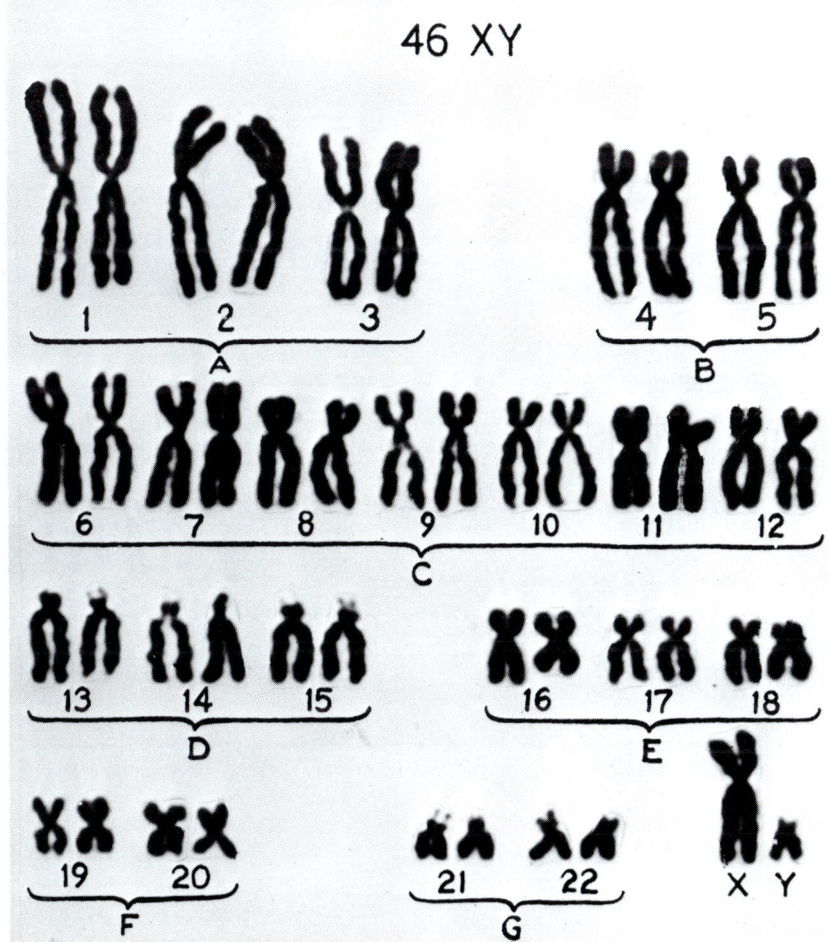

Chromosome of a human male organised in pairs. This is known as a karyotype.

STAYING ALIVE

WE'RE ALL DIFFERENT

As human beings, we share many physical features in common: the processes of respiration, digestion, excretion, not to mention similar physical features. However, we are all different in small ways: for instance hair colour and nose shape. People from the same family can be very similar in these terms but, apart from identical twins, even family members are different in some ways. The reason for differences is that we all have slightly different DNA (genetic information) in our bodies. This fact is put to good use in the field of forensic science as the following story describes.

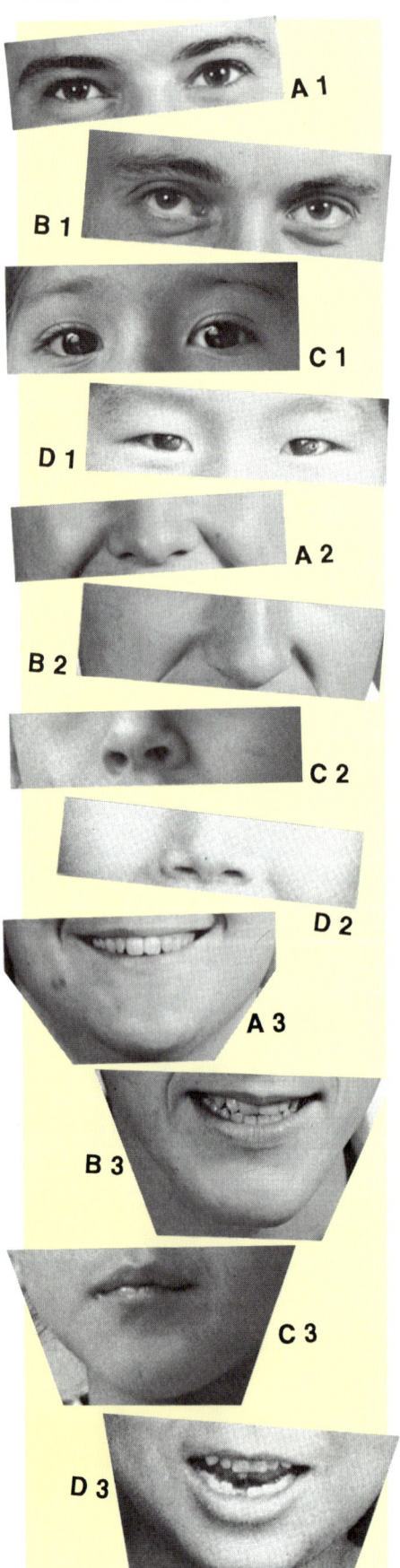

Police were called to take a closer look at an abandoned car at a local beauty spot.

A woman's' body was found.

"After close examination we have concluded that the woman was sexually assaulted before being killed."

Scientist found fingerprints on the car, but few were clear. Samples of hair, blood and semen found at the crime scene were analysed using DNA testing.

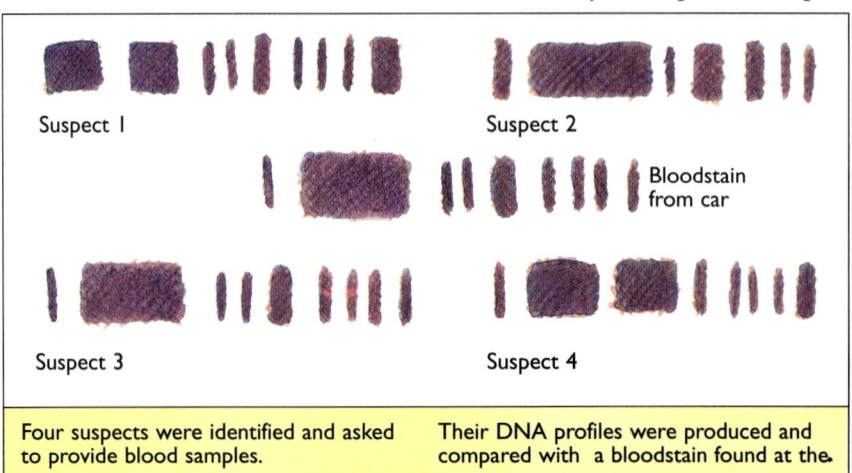

Four suspects were identified and asked to provide blood samples.

Their DNA profiles were produced and compared with a bloodstain found at the scene.

FROM ONE GENERATION TO ANOTHER

DNA PROFILING

Deoxyribose nucleic acid is the basic genetic material in cells. A person's DNA profile is produced through a variety of laboratory techniques. The profile looks rather like a barcode used on goods in supermarkets. It is unique to every person and can therefore be used for identification purposes.

DNA, GENES AND CHROMOSOMES

DNA is the molecule of inheritance. The discovery of its chemical structure in the 1950s revolutionized the study of genetics (the science of inheritance) since it helped to explain the observed differences in living things. The variety of life is a result of the different base sequences. A gene is a piece of DNA from 300 to several thousand base pairs in length. Each gene is responsible for a particular characteristic of an individual.

The genes are lined up on a chromosome which are the thread-like structures which can be seen in the nuclei of the cells when they are in the process of cell division.

1. Who do you think was the prime suspect in the murder? Give your reasons.
2. DNA profiling alone is not thought to be total proof of someone's guilt. Why?
3. Explain why DNA profiling would be impossible in the following cases:
   a semen from a man who had had a vasectomy
   b hair cuttings from a hairdresser's floor
4. Why do identical twins have the same DNA profiles?

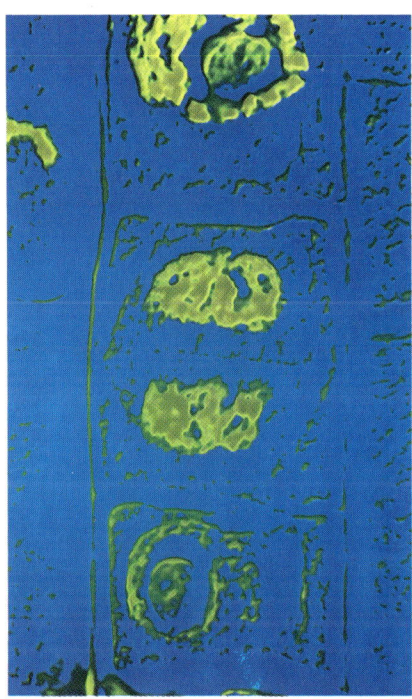

Cells undergoing mitosis in a root. What stage do you think they have reached?

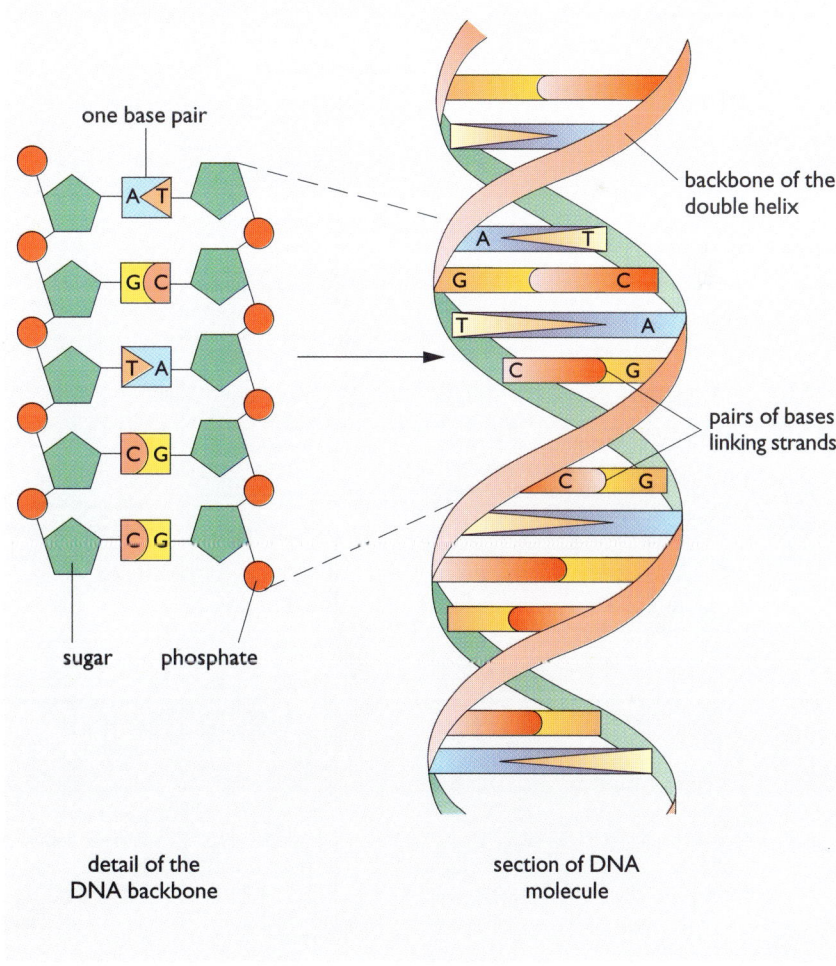

detail of the DNA backbone

section of DNA molecule

5. The illustration (right) shows the link between DNA, genes and chromosomes in diagram form. Use your own words to describe this link.
6. Find out more about the scientists who proposed the double helix model of DNA.

STAYING ALIVE

FROM PARENTS TO CHILD

The Smith family have many physical characteristics in common. There are also features which they do not share. Can you pick out which are the maternal and which the paternal grandparents of Paul and Kate? The diagrams on this page help to describe how the features of the Smith family are passed from generation to generation.

BODY CHROMOSOMES

In the nuclei of the cells of each Smith there are 46 chromosomes. This is the case for every body cell with two exceptions: red blood cells which have no nuclei and no chromosomes, and sex cells (eggs or sperm cells) which have exactly half the normal chromosome number.

Take Paul for example. His 46 chromosomes can be paired according to shape and size. Each chromosome pair is made up of one chromosome from his mother and one from his father. Paul has 22 pairs of chromosomes plus X and Y sex chromosomes. Kate, his sister, will have 22 pairs plus two X sex chromosomes.

The Smith family. The youngest members are Paul and Kate.

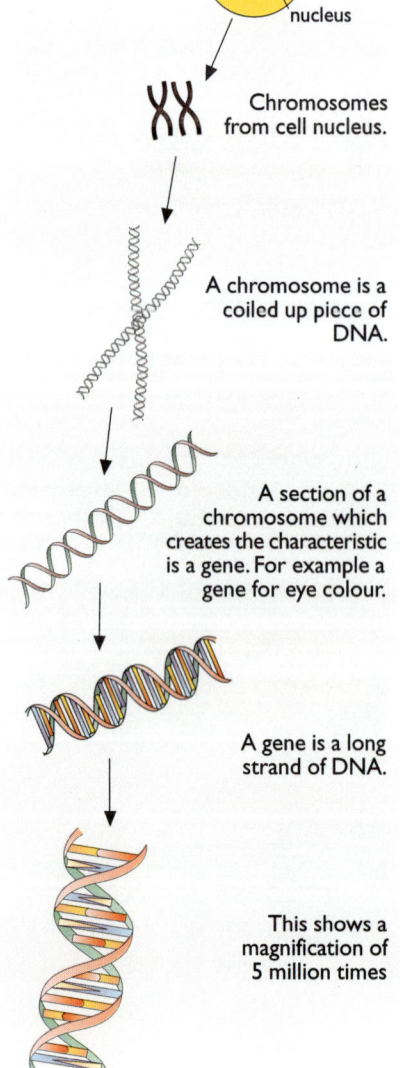

FROM ONE CELL TO MILLIONS

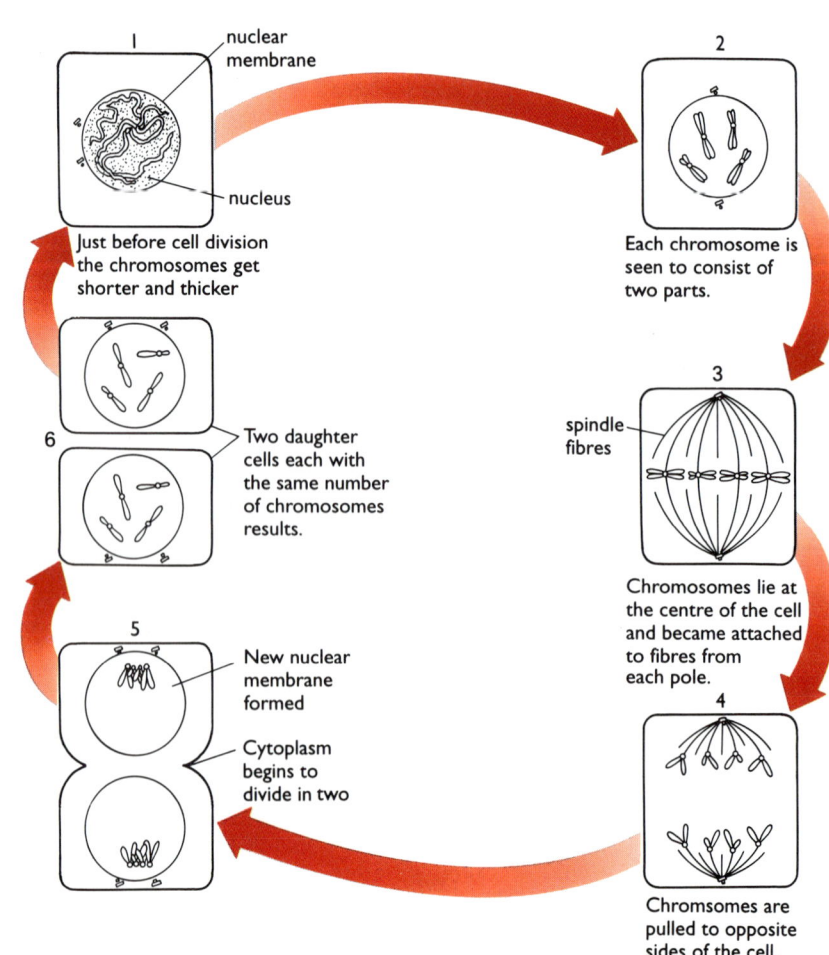

FROM ONE GENERATION TO ANOTHER

1. Which sex chromosomes will John and Sheila each have in their body cells? Where will each have come from?
2. Why do you think that sex cells have half the chromosome number of other body cells?

All the Smiths started life as a single fertilised egg – now look at them! Each of their bodies is made up of millions of cells which originate from that first cell by the process of cell division or **mitosis**. In the developing embryo of any animal or plant, mitosis proceeds very rapidly. In Kate's body there is still considerable cell division taking place. She grows by increasing the length of her bones and the size of her muscles not to mention her overall skin size to keep it all in! The diagrams opposite help to explain mitosis in Kate's body but only two pairs of Kate's chromosomes are shown to avoid confusion.

Notice that the chromosomes double before the cell divides. This means that the two cells produced (called daughter cells) are exactly the same as the original cell. The chromosomes are able to do this by DNA replication. The DNA double helix molecule unwinds and a new DNA strand is formed on each original stand. So *two* DNA molecules are formed and thus two chromosomes form from one.

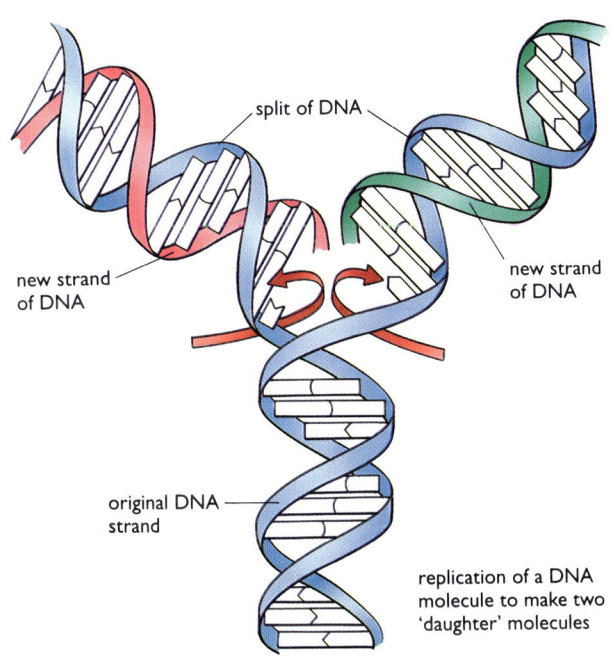

replication of a DNA molecule to make two 'daughter' molecules

3. Produce your own DNA molecule models from beads or plasticine. Show how replication takes place.
4. Write a suitable caption for each stage in the mitosis process shown in the diagrams.
5. Mitosis continues even in fully grown human adults. Which cells continue to divide?
6. Find out where cell division takes place in plants.

PRODUCING EGGS AND SPERMS

The fertilisation of an egg by a sperm cell brings together chromosomes from both parents: 23 from the mother and 23 from the father. For John and Sheila to produce sex cells with half the normal number of chromosomes, cells in their sex organs have to divide in a different way from mitosis. They divide by **meiosis**. Meiosis creates eggs and sperms with half the chromosome number of other body cells. Meiosis means that the chromosome pairs are split between two cells.

7. In which organs would meiosis be occurring in:
   a. a human female?
   b. a human male?
   c. a pea plant?
8. Draw diagrams to show how the sex of a baby is determined by the father's sperm.
9. Draw sketches to demonstrate how you think meiosis occurs.

STAYING ALIVE

WHEN THINGS GO WRONG

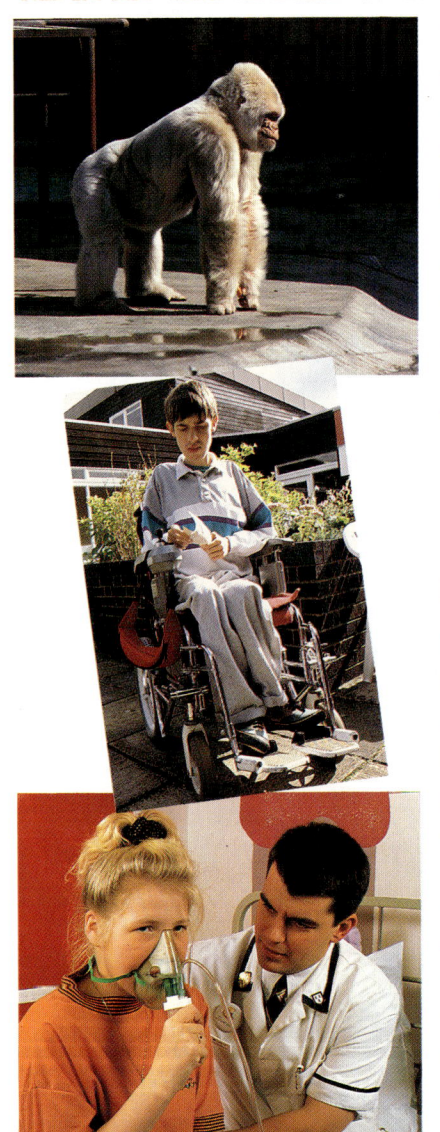

The photos on the left give some ideas of what happens when things go wrong with individual genes. It is questions about the causes and cures of such diseases which have led to **The Human Genome Project.** This is a massive, world-wide research effort to plot the position of human genes on the 23 pairs of chromosomes. At the same time the scientists are working out the DNA sequences of key genes which cause inherited diseases. One of the first genes to be tackled has been the gene which causes cystic fibrosis. This disease affects the digestive and respiratory systems. Sufferers need regular therapy if they are to remain healthy, and their life expectancy is considerably lower than normal. The gene sequence for the 'normal' gene has now been worked out and trials are underway to introduce this normal gene into the bodies of cystic fibrosis sufferers.

MUTATION OF GENES

How do genes go wrong? The answer is that at some point the DNA sequence has altered by mistake causing what is known as a **mutation.** For example, a change in just one base for a gene called PKU can cause the development of a genetic disorder called phenylketonuria. This disease causes serious growth disorders in children.

Mutations can occur in the copying process when an egg or sperm is being made. This mutation may then be recopied through each generation although the disease may not be present. (Find out why from pages 14–18) The causes of mutations are many and varied and cells do have their own ways of checking. However, mistakes aren't always picked up even with close checking.

A well known cause of mutations is radiation. For example, some of the sun's electromagnetic radiation can increase the likelihood of mutations. Extreme examples of the mutation effects of radiation are now being experienced by the survivors of the Chernobyl nuclear disaster. It is expected that the descendants of Chernobyl survivors will have a much higher incidence of birth defects than is usual.

Chernobyl nuclear power station.

FROM ONE GENERATION TO ANOTHER

Many of the laws of genetics have been worked out using organisms with natural mutations. *Drosophila melanogaster*, a fruit fly not much bigger than a pinhead, has four pairs of chromosomes and has revealed many of the secrets of inheritance. The differences between the individuals in these photographs are due to single gene mutations.

CELL DIVISION GONE WRONG

This child has **Down's syndrome** caused by the fact that his/her body cells have 3 copies of chromosome 21.

Fruitflies with different eye and body colours. These flies have a mutation for wing development body and eye colour. All these differences are caused by mutation of the genes responsible for each characteristic.

This genetic defect is present in 1 in 800 live births and results in the individual having learning and physical difficulties throughout life. Down's syndrome is the most common example of abnormal chromosome numbers in children. Most other abnormal chromosome combinations are lethal and affected embryos rarely survive. An estimated 40% of all miscarriages are due to chromosome abnormalities. Today we can test for many genetic abnormalities by performing amniocentesis tests in early pregnancy.

Abnormal chromosome numbers are caused by mistakes in meiosis: the cell division which produces the sex cells. Problems with mitosis (cell division in body cells) can result in other physiological difficulties. Cancer, one of the most common diseases in developed countries is the result of mitosis going wrong. Growth and division are carefully controlled in healthy cells. In cancerous cells, cell division runs out of control and a bundle of cancerous cells called a tumour is formed. As the tumour grows, it invades the tissues and organs and interferes with normal body processes. Scientists are still not sure how a cell becomes cancerous. Some chemicals have been linked to the development of specific cancers and are called **carcinogens.** For example, the hydrocarbons of cigarette smoke are known to cause lung cancer.

1. Draw a diagram to explain how Down's syndrome is caused.
2. Why must a surgeon remove all traces of cancer cells in an operation to remove a tumour?
3. The incidence of skin cancer (melanoma) has increased significantly in the last 30 years. Suggest reasons for this.
4. Explain why the children of Chernobyl survivors are at risk from genetic diseases.

STAYING ALIVE

LIKE MOTHER... OR FATHER? 1

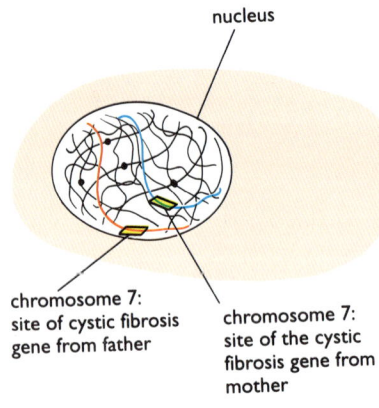

Adam Hill has the genetic disease cystic fibrosis. Other members of his family are all healthy.

How is it that Adam Hill who has cystic fibrosis can be born to parents who don't have the disease? It may be that a mutation has occurred during egg and/or sperm formation but the chances of that happening are very, very remote (more than one in a million). It is more likely that Adam's parents are both carriers of the mutant gene. It is estimated that in Britain there are 2 million people who carry the gene for cystic fibrosis.

Remember that the body cells contain chromosome pairs. Each pair contains one chromosome from the mother and one from the father. The cystic fibrosis gene is found on chromosome 7.

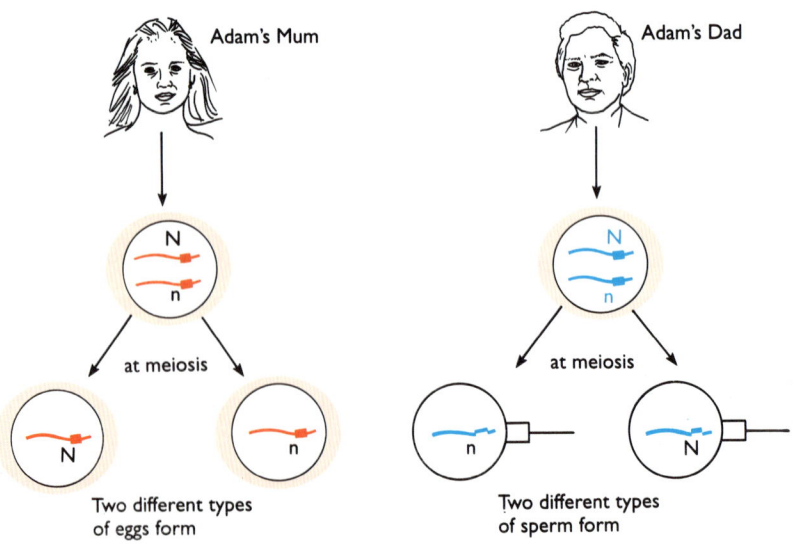

The formation of sex cells. 'n' is used to denote the cystic fibrosis gene and 'N' is used for the normal gene

FROM ONE GENERATION TO ANOTHER

Adam's father will have one normal gene and one cystic fibrosis gene. So will Adam's mother. Because the normal gene dominates the cystic fibrosis gene, both parents are free from the disease. However, look what happens when their bodies produce sex cells.

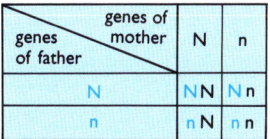

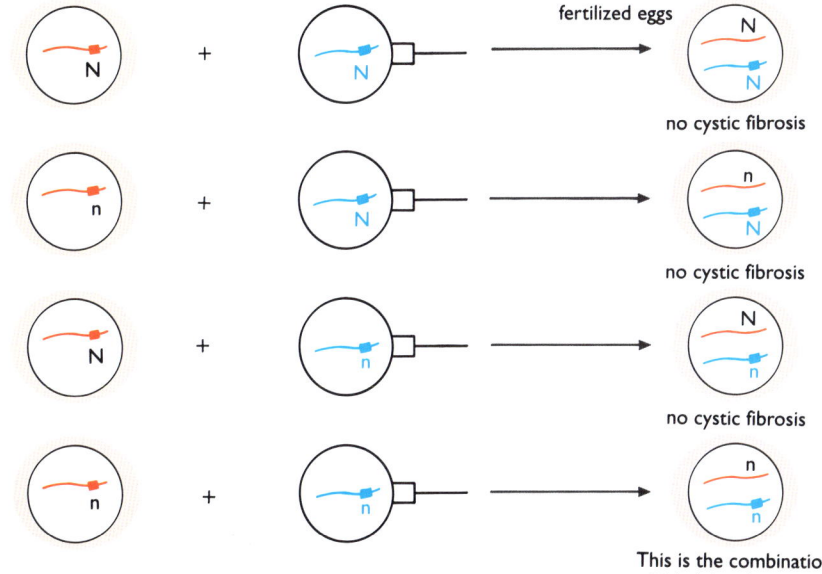

If a sperm with an **'n'** gene meets an egg with an **'n'** gene then the child will have two **n** genes. This is what Adam has.

The cystic fibrosis gene **'n'** is called a **recessive** gene. It only reveals itself if the normal, **dominant** gene (**N**) isn't present. This idea of dominant and recessive genes is helpful in understanding other inherited characteristics. Eye colour can be partly explained using these ideas: the gene for brown eyes is dominant to that for blue eyes. However, human genetics tends to be complicated; green and hazel eyes are controlled by a mix of genes. Many human characteristics tend to be controlled by more than one gene. This explains why until recently, geneticists have tended to work with very simple organisms like bacteria and fruit flies which have a small number of genes.

1 a Draw diagrams to explain why Helen, Adam's sister, has not inherited cystic fibrosis.
  b Explain why Helen may have children who suffer from cystic fibrosis.
2 What is the probability that the Hills might have another child who suffers from cystic fibrosis?
3 Explain the following observations in terms of dominant and recessive genes:
  a Two healthy parents have a child with the disease galactosemia, a disease which causes incomplete digestion of milk
  b When a normal winged fruit fly and one with deformed wings are crossed, all the offspring have normal wings.

STAYING ALIVE

LIKE MOTHER... OR FATHER? 2

SEX-LINKED INHERITANCE

Some inherited diseases are found more frequently in males than females. For example there are many more men than women who are red/green colour-blind. This is because the gene for normal colour sight is on the X chromosome. Women have two X chromosomes whereas men have one X and one Y.

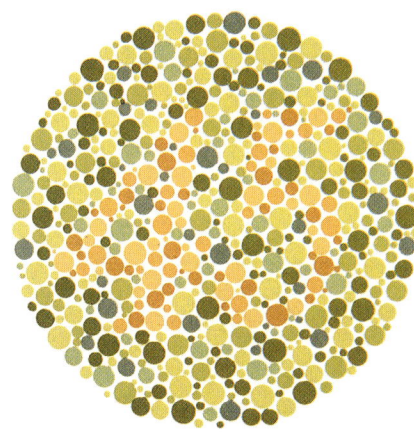

Can you see a number in this illustration? People with normal vision can see 45. This is one of a series of tests to identify colour blindness

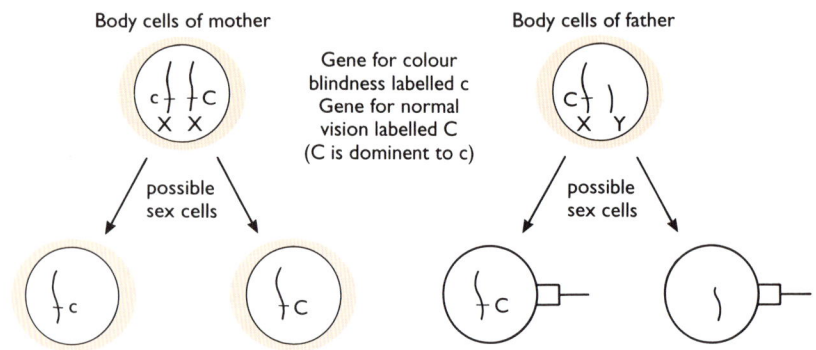

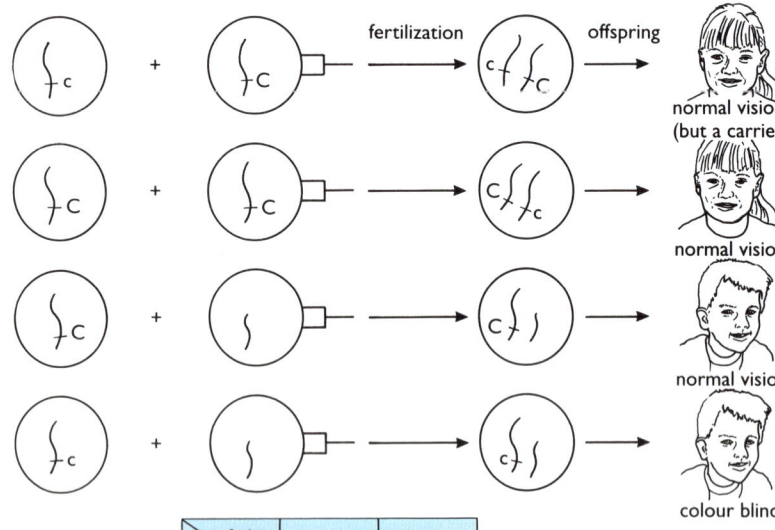

4 Look at the diagram (right). Explain why colour-blindness is more common in men than women.

5 Use diagrams like those shown on the right to show the possible gene combinations of the children of a colour-blind father and a normal sighted mother who is a non-carrier.

mother \ father	X^c	Y
X^C	$X^C X^c$	$X^C Y$
X^c	$X^c X^c$	$X^c Y$

FROM ONE GENERATION TO ANOTHER

GENETIC SCREENING

For couples whose families have a history of inherited disease, genetic counsellors can advise on the chances of their children inheriting the disorder. Given the facts, the couple then have to decide whether they wish to have children.

You may remember learning about amniocentisis in Book 1. This test is usually carried out only on women over 30, to detect inherited diseases in the developing embryo such as Down's syndrome. Some of the amniotic fluid surrounding the embryo is removed at the 15th or 16th week of pregnancy and the cells are tested for more than 100 genetic diseases. Early detection means that medical treatment for some diseases can begin long before birth. In some cases parents may choose to have the embryo aborted.

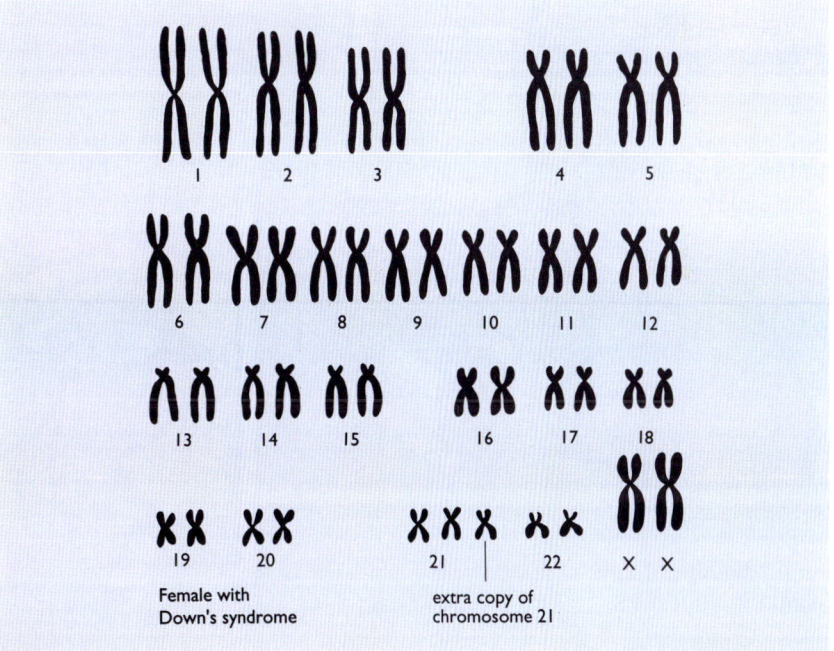

The karyotype for a Down's syndrome female.

6 Discuss the following questions in a group and prepare a short presentation of your views:
   a Should abortions be available for couples who discover their unborn baby has an inherited disease?
   b Should there be laws which forbid someone with an inherited disease to have children?
   c Should genetic screening be compulsory for all newborn babies?

7 There are religious and national laws which prevent marriage between close relatives. Suggest why this might be.

8 Haemophilia is an X-linked inherited disease like colour-blindness. The blood of haemophiliacs does not clot which causes problems when they cut or bruise themselves. What sort of genetic counselling might be given to couples where:
   a the woman has a haemophiliac brother and her husband isn't haemophiliac?
   b the man is a haemophiliac but the woman has no family history of haemophilia?

9 Huntington's chorea is a genetic disease of the nervous system. It does not develop until later life and causes dementia and involuntary jerky movements. It is caused by a dominant gene.
   a What are the chances of developing the disease if one of your parents suffered from the condition?
   b Would you wish to know early in life that you carried the gene? Give your reasons.

STAYING ALIVE

DNA: THE LIFE MOLECULE

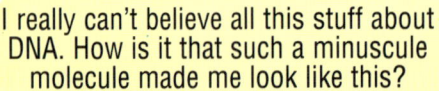

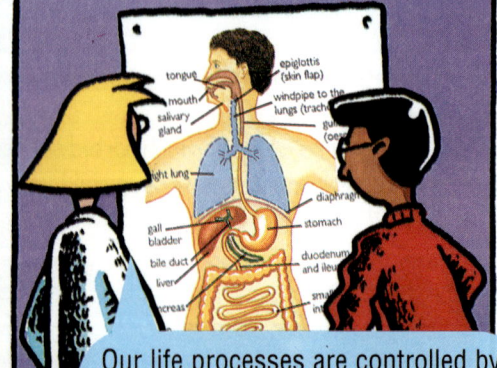

FROM ONE GENERATION TO ANOTHER

1. Make list of as many life processes as you can think of. What is the link between DNA and these life processes?
2. **a** What is the name given to a mistake in copying a base sequence?
   b Look at the photos of the flies on page 13. Use the explanations in the diagrams on the left to describe how radiation caused this change in fruit fly appearance. Use the words DNA, base sequence, protein, mutation, gene.

USING DNA IN INDUSTRY

The manufacturing industry has been quick to make use of genetics. Today, insulin for diabetics can be made in large quantities using DNA. The DNA which codes for human insulin is inserted into the DNA of a bacterium which becomes an insulin production 'factory' as shown in the diagram. This gene transfer between different species is called genetic engineering and is one of the fastest growing modern industries. Chymosin, the enzyme used by cheese-makers in large quantities to curdle milk, is another protein which is manufactured using genetically engineered microbes.

Genetically altered sheep are being used in the manufacture of certain antibiotics. DNA which codes for the antibiotic is introduced into the sheep's cells. The cells produce the antibiotic which appears in the sheep's milk. (Find out more about this process on page 22.) Current research into gene transfer between humans and pigs could result in the production of human-like organs for transplants in the future.

3. Predict the kind of conditions which will produce the best results in the manufacture of insulin using microbes.
4. Individuals with a deficiency of growth hormone have relied until now on hormone extracted from dead bodies. Suggest three advantages of using genetic engineering to help them.
5. Genetic engineering could mean a change in the way farm animals and plants are used in manufacturing. Use your imagination to write about a farm of the future.

STAYING ALIVE

EXPLAINING EVOLUTION

Knowing about genetics will help you to understand the theory of evolution. You are certainly in a better position than Charles Darwin and Alfred Wallace, the two scientists who first proposed this theory. They developed their theory of evolution long before the discovery of the gene and a century before the model for DNA was proposed.

Darwin and Wallace both spent years observing living organisms. Darwin did much of his research in the Galapagos Islands off the west coast of South America while Wallace's work centred on Indonesia. Both men arrived at the same theory quite independently and presented a joint paper to the Linnaean Society in 1858. A year later Darwin published *Origin of Species*, a book which had a tremendous impact on society.

Charles Darwin (top) and Alfred Wallace.

THE THEORY OF EVOLUTION

A theory is used to explain a lot of apparently unconnected facts. From their work Darwin and Wallace made the following observations:

1. There is variation between individuals in a species.
2. Many offspring are produced.
3. Only organisms best fitted to their environment survive.

They concluded that:

All living organisms struggle to survive. Since there aren't enough resources to maintain all the offspring and there are predators which attack them, some offspring lose the struggle for existence and die prematurely. Therefore those individuals whose features best fit them to exist in their environment will be most likely to survive.

FROM ONE GENERATION TO ANOTHER

1. Explain variation in terms of genetics.
2. How will mutations affect evolution?
3. 'Fitness' does not mean the same as the everyday explanation of the term. What does it mean in terms of species survival?
4. Use the theory of Natural Selection to explain how camouflage develops in a species of bird.

This idea of the 'survival of the fittest' is called the theory of **natural selection.** Taken further, this theory points to how life has evolved on Earth. It suggests that all living things share common ancestors and that the living world is in a constant state of change.

Many Victorians were scandalised by the ideas in *Origin of Species*. Accepted wisdom at the time was that living things had remained the same since Creation. How were people to accept that they shared a common ancestor with all animals?

CURRENT IDEAS ABOUT EVOLUTION

The ideas of Darwin and Wallace are now widely accepted among the scientific community. Scientists have developed ideas about the mechanism of evolution from the time when life first appeared on Earth about two thousand million years ago. It has been shown that the molecules of life such as DNA and proteins could have been formed in the conditions existing on Earth at that time. These molecules formed into very simple one-celled plants, followed by animals. The possible evolutionary development after this can be seen on the diagram on page 3.

Darwin on Species

Hear how selection was the efficient cause
(To form and species of transmuting laws):
There was a time when short-legged, lumbering dogs,
Could only catch the rabbits and the hogs;
The lighter creatures, and the fleeter prey,
Mocked their pursuers as they ran away.
At length the rabbits and the pigs declined,
Till scarce one specimen was left behind;
Then was the breed canine in doleful dumps,
Mourning short commons, and their shorter stumps,
Whilst bounding hares, at which they barked in vain,
Swarmed in the woods, and frolicked on the plain.
At last some turnspits of superior mind
Tried hard the chase, some sustenance to find;
Short-legged, short-winded, much they puffed and blew,
Whilst the fleet game escaped their eager view;

But they, with 'plastic' limbs and watchful care,
In fifty thousand ages caught a hare!
The others died that did not like to run,
Nor was man there to help them with his gun.
Those that remained in time's long cycles found
The way to change a turnspit to a hound;
The sturdy hound, improving on the plan,
Lengthened his legs, and as a greyhound ran:
Thus does *selection's* powers elaborate
Great things from little, little things from great,
To reach the wants of each peculiar state.
In million ages lions grew from cats,
In million ages seals fined down to sprats;
And black bears dabbling in the sea for play,
Lapsed into whales, and grandly swam away.

Anon (mid-19th century)

5. **a** Using the poem above draw a flow chart to show how the writer felt greyhounds had evolved.

   b The last four lines of the poem suggest that the writer hasn't quite understood the mechanism of evolution. How would you explain the errors to him/her?

STAYING ALIVE

INTERFERING WITH EVOLUTION

Human beings had been interfering with evolution long before the publication of *Origin of Species*. The 'artificial' selection used by animal and plant breeders provided Darwin with an important clue in his search for a theory. The animals and plants in the illustrations are unlikely results of evolution. They have been developed by *human* selection. Breeders produce the kind of organism they want by selecting organisms for breeding which have the characteristics they are looking for. Often many reproductive crosses over several generations are carried out in order to get organisms with specific characteristics they require. For example, horsebreeders imported three stallions into England in the 17th century because they had the qualities they were looking for. Now all the thoroughbred horses in the world are related to these stallions.

1 The variety of rose in the photo above right can be traced back to the dog rose growing 'wild' in hedgerows.
   a What living things in the wild might the other organisms be traced to?
   b If breeders wanted to develop a new breed of sheep for a cold environment,
     i what sort of characteristics do you think they'd look for?
     ii how do you think they would go about producing the sheep they want?
2 The owner of the prize bull in the photo can charge hundreds of pounds for this bull to serve a cow. Why?
3 In order to breed the right kind of dog, breeders may be tempted to carry out inbreeding. This means breeding between close relatives such as a sister and brother. Why do you think the Kennel Club has rules which prevent this? (Hint: look back to page 12).

INTERFERING WITH GENES

As we learn more about genetics, more opportunities arise for human intervention in evolution. It is now possible to transfer genes from one species to another species without breeding over several generations, which has been required in the past. Harmless viruses are sometimes used as the agents of gene transfer. The selected DNA from one species is attached to the virus which is then able to penetrate an egg cell of another species and thus introduce the new DNA. The transfer mechanism is rather like the one described on page 19. This kind of genetic modification has enormous potential.

FROM ONE GENERATION TO ANOTHER

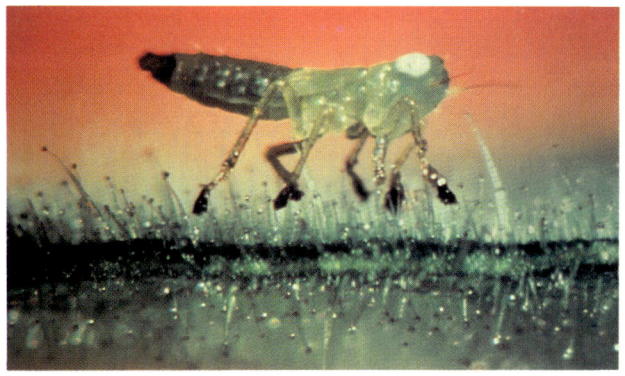

The International Potato Centre in Peru in collaboration with Cornell University hope to develop an insect resistant potato. They have identified genes from a wild species which cause hairy leaves. These hairs act like flypaper in trapping insects. Therefore if such a gene was introduced into potato plants, these plants could be grown without the use of pesticides.

Recently the Dutch government approved experiments in which a copy of a human gene has been introduced into cows. The idea is that this gene which prevents mastitis (an infection of the milk producing glands) in women, will have the same benefits for cows.

CLONING

Plant breeders may develop an organism with all the right characteristics. For example a plant from the tropics, such as coconut palm, may produce high yields and be able to resist pests. How do breeders then produce sufficient qualities of these palms? Sexual reproduction stands the risk of introducing other unrequired genes.

Growing plants from cuttings is an accepted way of producing offspring with the same genetic makeup. These days however scientists have gone a stage further in being able to produce a new plant from a single cell via tissue culture. A tiny piece of plant tissue is cut from the chosen plant. This tissue is grown on the correct nutrients on an agar plate and gives rise to many thousands of identical offspring. Acres of vegetables or trees can be established from one parent. This ensures the same quality product from each plant. There is one snag however: if the genes are all the same it will mean that all plants will have the same response to disease, pests or a change in environmental conditions.

The effects of lack of variety in a crop were experienced in the 1840s in Ireland. The fungal disease of blight (*Phytophera infestans*) which attacked potato crops spread quickly throughout the country. Because of the genetic similarity of the potatoes and the lack of variety of crops in general, a massive famine and economic disaster ensued.

Cloned coconut palms, above and below.

Name of Method	What is involved?	Advantages	Disadvantages
Selective breeding			
Gene transfer			
Cloning			

4 Copy and complete this table of information about different methods of altering the genetic make-up of animals and plants.

5 As a group, discuss your feelings about human interference in evolution. What are the potential advantages and disadvantages for the planet?

STAYING ALIVE

QUESTIONS

1 A grower had a rose with a large pale yellow flower and another with a small bright yellow flower. He wanted to produce a new variety with large bright yellow flower. He crossed the roses, collected the seeds and grew them.

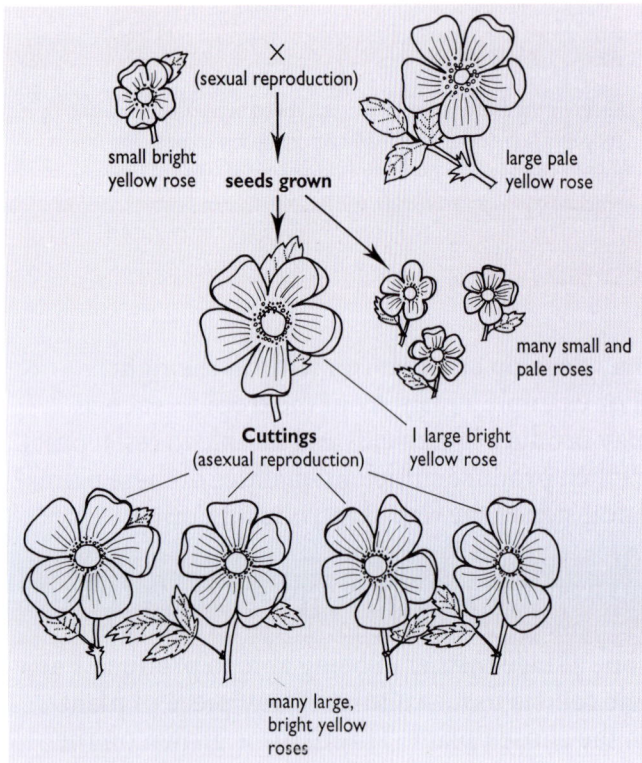

a Why did the grower use sexual reproduction to produce the large bright yellow rose?

b Why did the grower use cuttings (asexual reproduction) to produce lots of the new large bright yellow roses?

2 The diagram shows the inheritance of coat colour in a family of mice. **B** is the dominant gene (allele) for black coat and **b** is the recessive gene (allele).

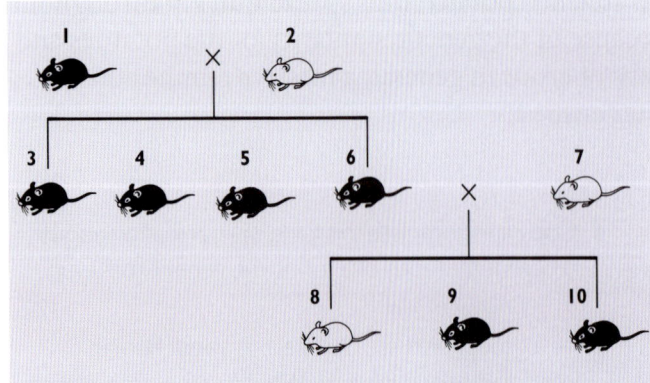

a i Which mouse is most likely to have the combination of alleles (genotype) **BB**?

ii What is the probability that the next mouse born to parents **6** and **7** will be black?

b i Write down the genotypes of mouse **3** and mouse **9**.

ii Write down the possible combinations of genotype which could result from a cross between mouse **3** and mouse **9**.

iii What proportion of offspring resulting from the mating of mouse **3** and mouse **9** would you expect to have black coats?

c After several generations of mice have been bred from those shown in the diagram, a mutant mouse is born whose coat colour is white with black patches. Suggest what could have happened to cause this.

d Describe the similarities and differences between male and female gametes of mice. You may assume that the sex of mice and of humans is inherited in similar ways..

3 Pure-breeding fruit flies were exposed to X-rays for a short period of time. The original flies had long, straight wings, red eyes and grey bodies. When allowed to interbreed, some of their offspring were like this but others had yellow or brown eyes, short or curled or no wings or black bodies. This is an example of:

A evolution
B genetic engineering
C mutation
D natural selection.

4 The table gives some details about a family:

	Mother	Father	Child
Number of chromosomes	46	46	47
Number of X chromosomes	2	1	1

Which one of these statements about the child is correct?

a The child is a boy not suffering from Down's syndrome
b The child is a boy suffering from Down's syndrome
c The child is a girl not suffering from Down's syndrome
d The child is a girl suffering from Down's syndrome

2 BEHAVING TO SURVIVE

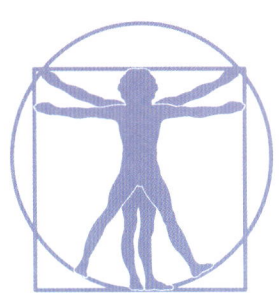

Contents
Sensing the Environment
Light detection
Plant responses
The movement response
Finding the way home
Questions

Detecting and responding to danger is vital for survival. In this chapter we adopt a naturalist's approach to the study of the ingenious methods adopted by a variety of animals and plants in their battle to stay alive.

A cougar pursues a snowshoe hare.

STAYING ALIVE

SENSING THE ENVIRONMENT

We experience our surroundings through the five senses of sight, hearing, touch, taste and smell. For centuries people assumed that other animals had the same senses. Any strange animal behaviour was put down to a mystical 'sixth sense'. For example, the ability of snakes to appear out of nowhere and deliver a lethal strike in total darkness meant that they were treated by many people as supernatural creatures. In fact, snakes like the boa constrictor or the green pit viper can detect the infra-red radiation of warm-blooded animals.

The senses have evolved to enable living organisms to pick up cues from the environment and respond if necessary. Much of the evidence that Darwin used in formulating his theory of natural selection came from examining the structures of living organisms. Study of the senses provides further evidence of the evolutionary links between different organisms. Darwin actually did carry out research into the sensitivity of plants and some of his work is described on page 30.

You will have had some opportunity already to investigate your own senses. The illustrations on these pages gives you an insight into some lesser-known senses in the living world.

1 INFRA-RED

The bat pictured (right) has a heat sensitive patch on the end of its nose. This 'nose-leaf' is a flap of skin separated from the rest of the body which is 9 °C cooler than the rest of the body. Using the nose-leaf, the bat can detect infra-red radiation from the warmth of an animal's body 16 cm away. This makes it an efficient hunter. Some snakes have their heat sensitive organs between the eyes and nose. Infra-red rays are focused by this pin-hole sized organ onto a grid of over 7000 nerve endings to produce an accurate 'heat picture' of the prey.

Infra-red

Magnetism

2 MAGNETIC RADIATION

Magnetism is thought to influence the activities of bees. A magnetic material called magnetite has been found on their abdomens. Some experiments also showed that bees can be trained to come to sugar solution if a magnetic field is applied. (See right.) Honeycomb building is also thought to be influenced by a magnetic field. A new swarm will tend to orientate new combs in the same direction as the parent hive. This orientation can be changed by applying a magnetic field.

BEHAVING TO SURVIVE

3 WEATHER

Some plants and animals have been used as barometers since early times. For example in Provence in France, green tree frogs are kept as rain monitors as their mating croaks warn of rain. Certain flowers such as marigolds only open their petals in fine weather. Many animals are sensitive to the electromagnetic waves created by a storm. Pigeons are known to be sensitive to small changes in air pressure which helps them to predict weather and maintain altitude.

Use the information on this page together with your own knowledge to produce a table to summarise information on animal senses. Use a table like the one below to help you.

Organism	Stimulus	Receptor	Survival Value
Pit viper	infra-red	Sense organs in head	Catches warm-blooded prey

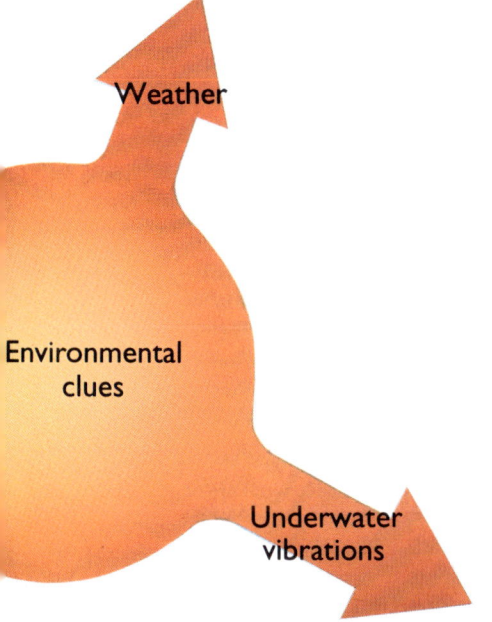

4 UNDERWATER VIBRATIONS

Many fish have lateral line organs along their head and bodies. Each organ consists of sensitive hairs attached to a jelly-like rod which bends in the direction of any water movement. Any disturbances in the water by predators or prey are detected. For shoaling fish, like herrings, these organs are buried along lateral lines and help them to keep their position in the shoal.

Hunting sharks are most sensitive to vibrations of 200 hertz, which happens to be the same frequency produced by a hovering helicopter. This means that air-sea rescues may act as dinner-bells for hungry sharks!

STAYING ALIVE

LIGHT DETECTION

We rely on light cues more than any other stimulus to help us sense our environment. Light is only a small part of the electromagnetic spectrum of radiation and covers waves 400–700 nanometers long. A few animals can 'see' radiation of higher and lower wavelengths as shown in the diagram. However, it must be remembered that humans have invented equipment which can detect all these wavelengths.

Animals rely on the photo-sensitive chemical **rhodopsin** to detect light. Rhodopsin is rather like the chemicals on a roll of photographic film, it changes when it comes into contact with light. Animals with eyes have specialised photo-sensitive cells containing rhodopsin.

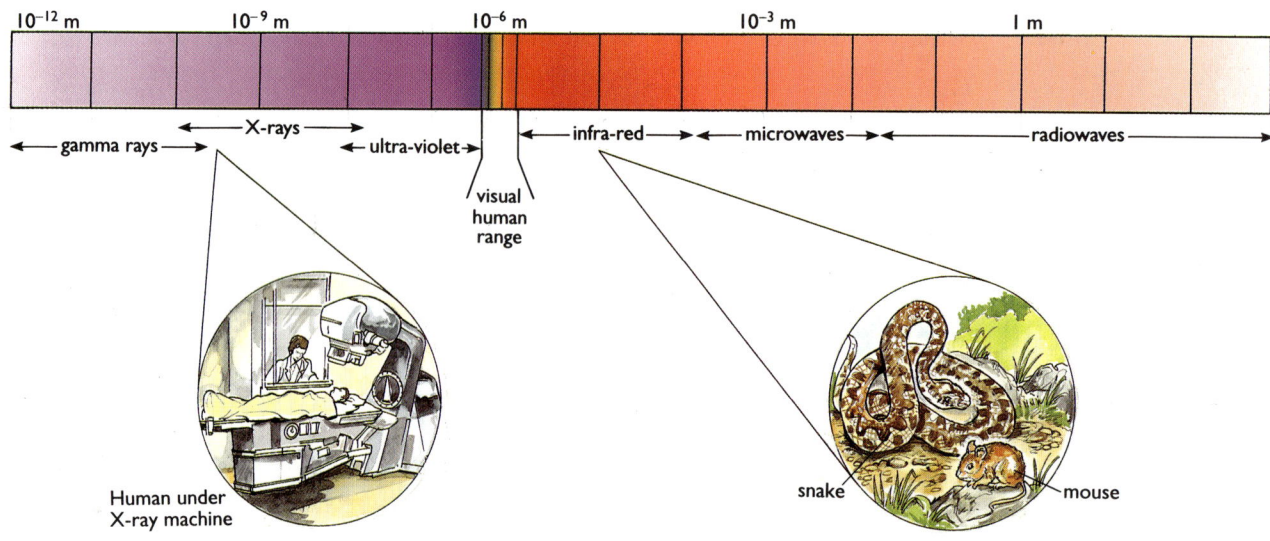

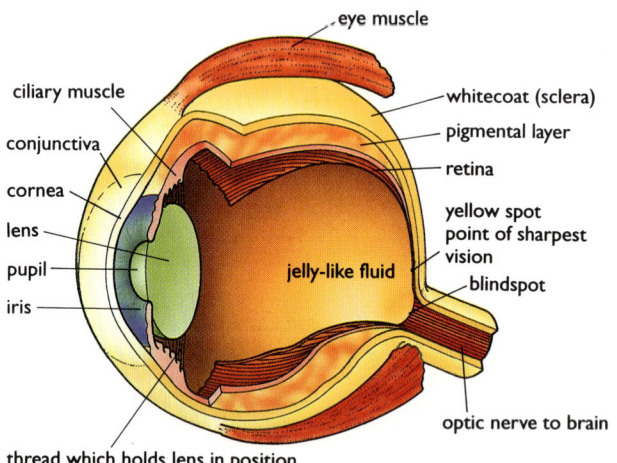

THE CAMERA EYE

Vertebrates have camera eyes, so-called because they resemble this equipment. The diagram on the left shows the inside of such an eye.

SEEING IN COLOUR

We have two sorts of light receptors in our eyes: **rod cells** and **cone cells.** Only the cone cells can distinguish between different wavelengths of light so they are for detecting colour. There are three types of cone cells, to detect red, blue and green light. The cells detect the light and send

1. Make a sketch of a cross-section of an eye. Link the following jobs to the different structures.
   - focuses light
   - contains light sensitive cells
   - carries nerve impulses to the brain
   - controls the amount of light hitting the retina
   - protects the eye (several labels)
   - area of most concentration of light cells

2. Produce your own 3D eye using different coloured plasticine. To see if you've got it right, cut a section through to see if it looks like the diagram.

BEHAVING TO SURVIVE

messages to the brain which does the colour mixing. Other primates, like apes, have the same combination of cones but many mammals like dogs and squirrels have only two pigments. Many nocturnal animals have a low concentration of cone cells altogether while stickleback fish have five pigments in their eyes.

GETTING IN FOCUS

Focusing light from objects at different distances is called **accommodation.** It is possible by any of the following methods:

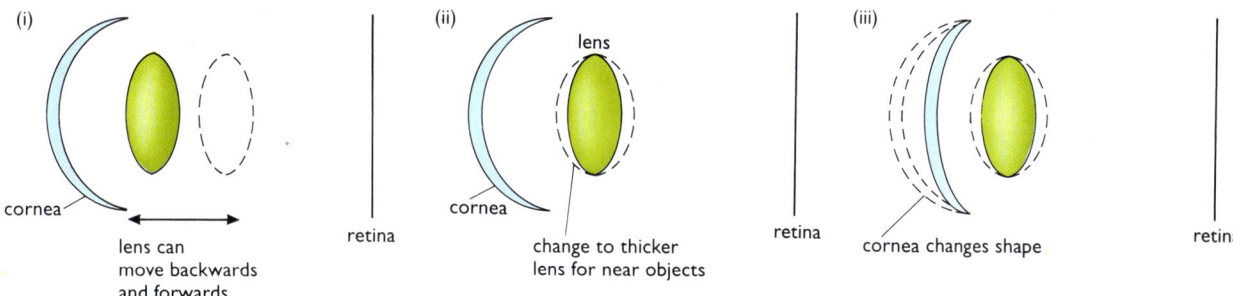

1 Changing the distance between the lens and retina, a method used by fish and octopuses.

2 Changing the shape of the lens as mammals do.

3 Changing the shape of the cornea. Pigeons and chickens can do this while also changing the lens shape.

Eagles have an extra skill. They have evolved the ability to magnify an image by two times rather like the telephoto system of a camera.

FIELDS OF VIEW

The differences between the positions of the eyes in predators and prey is quite marked. Look at these pictures of the fields of vision of different animals.

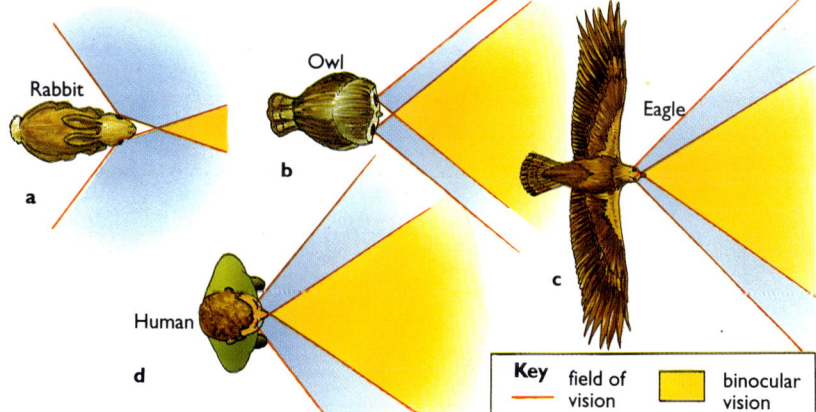

3 The diagrams above show the muscles involved in changing lens shape.
  a What shape of lens is needed to focus on a distant object?
  b Which muscles will contract to achieve this shape?
  c Suggest why some people may need reading glasses as they get older.
4 What is the different between the eyes of predators and prey? Explain the evolutionary advantage of each.
5 What different types of equipment have been developed to assist blind people?
6 Find out about the shapes of lenses which correct short and long sight.

FAILING EYESIGHT

Organisms born in the wild with poor vision will be at a considerable disadvantage in the survival stakes. For humans, technologies to overcome sight problems are continually being developed. One new technique uses lasers to change the shape of the human lens. The laser is able to remove a thin slice from the lens and so correct short-sightedness (myopia).

STAYING ALIVE

PLANT RESPONSES

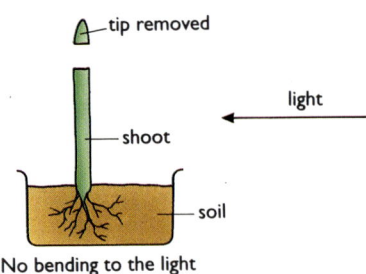

No bending to the light

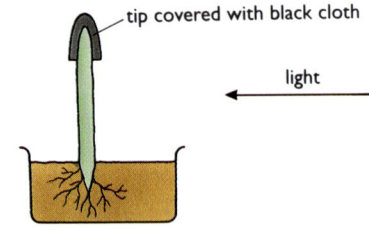

No bending towards the light

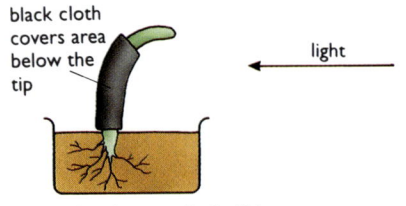

Shoot bends towards the light

Plant 'behaviour' isn't as obvious or dramatic as animal behaviour but it is vital for survival. It is easy to relate a plant's responses to photosynthesis:
- shoots grow towards the light.
- leaves can move quite quickly to face the sun so that they have a large leaf area exposed to the sun's radiation.
- roots grow downwards in search of water

What are the mechanisms for these kind of responses? A series of ingenious experiments by a number of scientists since the late 19th century have provided many clues.

The story begins in 1880 with Charles Darwin and his son Francis. They noticed that growing shoots did not bend towards the light if their growing tip was removed. They tried this with many types of shoot and all of them responded in the same way. For further experiments they chose to work with shoots of grass seed. Their results are shown in the diagram on the left.

1. What control experiments would the Darwins have used?
2. Try to explain the bending of the shoot in terms of
   a uneven growth.
   b what's happening to the cells.
3. What do you think the Darwins' hypothesis might have been when they set up their experiments?
4. What explanation can you offer for the Darwins' results?

In 1913, the Danish scientist Jensen took up the research. His hypothesis was that there is a chemical link between the tip of the shoot and the growing area below it. He used a thin impervious sheet of mica to test this idea.

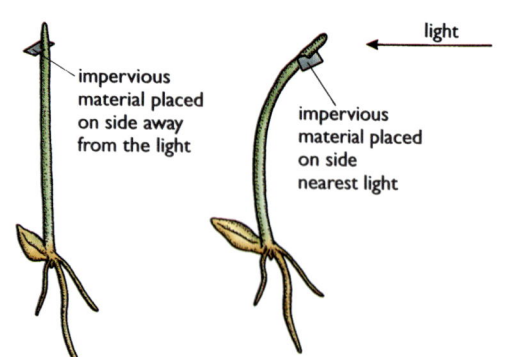

5. What was the effect of impervious material in both cases?
6. Explain the results in terms of Jensen's original hypothesis.

Further work by Went in America added weight to the idea of a chemical growth hormone being responsible for the results. A famous experiment is described in these diagrams.

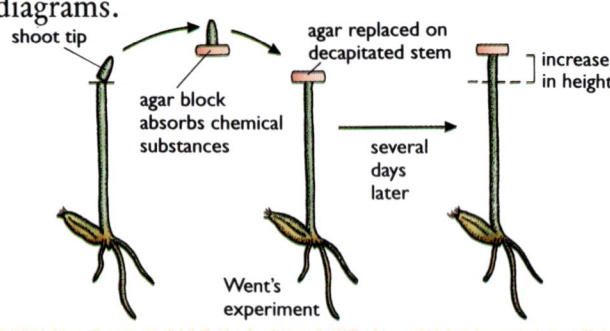

Went's experiment

7. What is a hormone?
8. What do you think has caused the growth of the shoot?
9. What does the experiment suggest about
   a where hormone is produced?
   b where the hormone acts?
10. What control experiment might Went have used?

BEHAVING TO SURVIVE

USING GROWTH SUBSTANCES IN AGRICULTURE

Eventually a chemical which appeared to affect growth was extracted from plants. It was given the name **auxin**. Today scientists have extracted and identified many different chemicals which all affect plant growth. These chemicals all go under the general name 'auxin'. Interestingly, one of the most potent auxins has been extracted from human urine!

Auxins are now produced synthetically and used in agriculture to improve crop yields. The actions of these auxins aren't as straightforward as some of the experiments on this page suggest. Auxins can slow down, as well as encourage, growth depending on their concentration and the type of cells they are applied to. Examples of some of the applications can be seen in the photographs.

a. Rooting powder Auxin promotes the growth of roots and is applied to cuttings to get them established.

b. Improving fruit production Spraying tomatoes with auxin stimulates the development of fruit even if the flowers have not been pollinated. It also allows the farmer to ripen all the plants at the same time and therefore harvest them together. Auxin sprays are used by other fruit growers to prevent fruit falling before they are ready for picking.

c. Preserving vegetables Near the end of the season, old potatoes start to sprout. Spraying with auxin can delay this for up to 3 years so the potatoes can be kept for much longer than usual.

Some very old gardening tricks have been shown to have a hormonal explanation. For example, gardeners place bananas with green tomatoes to get them to ripen. The trick works because ethylene from the banana is the naturally occurring hormone which promotes ripening.

Other hormones with quite different chemical compositions have been isolated and are now widely used in agriculture and horticulture. **Giberellins** are used to increase flower production and **cytokinins** to increase plant resistance to low temperatures and virus infections.

Research has shown that auxins are not the only chemicals to affect plant growth and development.

STAYING ALIVE

THE MOVEMENT RESPONSE

Developing highly-tuned senses is important for any animal but an ability to respond appropriately is also vital for survival. In Book 1 we looked at how the nervous and hormonal systems bring about responses. These activities help remind you of this work.

Look at the photo on the left.
1. Suggest which receptors the springbok and zebras used to sense the presence of the lion.
2. What were the effectors in both lion and springbok and zebras?
3. Draw a diagram to show how receptors and effectors are linked in one of the animals in the diagram (page 56-7 in Book 1 may help).

HOW WE MOVE

Of course not all our body movement is in response to danger. Your choice to pick up and read this book could well be because it looks so interesting! But movement always requires the interaction of three types of tissue: nerves, muscles and bone. The nerves carry an impulse to the muscles which respond by contracting and thus get shorter. Since the muscles are attached to bones, their contraction will create a pulling force on the bone and make it move. Look at the diagram showing the arrangement of muscles and bones in the arm. The two muscles work in opposite ways to bend and straighten the arm. When one contracts, the other relaxes.

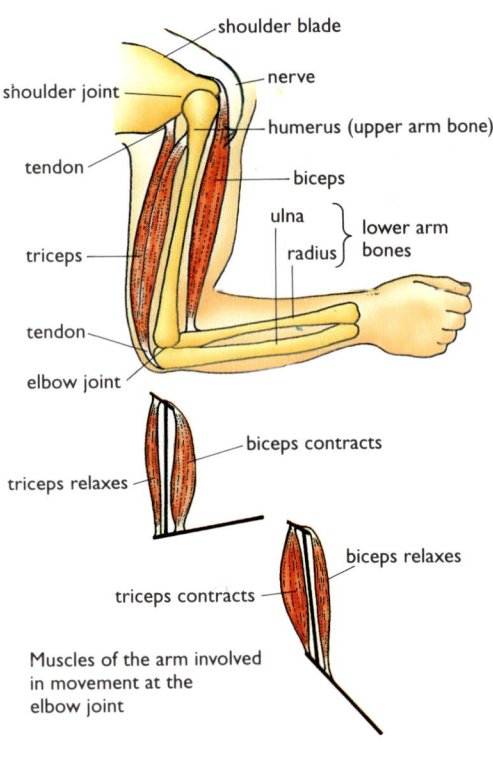

Muscles of the arm involved in movement at the elbow joint

THE JOINTS

A skeleton is made up of many bones joined in different ways. There are ball and socket joints which allow very free movement, hinge joints which allow more limited movement, and immovable joints which are pretty solidly fixed. Movement at joints creates friction which is kept to a minimum by the design of the joint. Each bone is covered at the end by smooth cartilage and between the bones is the lubricant, synovial fluid.

4. Copy and complete the following sentences by filling in the missing words:
   When an impulse in the _____ stimulates the biceps muscle it contracts while the _____ _____ relaxes. Now the arm will be _____.

5. Examine a human skeleton and identify the different bones
   a. List examples of the different types of joints
   b. List bones which protect the body organs and say which organs are protected.

BEHAVING TO SURVIVE

OTHER WAYS OF MOVING

Vertebrate animals have different sizes and shapes of muscles and skeletons but the basic principle of movement is the same for fish, birds, reptiles, mammals and amphibians. For animals which do not have this internal bone skeleton, the problem of movement has been solved in different ways.

LOOK NO LEGS!

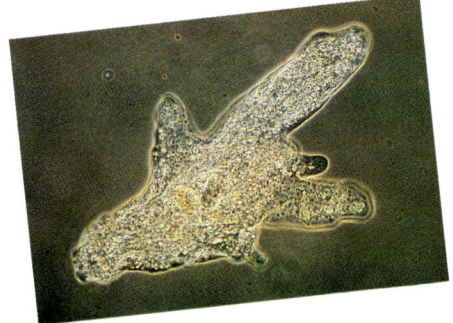

Amoeba movement: The electron microscope has revealed fibres of two different kinds of protein, actin and myosin. Actin acts as a kind of cell 'skeleton' which is moved by the contraction of myosin fibres. In fact this is the same kind of system which exists in human muscle cells which enables them to contract and relax.
Paramecium have tiny hairs or cilia that flick backwards and forwards like a whip to propel the cell along.

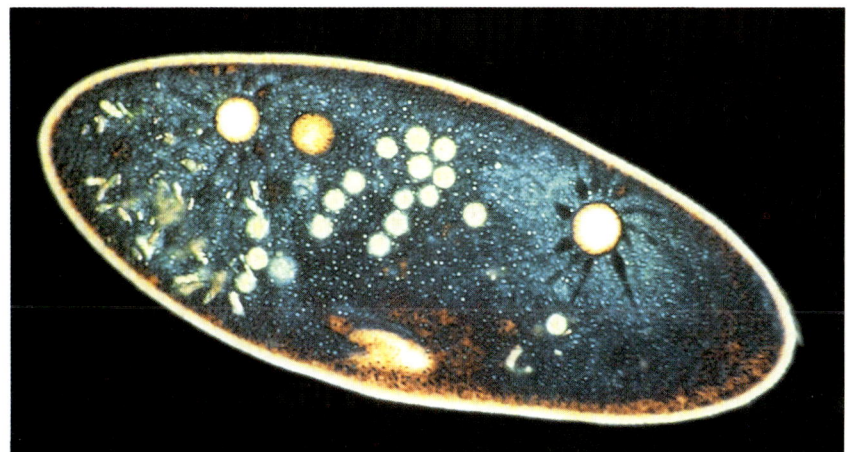

Paramecium use cilia for movement.

Earthworm: The separate segments of the earthworm body can be long and thin or short and fat. The diagram shows the sequence for crawling. A wave of contraction once begun moves backwards along the body.

Outside skeletons: The Arthropods are the group of animals with external skeletons – exoskeletons – and jointed legs, such as insects and crustaceans. Their muscles are attached internally to the external skeleton and are arranged in pairs like those of vertebrates.

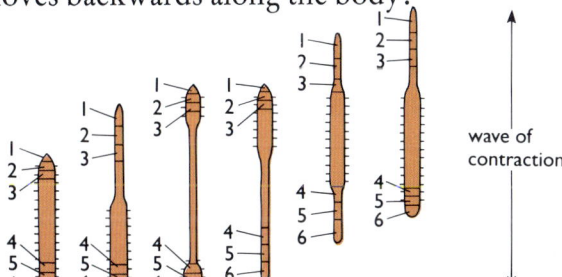

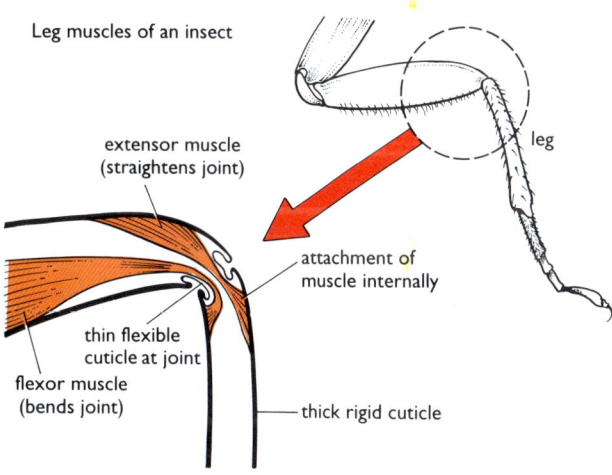

6 Choose an animal from one of the invertebrate groups which are listed. Prepare a presentation about how it moves.
7 Which muscles contract and which relax when an insect bends its leg?

33

STAYING ALIVE

FINDING THE WAY HOME

The Manx Shearwater is one of many species of birds which nest on islands around the British Isles. They migrate to a warmer, equatorial climate in the winter. The ornithologist R.M. Lockley observed that birds reared in his island home of Skokholm returned to breed there. How did they find their way and could they locate home when they were off the normal migration path away from other birds? The investigation carried out by Lockley involved ringing adult birds. These birds were then released from the different locations labelled on the map. The majority of the birds orientated themselves very quickly in the direction of Skokholm and returned safely. The normal flight path of the shearwater is almost entirely over the sea but those birds with a land journey in the experiment had no difficulty. If birds took time to point themselves in the right direction, it was because weather conditions were overcast. This suggested that the birds were using the sun's direction to orientate themselves. This is called **solar navigation**.

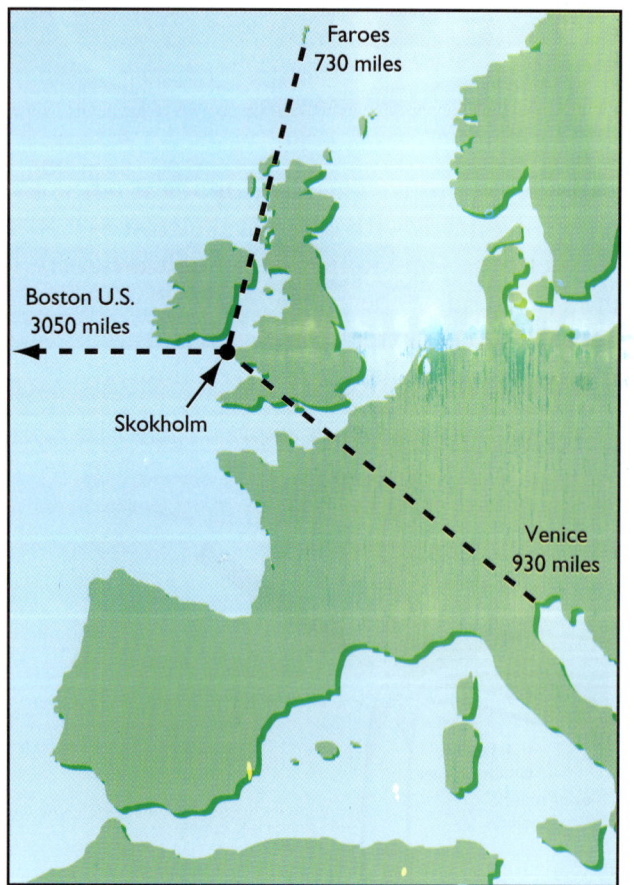

1. Suggest reasons why:
   a shearwater birds migrate in winter.
   b shearwaters return to the British Isles rather than stay near the equator.
2. List other groups of animals, other than birds, which migrate.
3. Do you think a bird's ability to orientate itself is learned from parents or is genetic? Suggest possible experiments which might test your ideas.

BODY CLOCKS

You may well have identified a problem that the Manx Shearwater has to overcome in solar navigation. How do the birds compensate for the sun's movement? The answer lies in the fact that like most living organisms, the birds have a body clock geared to the daily sun cycle. Every cell in the bird's body 'ticks' in what is called a **circadian rhythm.** The shearwater's internal clock enables it to maintain the correct bearings even though the sun moves across the sky.

Body clocks provide another survival 'sense' for living organisms. The rising and setting of the sun causes changes in temperature, humidity and light conditions. Being aware of these changes through an internal body clock helps an organism to avoid extreme conditions.

BEHAVING TO SURVIVE

Another advantage is that organisms can work in different time zones so that they avoid competing with each other. For example moths are active at night while their relatives, the butterflies, make maximum use of the daylight.

OTHER METHODS OF NAVIGATION

Not all animals rely on the sun for navigation. Many birds migrate at night. Evidence that the stars act as the guide comes from a series of experiments carried out in the Bremen planetarium in Germany. A husband and wife team, the Shauers, watched the way in which caged warblers orientated themselves under a projection of the night sky onto the planetarium roof. If the direction of the projection was changed, then the birds reorientated themselves. They were able to simulate the night sky for several of the places on their route to the wintering grounds and the birds always directed themselves appropriately. That was until the star pattern of the sky above the south Nile was projected. At this point the birds went to sleep. As far as the birds were concerned, they had 'arrived' at their final destination even though they were still in Bremen.

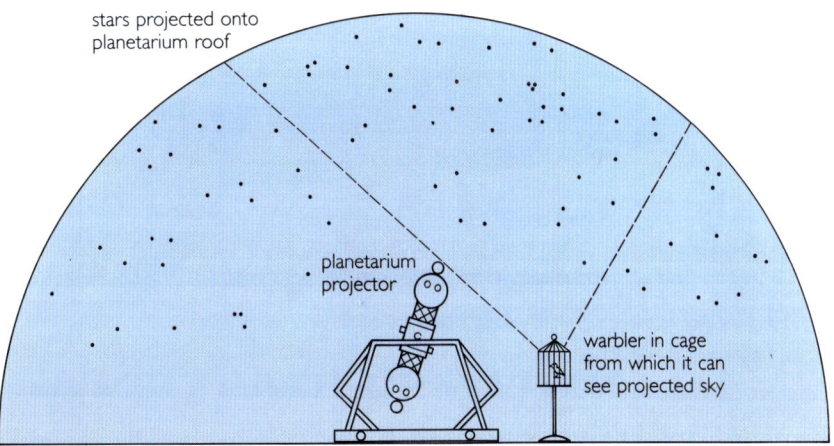

4 The reference in this section to the sun's movement isn't scientifically correct. Why?

5 Living organisms respond to changes in day-length. Carry out research into one organism's response. Identify the stimulus, sensor, co-ordinator and effector.

6 Design an experiment which might test a homing pigeon to see if it navigated using magnetism.

SENSORY BACK-UP SYSTEMS

Some birds have to postpone their flying when the sky is overcast because of their dependence on the sun or stars. Other birds, like robins and pigeons, have been found to have a magnetic sense which enables them to continue navigation using the Earth's magnetic field.

STAYING ALIVE

QUESTIONS

1 The diagrams show the same eye in different conditions.

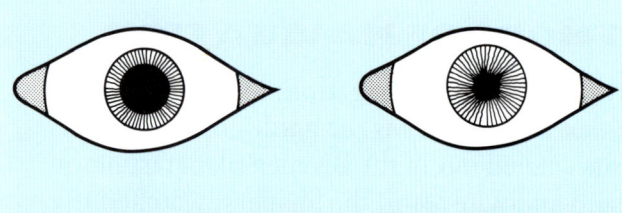

a i Copy the diagrams and label the pupil on one of the eyes.
ii What may have caused the eye to change? Explain why this response is necessary.
iii How much control do you have over this change?

b The part of the eye which is shaded in the diagram is blue. The dominant gene (allele) for eye colour is brown (represented by B). The recessive gene (allele) for eye colour is blue (b).
i Write down what 1, 2, 3 are.

	gene from		
child	father	mother	genotype
W	B	B	BB
X	B	b	1
Y	b	2	Bb
Z	b	b	3

ii What colour eyes do the mother and father have? Explain why.
iii Which child (if any) could have blue eyes? Explain why.

2 The diagram shows three plant stems, **A**, **B** and **C**, at the start and end of an experiment.

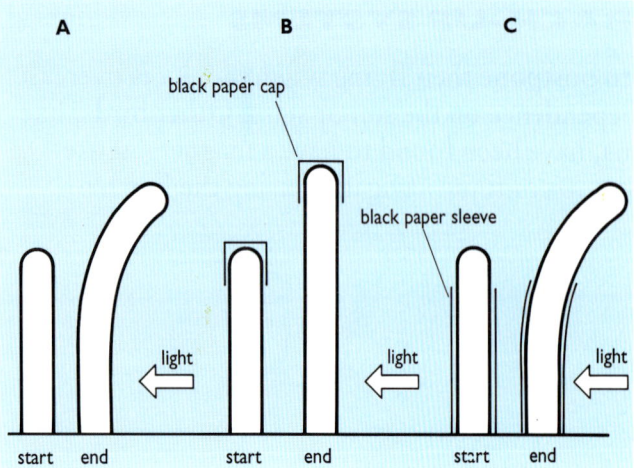

a What does this experiment suggest about which region of a plant stem is sensitive to the stimulus of light? Give reasons for your answer.
b Explain what causes the plant stem to bend towards the light.
c Suggest how this response is beneficial to plants.

3 The diagram shows the skeleton and some muscles of a human arm.

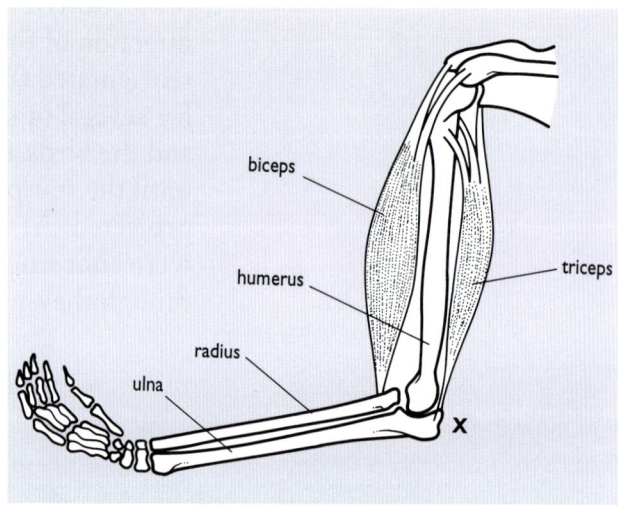

a Which labelled part bends the arm.
b Explain, using names given in the diagram, how the bent arm could be straightened again.
The diagram below shows a simplified synovial joint similar to the one found at **X**.

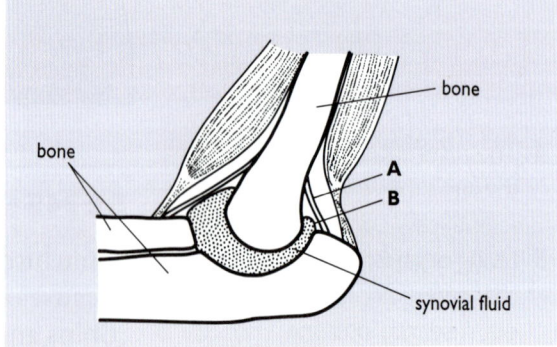

c i Where does the cartilage occur?
ii What is the function of the cartilage?
iii Suggest names for **A** and **B** on the diagram.
iv Suggest what might happen if the synovial fluid was not there.

3 WHAT FUTURE FOR LIFE?

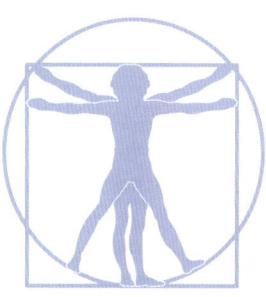

Contents
Evolution via technology
What future for elephants?
The sea: a healthy future?
Enough food for everyone?
How long will you live?
A question of research?
Questions

Human beings have altered the Earth's environment to such a degree that many people fear for the future. This chapter takes a case study approach to some of the more pressing health and environmental problems which face us. It provides an opportunity to apply some of your existing knowledge in new ways.

The human created environment of Hong Kong.

STAYING ALIVE

EVOLUTION VIA TECHNOLOGY?

1. Few people would disagree that humans (Homo sapiens) have been one of the most successful species on Earth. Although a relative newcomer to the planet, Homo sapiens have managed to survive in every ecosystem on Earth as well as in space.

2. The body of humans evolved through natural selection. However, because of their enlarged brain, Homo sapiens have been able to take things a step further and have developed technologies which enable them to take more control of their own environment. Early humans were able to develop tools which assisted them in improving their adaptation to the 'Hunter-gather' life. The development of settled agricultural communities was possible because humans had learned to domesticate animals and plants. The development of language and writing meant that learning could be passed from generation to generation.

3. Scientific investigations mean that we are improving our understanding of the physical, chemical and biological processes all the time. This understanding has been used to overcome the limitations of our bodies. For example the development of optical instruments like the telescope and microscope mean we can 'see' much more than our ancestors, the development of transport systems means that we can move at speeds our great grandparents would have thought impossible.

4. This human-created 'evolution' continues at an even faster pace. Developments particularly in microelectronics and genetic engineering are changing our world by the minute. For many people such technological changes are welcomed as 'progress' for humankind. Other people say that these developments make them worry about the future of life on Earth.

Genetic engineering could help feed the world claim scientists

Concern over new developments in embryo research

Artificial intelligence: could it replace the human brain?

WHAT FUTURE FOR LIFE?

1 In simple terms, describe the processes which will have led to the evolution of *Homo sapiens*. (see page 3)

2 Brainstorm a list of technologies which affect our lives. (e.g. electricity, immunisation, the petrol engine). Identify the advantages and disadvantages to you and your family.

TECHNOLOGY . . . GOOD OR BAD?

Here is a list of viewpoints about the future of the Earth.

h. Developments in genetic engineering mean that new breeds of cattle, sheep, cereal, vegetables and fruit can be produced. It will mean more food with greater variety for everyone.

e. Our over-consumption of fossil fuels means that the world will be seriously short of energy within our lifetime.

d. There is more and more waste that isn't bio-degradable. I don't think it will be very long before the countryside becomes one big rubbish dump.

k. Acid rain and greenhouse gases are threatening life on the planet.

l. Better education for more people will reduce the problems of over-population because people won't need or want big families.

a. Because of our exploitation of the environment, the number of species which are disappearing is increasing at an alarming rate.

j. Population control will be achieved through natural means as it has done throughout history. Famine is not a new phenomenon and these days we have AIDS instead of plague that's all.

f. Developments in fuel cell technology, wind and solar power mean a future of cheaper, safe power sources.

i. Its great how recycling has really taken off in this country. Did you know that they are even breeding bacteria to digest plastics these days?

c. Remember the smog in the '50s? New laws and new anti-pollution equipment mean that we all live in a much cleaner environment now.

g. There is a world population explosion which will mean too many mouths to feed and not enough food to do it.

b. The potential for stimulating evolution is enormous since scientists have learned how to create new organisms by transferring genes between different species.

3 **a** Group the statements above into optimistic and pessimistic views.

b Pair statements from each group so that each pair represents opposing views on an issue e.g. *a* and *b*.

c For each pair of opposing views show where you stand on the issue using a 4 point scale as follows:

Pessimistic	1 2 3 4	Optimistic
View a		View b

d Try to give reasons and provide evidence for your answers in **c**.

STAYING ALIVE

WHAT FUTURE FOR ELEPHANTS?

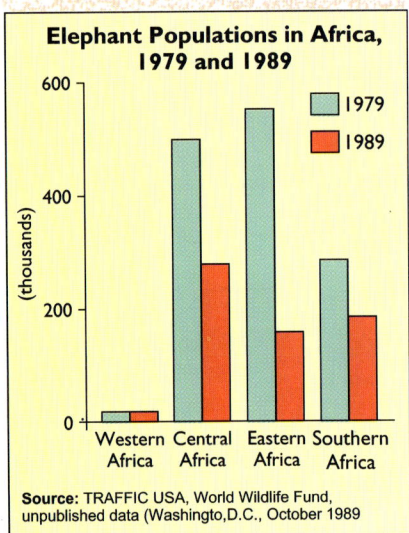

All the world's civilisations have used the products of wild animals and plants for their own ends. The problem is, can this be done without threatening the extinction of some species?

People have been worried about the future of the African elephant for many years. Look at the graphs which show the fall in population size. These figures led the Convention on International Trade in Endangered Species (CITES) to impose a ban on ivory trading in 1989 in an attempt to protect the African elephant, the world's largest land mammal. Conservationists believe that this ban has successfully stopped the mass elephant killings and ivory poaching which swept Africa in the 1980s. However, this is not the end of the story. By the mid 1990s there was pressure from some countries to reintroduce ivory trading in a limited way. The reasons are complex and are explained in the magazine article (left).

TO BAN OR NOT TO BAN?

July 1996

SOME archaeologists claim that it was hunting which pushed the North American mammoth to extinction. Today many conservationists feel that the mammoth's modern relatives, the African elephants could be in for a similar fate if the ban on ivory trading is lifted.

The row about banning the ivory trade won't go away. Now it is governments in Southern Africa who want to lift the ban because they claim that they now have too many elephants!

In Zimbabwe, scientists claim that in their conservation parks there are now 25 000 elephants too many. They fear that this will lead to destruction of the very environment on which the elephants rely. To make matters worse, some hungry elephant herds are now damaging and eating the crops of neighbouring farmers. The Zimbabweans plan to cull 5000 elephants a year which they argue is necessary to manage the population properly. Culling is seen as a necessary evil in much land management but the culling of elephants is seen by many to be a quite different issue. There has been international uproar about the action in Zimbabwe. This has been given further fuel after Zimbabwe and 5 other South African countries made a bid to alter the ivory trading ban. They want ivory trade to be permitted in a very regulated way. They argue that they need to make money by 'farming' elephants so that they can pay for their work in conservation. Other countries in East Africa feel that a return of the ivory trade will cause the return of poachers who did so much to damage their thriving tourist industry.

WHAT FUTURE FOR LIFE?

1 Why is culling a "necessary evil" in some game parks?
2 List the advantages and disadvantages of ivory trading.
3 Write a letter to the editor of a wildlife magazine to state your views on the subject of elephant conservation.

COUNTING ELEPHANT POPULATIONS

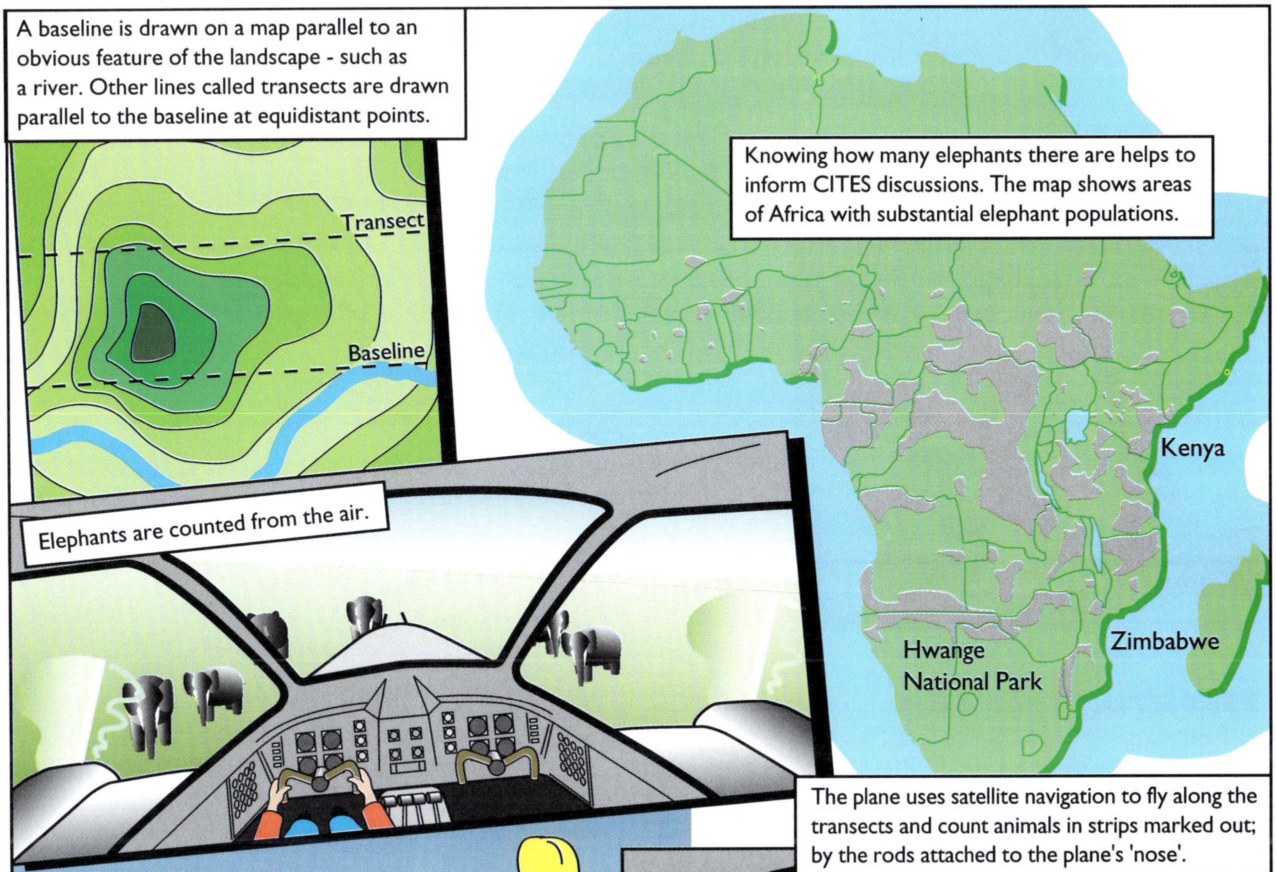

A baseline is drawn on a map parallel to an obvious feature of the landscape - such as a river. Other lines called transects are drawn parallel to the baseline at equidistant points.

Knowing how many elephants there are helps to inform CITES discussions. The map shows areas of Africa with substantial elephant populations.

Elephants are counted from the air.

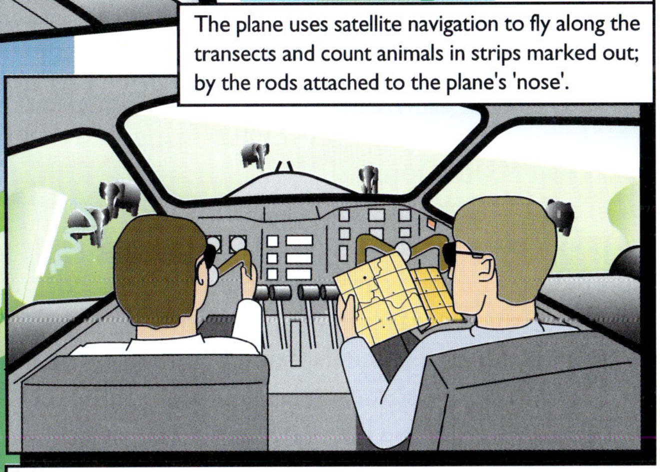

The plane uses satellite navigation to fly along the transects and count animals in strips marked out; by the rods attached to the plane's 'nose'.

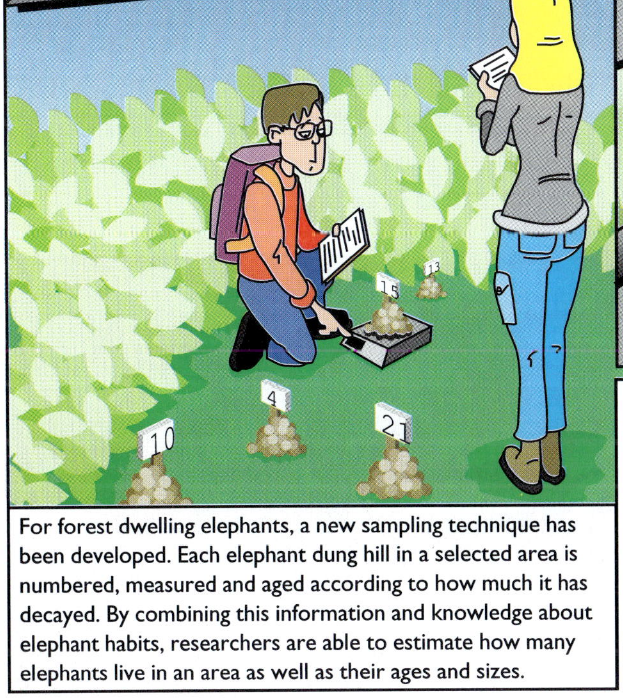

For forest dwelling elephants, a new sampling technique has been developed. Each elephant dung hill in a selected area is numbered, measured and aged according to how much it has decayed. By combining this information and knowledge about elephant habits, researchers are able to estimate how many elephants live in an area as well as their ages and sizes.

4 Why do scientists need to know the number and location of elephants?
5 Suggest reasons why the numbers of elephants along the river aren't counted.
6 List the different sampling techniques you have used to count numbers of animals in a habitat.

STAYING ALIVE

THE SEA: A HEALTHY FUTURE?

Since the sea is the world's largest ecosystem (occupying 70 per cent of the planet), its future could spell the future of the whole planet. For humans the sea acts as a hunting ground, a playground, a highway, a mine, a farm, a supermarket and a rubbish dump. Here we examine some of the environmental effects of one human activity: fishing.

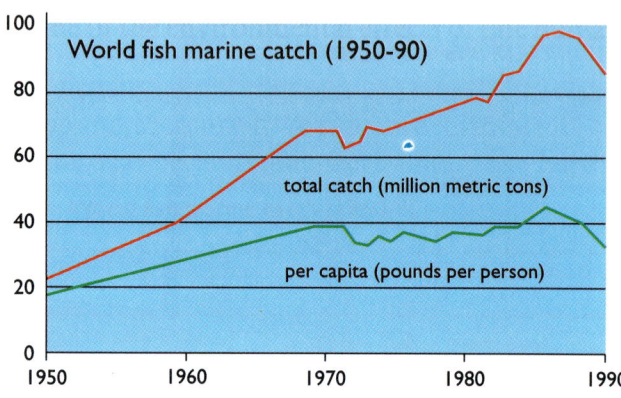

FISHING THE SEA

Look at the graph of the changes to the world marine fish catch. Increased catches do not mean that the numbers of fish in the sea have increased, it's just that fishing methods have improved. In fact several factors have resulted in changes to the wild fish populations:

a About 90 per cent of the world's fish population breeds along the coast. These breeding grounds are being rapidly reduced due to the increases in human population and the presence of industrial development.

b Coral reefs are some of the richest marine habitats. They are being destroyed by coral mining and blast fishing (where fish are forced from the coral cover by dynamite). Because they are filter feeders, increased sediment in the water is also killing coral with a knock-on effect to fish numbers.

c Increased competition between different countries to improve fish catches has caused fish numbers to fall. New fishing nets have much smaller holes to increase the catches too.

Such pressures have forced many countries to introduce a quota system to limit fishing in their coastal waters.

d Today the size of the average fish in many waters is considerably smaller. Scientists believe that this is a result of evolutionary pressure. The small fish are 'the ones that got away' and are therefore the fish who are successful in breeding.

WHAT FUTURE FOR LIFE?

FISH-FARMING

Many countries identified the problems of over-fishing in the 1980s and have invested in fish-farming. Today nearly 12 per cent of the world's fish catch comes from fish-farmers. Japan is the world's largest producer. Shrimps, salmon, prawns, bream and other species with a high market value are farmed along Japanese coastlines. Production has increased but so have some of the problems associated with any type of intensive farming.

The excrement from fish builds up around the fish cages (an average salmon farm produces the same amount of effluent as a town of 40 000 people). This waste, together with uneaten fish food, builds up to form a sludge which prevents the growth of the normal aquatic organisms. Instead it encourages the growth of toxic red algae which can kill fish and poison people who eat contaminated seafood. The Japanese have used antibiotics to deal with these problems. This has led to increased resistance of the harmful organisms to a range of antibiotics and has made people worry about the quality of fish from farms.

Another effect of intensive farming is the speed at which disease can spread through the farm population and then affect the wild population.

Fish hatcheries have been set up to try to overcome the hazards of intensive fish-farming. Here fish eggs are harvested in the wild, hatched and reintroduced to rivers whose fish populations are too low. Some environmentalists argue that this will mean further problems and result in a loss of species diversity.

1. Explain how natural selection is working to create smaller fish.
2. List reasons why the development of tourist industries can lead to decline in a country's fishing industry.
3. Conservationists say that tree felling on land causes increased sediment in the sea. Draw a flow chart to explain this link.
4. List the advantages and disadvantages of fish-farming.
5. Fertilisers affect the ecology of the sea in the same way as the rivers you studied in Book 1. Draw a flowchart to show what happens.
6. What is wrong with a reduction in species diversity
   a on the fish-farm?
   b in the wild?
7. Write sentences to list other environmental threats facing the sea.
8. Explain Rachel Carson's statement below.

Another way of looking at our link with the sea is reflected in the words of one of the first environmentalists, Rachel Carson:

> 'Each of us carries in our veins a salty stream in which the elements sodium, potassium and calcium are combined in almost the same proportions as in sea water. This is our inheritance from the day, untold millions of years ago, when a remote ancestor, having progressed from the one-celled to the many-celled, first developed a circulatory system in which the fluid was merely the water of the sea.'

STAYING ALIVE

ENOUGH FOOD FOR EVERYONE?

A farm is a man-made ecosystem which requires proper management if it is to provide for the needs of this couple. Examine the rest of the information on this page which identifies some of the management decisions that they will have to make.

How do we increase our crops so we can feed ourselves <u>and</u> raise cash for school fees?

How do we improve our yields <u>and</u> protect our land so that it continues to be fertile?

1 What are 'limiting factors' on photosynthesis?
2 The standing water of irrigation schemes present other environmental problems for the family. Explain what these might be.
3 Explain why microbes are important in compost production.
4 What problems might the couple create for the local environment if they begin to use chemical fertilisers?
5 Give some examples of different ways that plant hormones can improve production. (See Chapter 2).

PROBLEM 1: HOW TO IMPROVE OUR CROPS

There are several ways to do this:

a By increasing the rate of photosynthesis. For these farmers solar energy is not a limiting factor of growth. Irrigation schemes can help with water but these require investment of money and local planning agreements.

b By improving the availability of minerals needed for protein production. The couple do manufacture their own compost from the organic waste of the farm but there is not enough of it. They can buy industrial fertilisers but these are expensive.

c By applying plant growth hormones. Chemically produced auxins can increase the size of different vegetables but again, they are costly.

WHAT FUTURE FOR LIFE?

PROBLEM 2: HOW TO IMPROVE OUR ANIMAL PRODUCTION?

Some possibilities include:

a High protein foodstuffs. Again there is a finance problem. Not only is protein expensive but there is a big question about how cost effective meat is. To produce 1 kJ of energy from beef, 20 kJ of energy from grain is needed. Surely a poor family is better off being vegetarian?

b Hormone injections to increase yields. In the west there has been much controversy about the use of **anabolic steroids** by athletes. Similar hormones can be injected into animals to increase muscle size. Another hormone, **prolactin** is available which can produce increased milk production in cows.

6 What are proteins used for in an animal's body?
7 List the other foodstuffs which will have to be in the diet of an animal if it is to remain healthy. Write a sentence about the uses of each foodstuff for the animal body.
8 What is your response to the question about vegetarianism?

PROBLEM 3: BIOLOGICAL OR CHEMICAL PESTICIDE?

Pests are thought to destroy a third of the crops grown world-wide. Biological pest control was studied in Book 1. However, as we saw there, using the natural enemies of pests can get out of hand and cause even bigger problems for the farmer. Chemical pesticides have been an effective check on pests although in recent years there has been increasing concern because:

- the pest organisms have become increasingly resistant to the chemicals
- pesticides get into food chains and become more concentrated in the secondary and tertiary consumers. (For example DDT, which is still used in many developing countries has been shown to be responsible for the death of birds of prey in Britain.)
- pesticides can also kill the natural predators of the pests
- chemical pesticides can be harmful to humans who handle them
- chemical pesticides are costly for small farmers

PROBLEM 4: TRADITIONAL OR BIOENGINEERED CROPS?

In the 1970s people thought that the 'Green Revolution' would provide the answer to world hunger. High yield seeds were bred by artificial selection. Many scientists claimed that they would provide poor people with better crop yields. Unfortunately this dream was never realised because these varieties required more fertilisers and irrigation, something poor farmers in the Southern hemisphere couldn't afford. At the same time the new seeds had less resistance to the native pests which resulted in crop failure rather than increased production. Some people are worried that the new genetically engineered crops and animals will provide similar problems for poor farmers. Others believe that the lessons of the 1970s have been learned. They speculate that it will be possible to engineer crops which have a high resistance to drought, will have nitrogen-fixing bacteria attached to their roots and will have built-in resistance to disease.

9 Explain how pesticides can create problems for the tertiary consumers of a food chain.
10 Where do you stand on the issue of pesticides and why?
11 How might nitrogen-fixing bacteria in genetically engineered plants help reduce farming costs?
12 Describe with the aid of diagrams how a potato plant might be engineered so that it becomes more resistant to drought. (see page 23)
13 Use the information on this page to consider the future for this African family. What would you do to improve the farm if you were in their place?

STAYING ALIVE

HOW LONG WILL YOU LIVE?

	300 BC (Early Bronze Age)	150 BC (Iron Age)	650 BC (Classical Greece)	120 AD (Imperial Rome)	1400 AD (Middle Ages)	1820 AD (Post Napoleonic)	1990 AD (Today)
Male life expectancy	33.7	38.6	45.0	40.2	37.7	40.2	70.0
Height in cms	166.3	166.7	169.8	169.0	169.3	169.8	175.0
Female life expectancy	29.5	31.3	36.2	34.6	31.1	37.3	76.0
Height in cms	153.0	154.6	156.3	156.7	157.0	157.6	162.7
No. of births	4.0	3.7	4.3	3.7	4+	3.8	2.2
No. of survivors	1.9	1.5	2.7	2.0	1.6	2.2	2.0
Dental lesions	4.9	6.0	1.0	24.0	10.0	36.0	8.0
World population	?	?	?	?250m	300m	900m	5,000m

How long do you think you'll live? Look at the chart showing life expectancy. What are your chances in comparison with your ancestors? The cause of ageing is still not known. One theory is that as you get older, you accumulate more and more errors in your DNA. This is probably due to background radiation, chemical oxidation and faults in copying made by dividing cells. Just like photocopying photocopies, the message carried by the DNA will become more and more blurred as the machinery ages!

Changed life expectancy has resulted in a different age profile in Britain (see the chart below).

1. Make a list of some of the reasons for changes in life expectancy between 1820 and 1990.
2. An elderly relative wants to know why their body isn't as good as it used to be. Writer a letter including diagrams to explain.
3. The change in the age profile has many consequences for the British economy. Suggest what some of them are.
4. Find out what the most common causes of death are in the Western world (see Book 1).

	1840	1880	1920	1940	1990
0-14	36%	36%	26%	24%	19%
15-29	28	26	28	19	22
30-44	18	18	21	23	21
45-59	11	13	15	18	20
60-74	6	6	8	12	12
75	1	1	2	4	6

NEW PARTS FOR OLD

The huge development in surgery have meant that we can 'replace' parts of our body. The diagram opposite lists some of the treatments which are now available.

5 a Surgery is expensive. If you controlled the health budget for a hospital, which surgery would you give priority to? Look at the types in the diagram and work out a priority list.

b Would the age of a person affect your decisions in part a?

WHAT FUTURE FOR LIFE?

Hair Transplant An instrument is used to remove pieces of scalp from hairier parts of the head and spread the growth of hair.

Bones of the middle ear Plastic replicas of these delicate structures can assist some people who are deaf.

Jaws These can be replaced with a plastic replica

Heart pacemaker This tiny battery operated device provides a reliable alternative for those patients whose natural pacemaker has slowed down. It is implanted in the chest and ensures a regular heart beat. (see page 176 in Book 1)

Elbow joints Porous metal implants are used in this complex joint. The living bone grows into this implant to form a strong bond.

Liver transplants These are still a developing area of surgery although the success rate is improving.

Finger joints Plastic implants can replace the bones damaged by arthritis

Vagina In male to female sex changes, the amputated penis can be turned inside out and sown into the lower abdomen to form a vagina.

Eye lens replacement Doctors cut a slit in the eye capsule and can then pop out the lens. A new clear plastic lens is then inserted.

Face Faces disfigured by cancer or accidents can be reconstructed. Tissue containing arteries and veins close together is taken from another part of the body. Blood vessels in the transplant are joined to those in the face.

Heart Transplants are now much more successful because of improved anti-rejection drugs.

Lungs Transplants are possible but are more successful when done in conjunction with a heart transplant because of all the complex plumbing between heart and lungs.

Heart valves These ensure the correct direction of blood flow in the heart. Transplants from other human or animal hearts are possible but artificial replacements are likely to last longer. The latest valves are made from polyester.

Kidneys These were the first organs to be transplanted successfully.

Hip joint Now a routine replacement (for more details see pages 162–3)

Penis Men who can no longer gain an erection can have an inflatable tube implanted in their penis. A fluid filled sac is then put inside the scrotum and the man is able to inflate his penis by squeezing the scrotum.

Knee joints Plastic surfaces are used to replace damaged or diseased natural ones.

Thermograph of a human body showing temperature variation.

STAYING ALIVE

A QUESTION OF RESEARCH?

Scientific research which uses living animals has always been a focus of controversy. Look at the three viewpoints represented on this page and use them to form your own opinion on the matter.

Anti-vivisectionists

We believe that all experimenting on animals is wrong. Animals have got rights as well as humans. They are living things just as we are, yet scientists treat them as if they are unfeeling bits of equipment. You've heard of racism, well scientists are speciesists! They wouldn't carry out their experiments on humans, why should they do it on helpless animals?

We know that people say that the animals save human lives in the end but surely a rat or a mouse is quite different to a human anyway. There are lots of drugs on the market which showed no benefits to animals and yet they help humans. Where is the logic?

Do you know about the Draize test for cosmetics and household products? It uses live rabbits and tests the products on their eyes! Apparently there are techniques now using human tissue cultures where you can do the tests on real human cells where no living thing needs to get hurt. Cosmetics are advertised which have not been tested on animals so why can't all companies adopt these methods? I bet the researchers would be horrified if someone did experiments on their own pets yet they are prepared to make other animals suffer.

There's another development in biotechnology which really worries us too. Now as well as factory farming for food, they are using the bodies of animals to produce drugs. There are sheep being engineered so that their milk contains drugs which can then be extracted and sold for medical purposes. Don't ask me how they do it, but I know its happening.

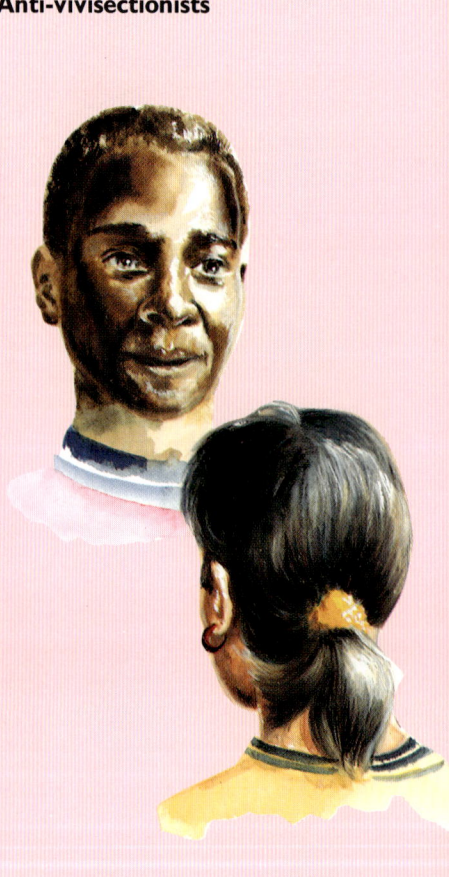

These animals rights people really don't know what they are on about. Don't they realise that the enormous advances in medicine in the last century have only been possible because of research using animals? The drugs we now have to control ulcers, strokes, epilepsy, high blood pressure and many other diseases have been possible because of animal experiments. How many of them suffer from asthma? We bet they wouldn't be without their inhaler which will have gone through animal tests. There is still so much illness and disease in the world. Stopping animal experiments would slow down the rate

Vivisectionists

WHAT FUTURE FOR LIFE?

There have been some very positive developments in the field of animal testing which have benefitted animals *and* humans. A new Act of Parliament in 1986 put much stricter controls on vivisection. All places where these experiments are carried out have to be registered and so do the scientists who are involved. There are inspectors who supply licences which allow each type of experiment to proceed. Experiments are only allowed if the balance of benefit to human suffering outweighs the animal suffering. These inspectors carry out regular checks to make sure that government guidelines in the Act are being followed. Animal houses have to be kept under specified conditions suitable for the animals. Laboratory animals have much better conditions than the average farm animal.

There's no doubt that the Law has reduced animal experiments so we feel sure that it is only those experiments which are really necessary which now take place. Today lots more research is done on human tissue culture. However, this isn't helpful when you want to look at some of the sophisticated systems of the body so there's going to be the need for vivisection in the foreseeable future.

Pragmatists

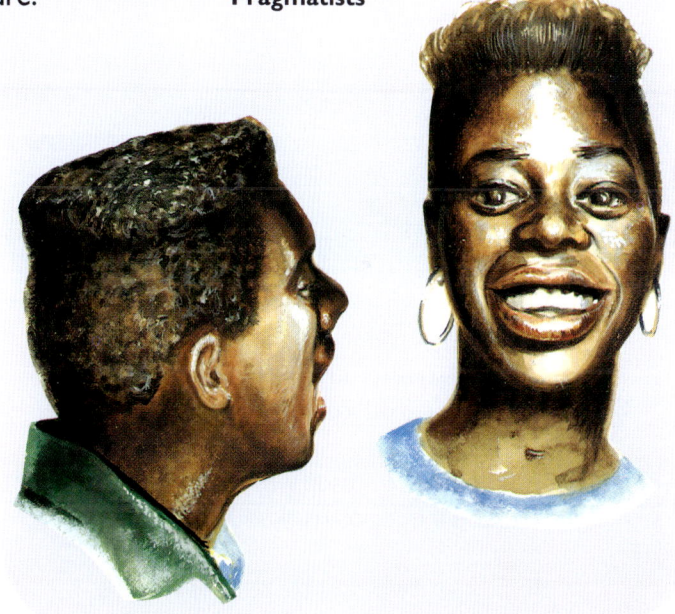

of progress in most medical fields. Yes we know that there are new tissue culture methods and even computer simulations but would 'tested on a computer and it worked' make you feel secure about a new drug? Anyway how far are these anti-vivisectionists prepared to go? Are they against using flies and worms or is it just the cuddly animals they object to? Did you know that a large part of what we know about genetic disease comes from studying and killing fruit flies? The animal libbers make a big thing of how equal animals are and yet they'd soon be round to the doctors if they had worms!

1 For each couple list the main points in their argument.
2 Try to match the arguments of the vivisectionist with opposing views of the anti-vivisectionist.
3 Carry out your own classroom debate on the issue. Where do you stand now?
4 Human tissue culture is mentioned several times. What is it?

STAYING ALIVE

QUESTIONS

1 The maps below show the distribution of the red squirrel and of the grey squirrel in 1940 and in 1970.

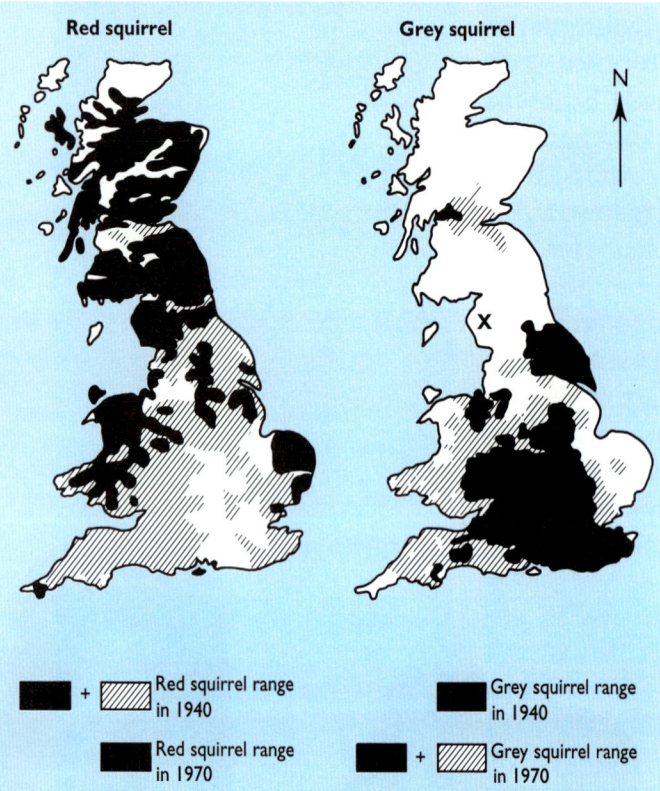

a What changes took place in the distribution of the red squirrel between 1940 and 1970?
b The red squirrel is native to Britain. The grey squirrel was introduced into Britain during the nineteenth century.
   i Suggest **one** reason why the grey squirrel is not found in the region marked **X** on the right-hand map.
   ii Suggest **two** possible reasons why the introduction of the grey squirrel into Britain might have affected the distribution of the red squirrel.
c Suggest **two** possible ways of making sure that the red squirrel does not die out in Britain.

2 At a plant breeding station, barley plants were crossed to produce improved varieties. Certain features of four varieties **A**, **B**, **C** and **D** are described in the following table.

Feature	Variety A	Variety B	Variety C	Variety D
Yield	very high	high	medium	low
Resistance to disease	low	high	high	low
Resistance to water shortage	low	low	high	low
Height (cm)	100	30	30	30

a Why would variety **A** be unsuitable in very windy regions?
b Use the information in the table above to suggest a variety most suitable for the following regions:
   i Very low rainfall, windy and a high number of pests
   ii High rainfall, very windy and a medium number of pests
   iii High rainfall, low wind and a low number of pests

3 The table below shows the concentration of a 'greenhouse gases' in 1850 and 1985 and their estimated concentration in 2050.

	Concentration in parts per million in each year		
Greenhouse gas	1850	1985	2050
Carbon dioxide	275	345	400–600
Methane	0.7	1.7	2.1–4.0
Nitrous oxide	0.29	0.30	0.35–0.45
CFC 11*	0	0.22	0.7–3.0

*CFC 11 is a chlorofluorocarbon   (adapted from Science, 1988)

a Give **one** reason why the concentration of carbon dioxide has increased since 1850.
b Which gas is estimated to have the greatest percentage increase between 1985 and 2050? (Work this out approximately, you do not need to do an accurate calculation).
c Suggest why there was no CFC 11 in 1850.
d Once source of methane is the burying of garbage (household rubbish) in huge landfill sites. Suggest one way in which garbage disposal could help conserve scarce resources.
e The projections to the year 2050 were made in 1988. Which projection do you think may now be much too high? Give a reason for your answer.

50

SECTION 2

MAKING MATTER

MAKING MATTER

IMPORTANT MATTERS

... and you've studied many of this century's famous scientists. This video clip you're going to see is about one of them, Richard Feynman. I know from your projects that one or two of you have seen the Horizon programmes which showed his life story, and some of you have borrowed his biography from the library.

When the clip finishes I'm going to ask you to discuss what Richard Feynman says, so listen carefully ...

If all scientific knowledge were lost in some terrible disaster, what single statement would preserve the most information for the next generation of creatures? How could we best pass on our understanding of the world?

I think I'd choose this statement: All things are made of atoms – little particles that move around in perpetual motion attracting each other when they are a little distance apart, but repelling upon being squeezed into one another.

Now I want you to break into groups of about 4. Someone in each group will need to be the group reporter. Discuss Richard Feynman's "super statement". Agree an explanation of what it means and give some examples of the statement in practice.

All things are made of **atoms**. Atoms are tiny particles, too small to see with the naked eye. The ancient Greeks first had the idea that you'd eventually get to a point where you couldn't break up a substance any more and that you'd be left with tiny unbreakable particles. That's where the name atom came from – from the Greek word for those unbreakable particles (atomos). It was many hundreds of years before we had any proof that atoms really exist. Atoms can join together in clumps called **molecules**. If the atom is in a molecule are the same, then the substance is called an **element**. Where *different* molecules are joined together the substance is called a **compound**.

52

MAKING MATTER

The elements can be arranged in the Periodic Table. That puts elements in order of **atomic number**, and the pattern of their position in the table summarises a great deal of information about their properties. We can use that information to make reliable predictions about the properties of compounds of the elements, too. the horizontal rows are called **periods**, the vertical colums are called **groups**.

Atoms have a nucleus surrounded by **electrons**, which are negative charges. Most of an atom is space: the electrons move around the nucleus almost like planets around the Sun. The paths of the electrons are called orbits: sometimes we describe them as energy levels or shells.

The nucleus is made up from particles called **neutrons** which have no charge, and **protons**, which have a positive charge. Protons and neutrons each have a mass of 1 atomic unit (**amu**): compared to them, electrons have so little mass that we ignore it.

In an atom the charges are balanced. There will be about the same number of electrons as there are protons. In the Periodic Table the atoms are arranged in order of the number of protons (the atomic number). So, as you move across the table from one element to the next, you know that there's one more proton and one more electron. The electrons are the ones involved in chemical reactions, so knowing about the number of electrons and how they are arranged, tells us something about the way in which an element will react.

In the same row (or period) of the table each added electron goes in the same energy level (or shell). By looking at the table, you know that the element in the first period will have one electron shell (which is full when it has two electrons). For period 2 atoms, electron shell 2 is being filled with electrons. So, you know that the third atom in period 2 will have 3 electrons: two electrons in shell number one, and one electron in the outer shell.

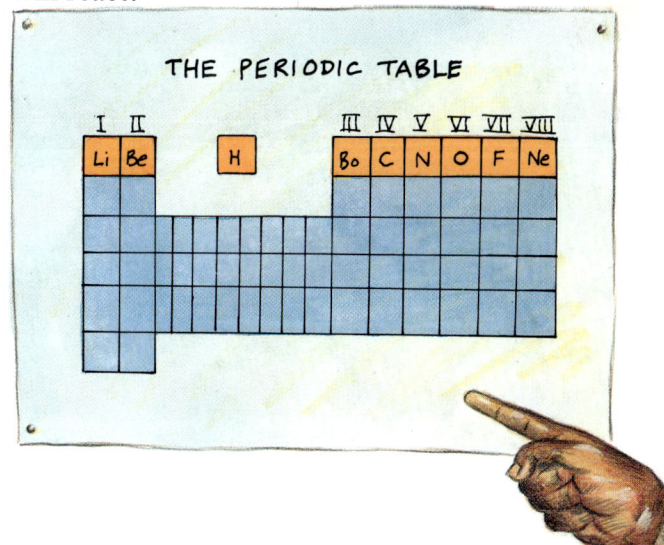

MAKING MATTER

The particles in substances are moving. This is called the **Kinetic Theory**. In solids the particles are close together and just moving. In a liquid, they are free to move, but are still quite close together. In a gas, the particles are very far apart and fast moving. Changing from the solid state to the liquid state is called **melting**. Boiling is what happens when a liquid changes to a gas (or vapour).

I can see that most of you have nearly finished. Recorders, make sure that you have a record of the explanations from your group. I'll give you a few minutes to get ready to present your ideas to the class. First, I want to set your homework. In the light of our discussions and any other research of your own, I'd like you to decide what statement you'd choose if you were asked the same question as Richard Feynman.

1. If you had been in the class as these pupils, you'd probably have made many of the same suggestions. For each suggestion the groups made, write a summary for yourself, adding any extra information you think should be there. (For some of them you might have to look back at work you've done before. That's allowed!)

2. The text didn't eavesdrop on any discussions about a number of scientific explanations. Imagine that you were in the groups where each of the following was being discussed: write down your own explanations for
   a metals and non-metals
   b polymers
   c chemical reactions
   d ions and electrolysis.

3. Look back to the homework that was set for the class. What statement would **you** choose? Why? Compare ideas with some others. If there is time you might be able to survey ideas and look for patterns in replies.

4. There is a story that the young Richard Feynman never got a satisfactory reply to this question that he asked his science teacher:
"How do sharp things stay sharp all this time if the atoms are always jiggling?"
How would you answer the question?

4 TAKE ONE PLANET

As time has gone by, humans have developed more sophisticated technology. This has helped us to build up whole-planet patterns of events on Earth. We have been able to study other planets and compare them to Earth, and sometimes improve our knowledge of Earth as a result.

In this chapter you will learn about our developing understanding of the planet Earth and its atmosphere. You will learn about our attempts to get information about other planets, and how this has affected our understanding.

Contents
Heavy weather
Predictable planets
Adventures in space
Space: the final frontier?
Planet Earth unmasked
In the melting pot
Questions

Ancient Chinese star maps.

MAKING MATTER

HEAVY WEATHER

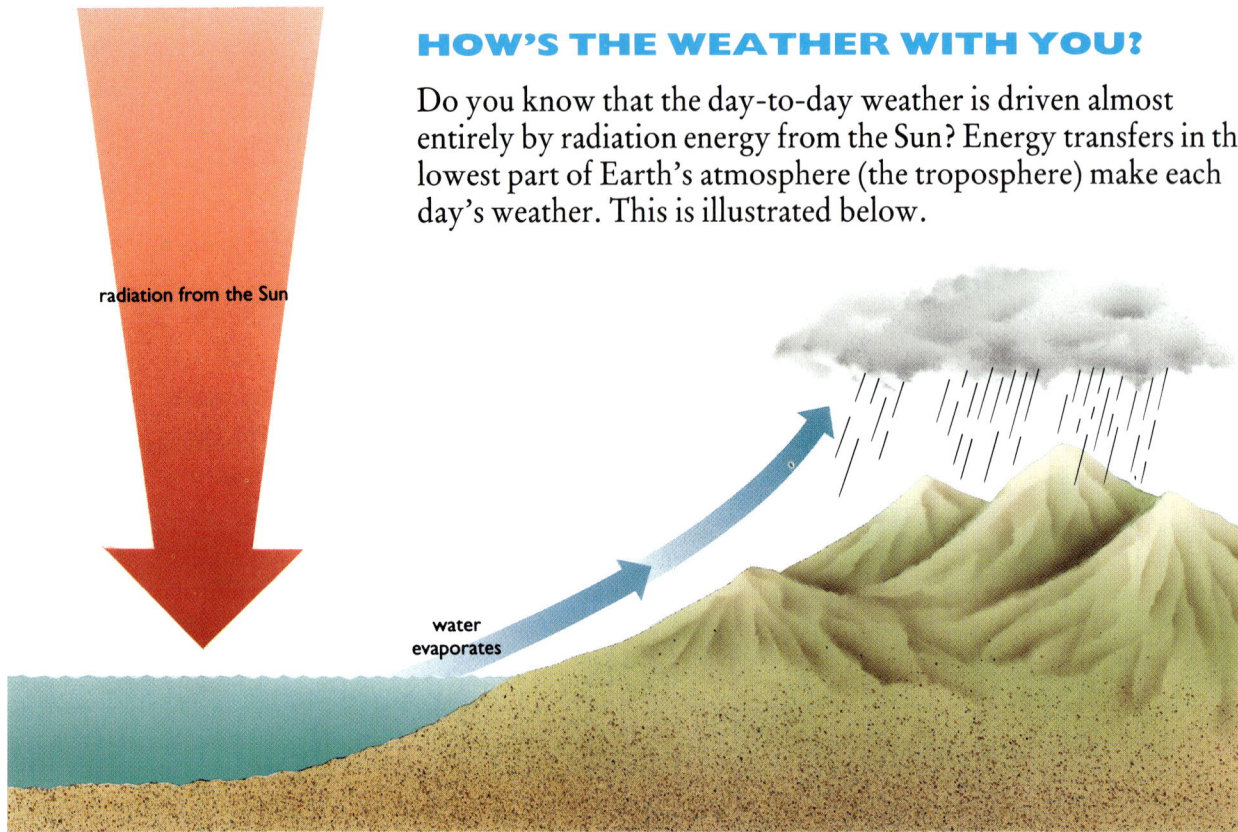

HOW'S THE WEATHER WITH YOU?

Do you know that the day-to-day weather is driven almost entirely by radiation energy from the Sun? Energy transfers in the lowest part of Earth's atmosphere (the troposphere) make each day's weather. This is illustrated below.

Circulating warm air in the picture above carries water vapour from the sea. The air stays clear until the water vapour begins to condense into drops. Small drops make clouds, bigger drops make rain. Air gets cooler as it goes higher. Where the air meets a hill and has to climb up, it gets cooler and rain falls.

Warm air rises and moves towards the poles. It is replaced by cold air moving towards the equator. These currents are the prevailing winds. The prevailing winds are overtaken by the rotating Earth. Instead of blowing at right angles to the equator, they blow diagonally.

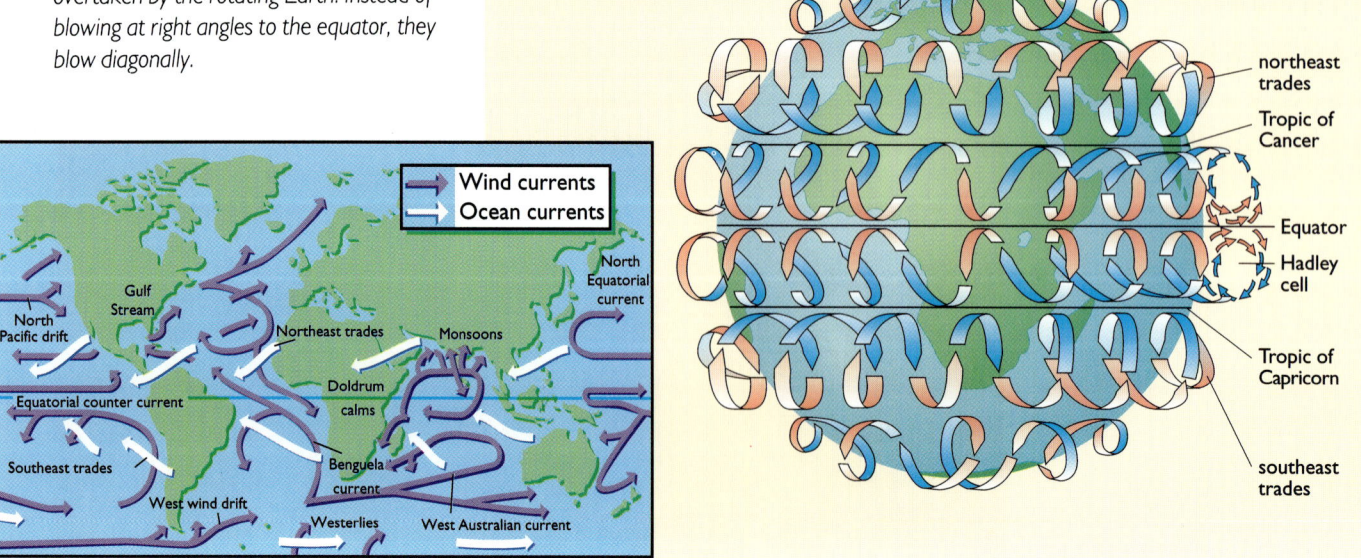

arrows show the pattern of air circulation

56

TAKE ONE PLANET

CIRCULATION WARS?

Energy from the Sun is absorbed mainly in the tropics and near the equator. Some of the energy causes circulation patterns in the atmosphere and the oceans. In the illustration you can see how ocean currents are affected by the land, and the way the prevailing winds are affected by the Earth's rotation.

THE CLIMATE JIGSAW PUZZLE

We now know that the oceans play a very important part in climate. There are currents at the surface and convection currents which transfer energy between the surface and the depths. Surface currents are caused by the prevailing winds blowing across the water. The Gulf Stream carries heat energy towards the north and east. It means that Britain has winters which are milder than most places at the same latitude.

In the Pacific, the circulation of atmosphere and ocean seems to have two different patterns. In one the surface water is warm in the west and cold in the east. In the other, the warm surface water is in the east, and the cold in the west. In both cases, the warm surface causes winds to blow into the warm region from the other side of the ocean. The winds push warm surface water into the warm region, exposing colder water from the deep ocean behind them. Scientists are still trying to understand why the circulation pattern changes, and to be able to predict when it does. The change of pattern brings far-reaching changes to the weather, as the following extract shows.

Drought hits Brazil as climate chaos spreads

WHAT links flooding in southern England, bush fires in New South Wales and famine in Brazil? The answer is El Niño: a reversal of winds and ocean currents across the Pacific which happens every four or five years. It usually lasts for about a year, but the 1991 El Niño is still going strong. This El Niño has been blamed for torrential rains from Japan to the Mississippi in 1993, droughts in southern Africa, New South Wales and northeast Brazil and record rains in Britain in January 1994.

The first signs of El Niño were when winds in western Pacific reversed in the summer of 1991. This brought drought and forest fires to Indonesia, and dry wheat fields in Australia. Other unusual weather conditions included a hurricane in Samoa in December, freak rainstorms and floods in California and Peru. In 1992 there were droughts in southern Africa.

By the end of 1993, some parts of northeast Brazil had had just a quarter of their normal rainfall since El Niño started in 1991. This is its worst drought this century and may bring the greatest suffering of the current El Niño.

Adapted from articles by Fred Pearce in New Scientist.

1 a Describe the energy transfers which take place at each stage in illustrations on these pages.
  b Explain what happens to the particles' spacing and energy.
2 If you stand on the sea-shore on a sunny day you can feel a cool breeze blowing from the sea.
  a Explain the air movements which cause the cool sea breeze.
  b Explain what you might notice if you stood in the same place when the sun had gone down.
3 a What were the first signs of El Niño?
  b From the data in the article, in which years should there be El Niños?
  c Explain how the changing currents could cause:
  i drought ii flooding.
4 In 1992 scientists were predicting that the 1991 El Niño was going to be severe. Were they correct? Explain your answer using evidence from as many sources as you can find. (You could work in groups to search out up-to-date information from the library or databases.)

MAKING MATTER

PREDICTABLE PLANETS

A view of Mars from the spacecraft Viking.

PROBING THE PLANETS

Before we had space probes, scientists used telescope observations to work out the size and mass of planets. The force of gravity with which a planet pulls on its moons, or on other planets, allowed scientists to work out its mass. Once mass and size are known its possible to work out density.

Earth, Mars, Venus and Mercury have similar densities. Scientists predicted this was because they were alike. Like Earth, they seem to be made of rock and may have an iron core. Jupiter, Saturn, Uranus and Neptune have such low densities that they must be mainly gases or liquids. Pluto is a planet that we know very little about yet. Scientists think it's small and solid, made of rock and ice.

As each year goes by, we learn more about the planets. The information comes from spacecraft and from instruments used on Earth. As technology improves, we can get better information.

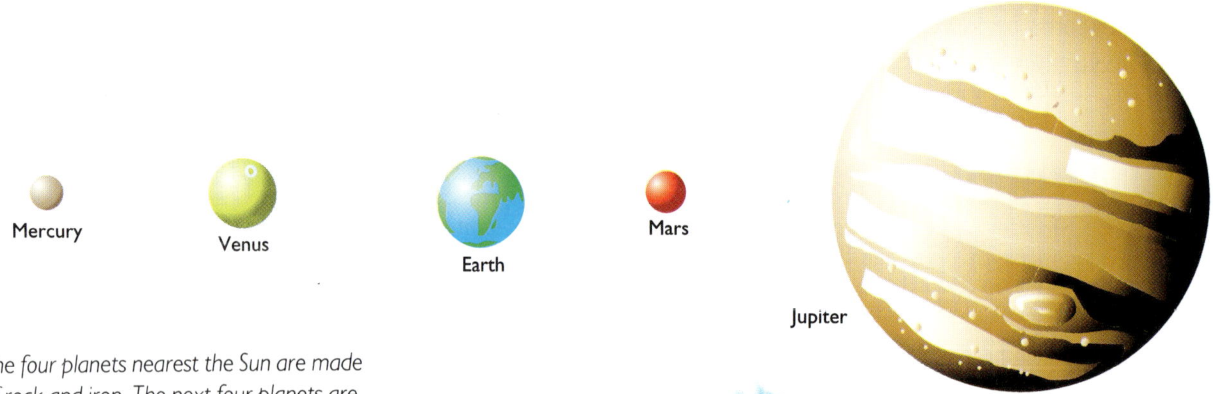

Mercury Venus Earth Mars Jupiter

The four planets nearest the Sun are made of rock and iron. The next four planets are made of gases.

Saturn and its satellites photographed by Voyager.

If I can just find an Ocean big enough, I can get Saturn to float in Water.

58

TAKE ONE PLANET

Table 1

	diameter (km)	mass (Earth = 1)	density (water = 1)	surface gravity (Earth = 1)	average distance from Sun (million km)	Number of satellites	Main satellites (diameter in km)	Rings?
Mercury	4878	0.06	5.42	0.40	57.9	0	–	no
Venus	12 103	0.81	5.25	0.90	108.2	0	–	no
Earth	12 756	1.00	5.52	1.00	149.6	1	Moon (3476)	no
Mars	6794	0.11	3.94	0.40	227.9	2	Phobos (22) Deimos (12)	no
Jupiter	142 800	318.0	1.32	2.60	778.3	16	Ganymede (5262) Callisto (4800) Europa (3138) Io (3630)	yes
Saturn	120 660	95.0	0.69	1.10	1427.0	17	Titan (5150) Rhea (1530)	yes
Uranus	51 400	15.0	1.26	0.90	2869.6	15	Titania (1590) Oberon (1560)	yes
Neptune	49 400	17.0	1.64	1.20	4496.7	8	Triton (2720)	no
Pluto	5900	0.002	2.1	0.20	5900	1	Charon (1200)	no

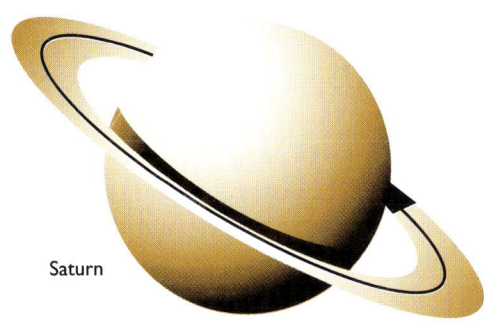
Saturn

Uranus

Neptune

Pluto

Table 2

	Time to spin on axis			Time to orbit Sun (years)
	days	hours	minutes	
Mercury	58	16		0.2
Venus	244	7		0.6
Earth		23	56	1.0
Mars		24	37	1.5
Jupiter		9	50	5.2
Saturn		10	14	9.5
Uranus		10	49	19.2
Neptune		15	48	30.1
Pluto	6	9	17	39.4

1 Mercury, Venus, Earth and Mars are described as **rocky dwarves**; Jupiter, Saturn, Uranus and Neptune are described as **gassy giants**. Explain why they have been given these descriptions.

2 Use the information in Table 1 to describe the patterns which link a planet's
   a density and distance from the Sun.
   b density and diameter.
3 Which planet does not fit the patterns in **2**?
4 Use the information in Table 2 to describe the pattern which link a planet's period of orbit and its distance from the Sun.
5 Study the cartoon. Do you agree with the character's view?
6 a Based on the information in Tables 1 and 2, on which planet apart from the Earth would humans find it easiest to live? Write down your reasons.
   b What other information would you need to decide whether human life was possible?
   c Compare you answers with someone else's.

MAKING MATTER

ADVENTURES IN SPACE

After a million and a half kilometre chase, travelling at 28 156 k.p.h the space shuttle Columbia catches up with a stranded satellite. Inside Columbia astronaut Bonnie Dunbar guides the mechanical arm to capture the satellite. It was January 1990 and the satellite was falling towards Earth at 800 m a day. Within weeks it would have burned up in the atmosphere, destroying all the data it had gathered.

Since the first satellite left Earth (a 'Sputnik' sent by the USSR) in 1957, humans have launched more than 3000 satellites. Now satellites fill the space around the Earth, kept there by the pull of gravity. As long as a craft moves at the correct speed to counteract the force of gravity it will stay up. Engineers design the craft, and its path, to do the job they need.

GETTING THE HANG OF IT

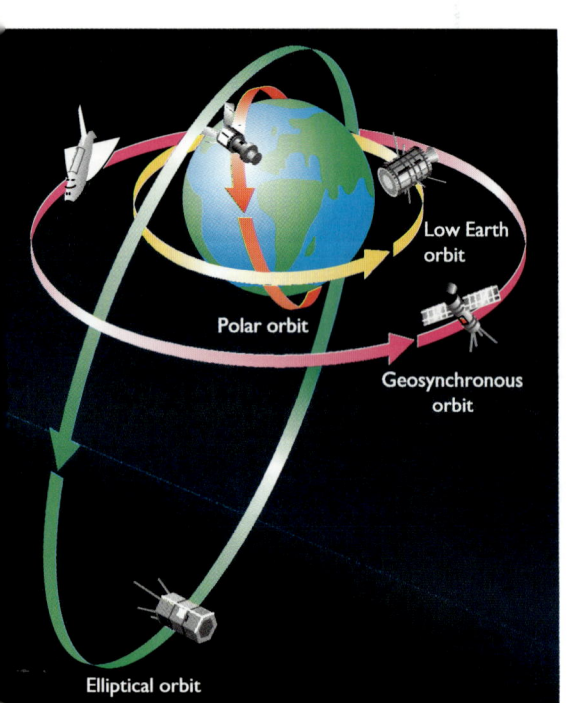

Geostationary (or geosynchronous) satellites orbit with Earth, so they stay over the same spot. A satellite with a low orbit will give detailed survey pictures of Earth. A higher orbit will allow it to survey larger areas.

If a satellite's speed is just enough to keep it up, its orbit will be nearly circular. Some satellites travel in an ellipse around Earth. A satellite like this will lose speed as it travels against the pull of gravity. At its furthest distance from Earth, gravity pulls it back: it accelerates towards Earth. By the time it gets to its nearest position to Earth, it is travelling fast enough to move away again. Using the interaction between gravity and the spacecraft's mass in this way is used to help long distance spacecraft reach the furthest planets.

The idea of geostationary orbit was first proposed in a story written by Arthur C. Clarke in 1974 and some people still call them Clarke orbits. In the film *Star Trek IV*, the crew of the Enterprise in a Klingon starship used an elliptical orbit of the Sun to build up enough speed to travel back in time!

TAKE ONE PLANET

Helen Harman answered an advert to be an astronaut with the Russian space programme. She was Britain's first 'cosmonaut'.

UP, UP

The diagram shows the path of two different balls. Ball A moves with the greatest speed. Now imagine a very high hill and a powerful ball thrower. The hill is so high you can see the curve of the Earth. Both balls still curve towards the Earth. The path of ball B follows the curve of the Earth. B is moving with the right speed and at the right distance to stay in orbit. Managing this trick on a much larger scale is the job of space engineers.

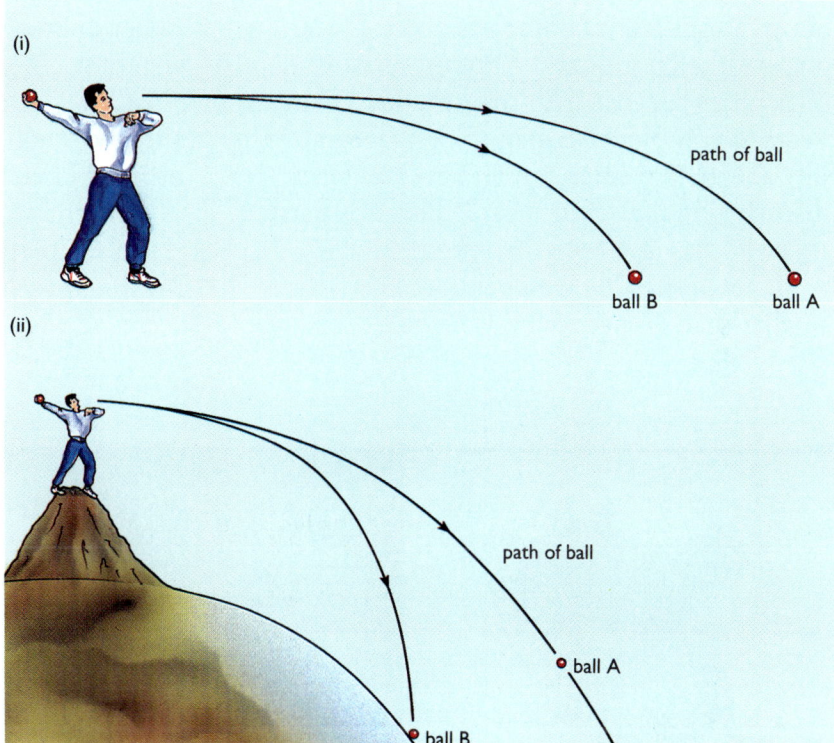

All rockets work on the same principle, though designs and fuel may differ. Burning fuels produces gases. The hot gases are forced through a nozzle to produce the force, or thrust. If the thrust is large enough the spacecraft will move away from Earth. Although the thrust may stay constant, the spacecraft will accelerate because its mass decreases as fuel is used and air resistance decreases.

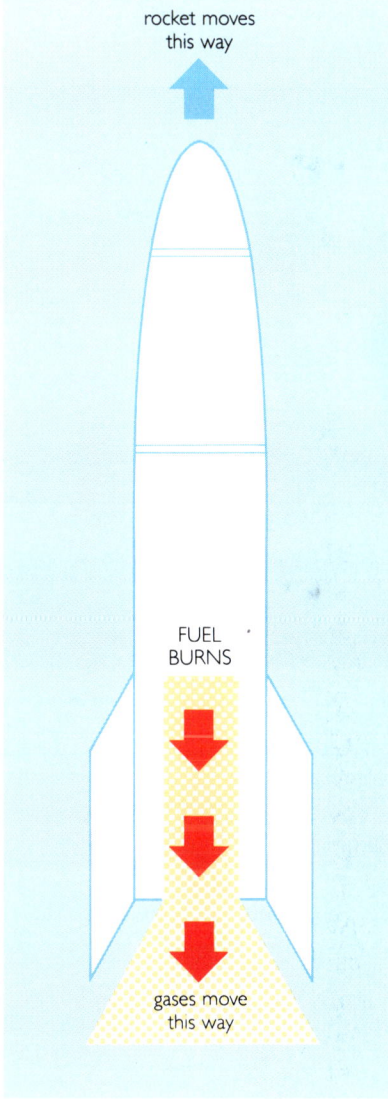

1. Use your understanding of force, mass and acceleration to explain why a spacecraft will accelerate as its fuel burns.
2. Explain why a craft like the satellite in the picture would burn up if it had not been rescued.
3. Imagine that you are one of the crew of the Enterprise, completing the ship's log during the time the spaceship is using the Sun's gravity to accelerate. Describe what is happening.

MAKING MATTER

SPACE: THE FINAL FRONTIER?

THE SEARCH FOR PLANET X

In the early 1900s Percival Lowell noticed that the orbit of Uranus seemed to be disturbed. He predicted that a new planet was causing the disturbance. He called it Planet X and estimated that its mass was 6.7 times greater than Earth's.

To calculate the orbit of planets scientists need observations from a complete orbit. Distant planets like Uranus and Neptune cause difficulties because their orbits take so many years to complete (see page 59). Spacecraft sent into the distant solar system have not been disturbed in their journeys. If Planet X existed, they should have been disturbed.

Planet X should be bigger than Earth but smaller than Neptune and Uranus. Its average distance from the Sun would be so great it would take a thousand years to make one orbit.

In 1983 the Infra-Red Astronomical Satellite (IRAS) made a survey of 70% of the sky. A Planet X big enough to disturb the orbit of Uranus should have produced enough infra-red radiation to be picked up by IRAS. There was no sign of it.

In 1989 Voyager 2 went to Neptune. Its data allowed scientists to explain Neptune's disturbed orbit. If Planet X exists it doesn't affect Neptune.

A recent prediction of Planet X's position puts it in a region of the sky surveyed by IRAS. Putting these two lines of research together seems to suggest that there is no Planet X.

Pioneer 10 and 11 were launched in the 1970s and are now on their way out of the Solar system. They have provided us with much new information on their journeys.

1 Some astronomers think that Pluto is not a real planet. What evidence could they use to support their argument?

2 **a** List evidence in support of Planet X.
   b List evidence against Planet X.
   c Do you think Planet X exists? Have you got enough evidence?

3 One explanation for the spacecrafts' undisturbed journeys was that Planet X would be too far from them. What do you think the reason could be, and why?

4 Find out more about Planet X, by going to the magazine section of a library, or a CD-ROM database. The Planet X story has been written about in New Scientist. (Try the issues of 22/29 December 1990 [Ken Croswell] & 30 November 1991 [Nigel Henbest]).

TAKE ONE PLANET

LIFE IN SPACE

For as long as we have been exploring space, many scientists have dreamt of space stations that could support life in space. The USSR made this a reality with the Salyut space station. Others' dreams have gone further . . .

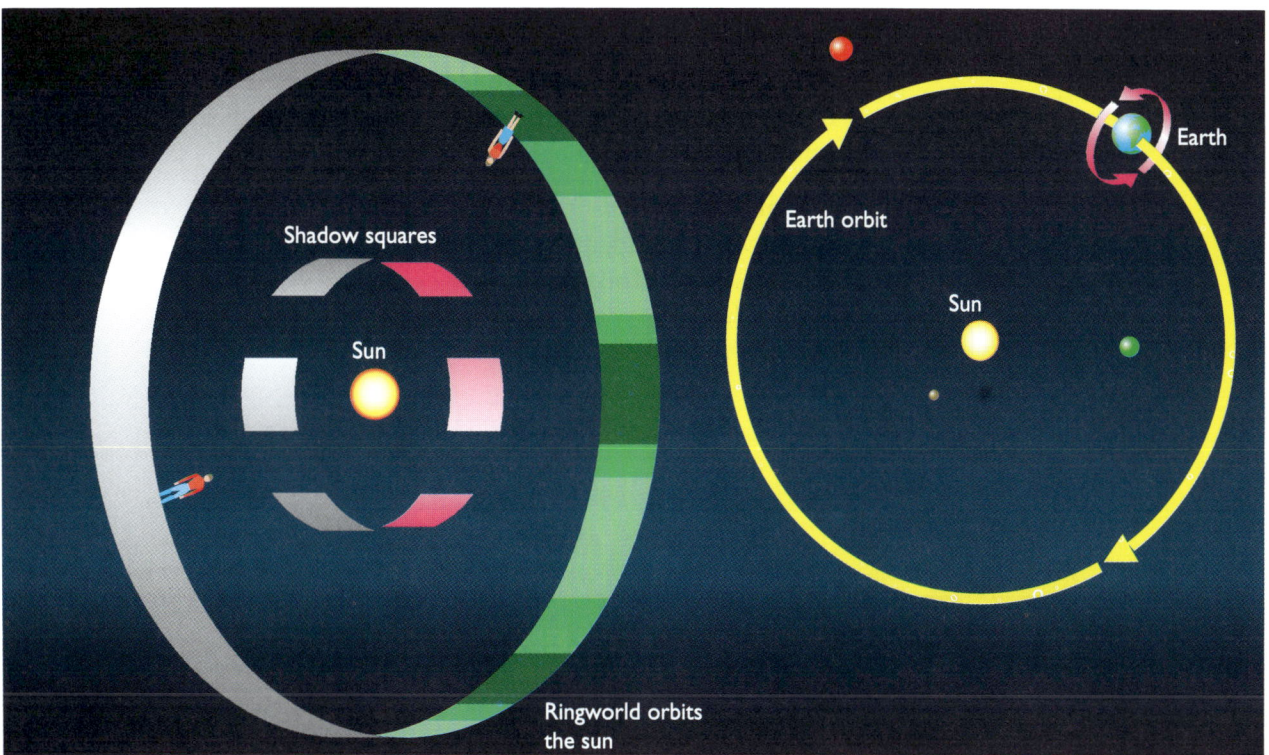

The diagram shows *Ringworld*, a design to support life as we know it on Earth. It is a giant ring, with a diameter of 1.6 million kilometres and a circumference of 940 million kilometres. The ring orbits the Sun so that it is the same distance from the Sun as Earth. The large mass of the ring, moving around the Sun, would create force of gravity. Just as gravity keeps us on the surface of Earth, *Ringworld*'s gravity would keep us on its surface. There is a difference, though. On *Ringworld* we would live on the inner surface of the ring, facing the Sun. To create day and night a ring of squares would be placed in orbit to block out sunlight for 12 hours at a time. The design means that life on Ringworld would be very like life on Earth.

5 What factors make it possible for Ringworld to have conditions like Earth? Explain how each factor helps.

6 The account misses out some important features needed for life on Earth to survive on Ringworld. Make a list of the missing features. Suggest how they could be made to happen on Ringworld.

7 Imagine that you live on Ringworld. Write an account of your life there:
 a over a day
 b a month
 c a year.

To find out more about *Ringworld,* go to the science fiction section of the library. *Ringworld* was invented by Larry Niven in a novel called *Ringworld Engineers*.

MAKING MATTER

PLANET EARTH UNMASKED

WHAT DO YOU KNOW?

We know more about the rocks on the surface of the Moon than we do about rocks 16 km under the Earth's crust. At its thickest the crust is 64 km: at its thinnest it is 10 km thick. Finding out what's happening under our feet is quite a task. The diagram below shows some of the observations and scientific ideas scientists use to help them. They:

- look for patterns in the observations,
- use scientific ideas to explain the patterns,
- make predictions from their explanations,
- look for more data to see whether it supports the explanation.

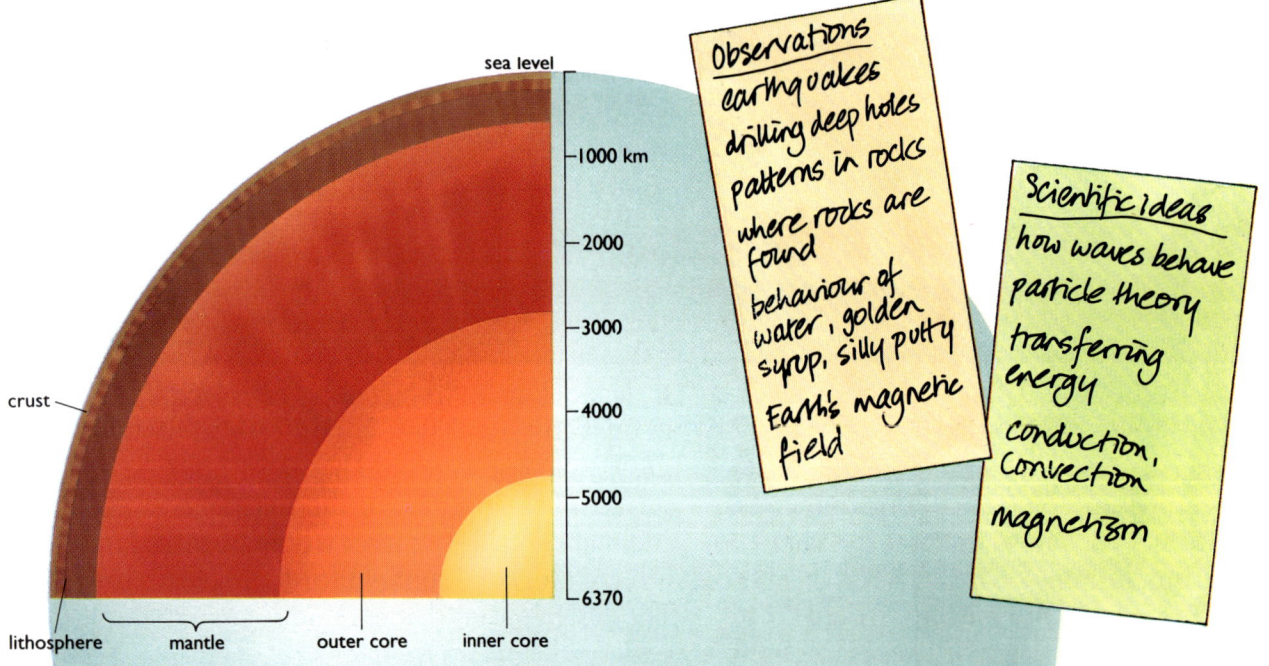

You do the same sort of thing when you carry out a scientific investigation. Scientists studying the Earth also use modelling, often using a computer to get a better, more complete picture.

It is very difficult to get direct information from under the Earth's crust. Scientists use information about the behaviour of things we know. Richter, for example, when studying the Earth's mantle, used a model employing golden syrup. By varying the temperature and pressure his team could make it flow or become solid. They made computer models of golden syrup's behaviour and linked it to observations of the Earth's behaviour. You can see from the diagram on pages 66–7 that this sort of computer from modelling has proved very useful.

TAKE ONE PLANET

A WHOLE LOT OF SHAKING GOING ON

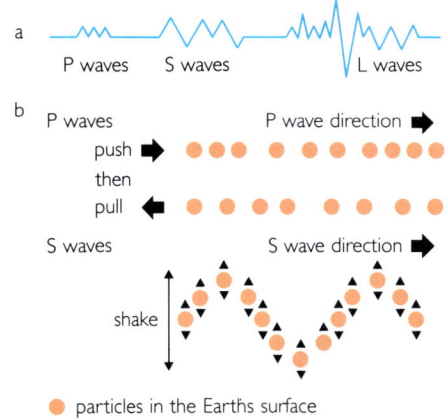

a) Seismogram recording of an earthquake
b) P, S and L waves: the particles' patterns of movement

Much of our information about Earth's structure has come from earthquakes. The energy from an earthquake is transferred through the Earth by **waves.** The speed, and direction, of these waves depends on the rock they pass through. Understanding how other waves behave allow us to explain what's happening. By studying the speed and path of waves, scientists have been able to build up a picture of the Earth's inner structure.

Energy from earthquakes is carried through the deep Earth by two different waves: *P* and *S* waves. Some energy is carried along the Earth's surface by *L* waves. It's *L* waves that cause earthquake damage. How *P* and *S* waves transfer energy from particle to particle through the Earth is shown on the left.

Earth Layer	approximate speed of P wave (km/sec)	approximate density of layer (g/cm3)
Crust	7	3
Upper mantle	8	3
Core-mantle boundary	14	5
Outer core	8	10
Inner core	11	13

The Deccan Traps.

TRAPPING THE SECRETS OF THE LANDSCAPE

Many scientists have studied the landscape to help explain what's happening under the Earth's crust. Places like the Deccan Traps in north-west India provide a lot of information. They have great amounts of rock called flood basalt. It looks as though flood basalt came from great lava flows. The Deccan Traps was produced by a single lava flow some 65 million years ago. The flow covered an area the size of Ireland in a week, with a sheet of lava at a temperature of 1200 °C. Studying the Deccan Traps and comparing observations with explanations of how matter behaves has given important clues to Earth's structure. The detective work continues and the illustration on page 64 shows the story so far.

The eruptions that formed flood basalts are bigger than any eruption known in history.

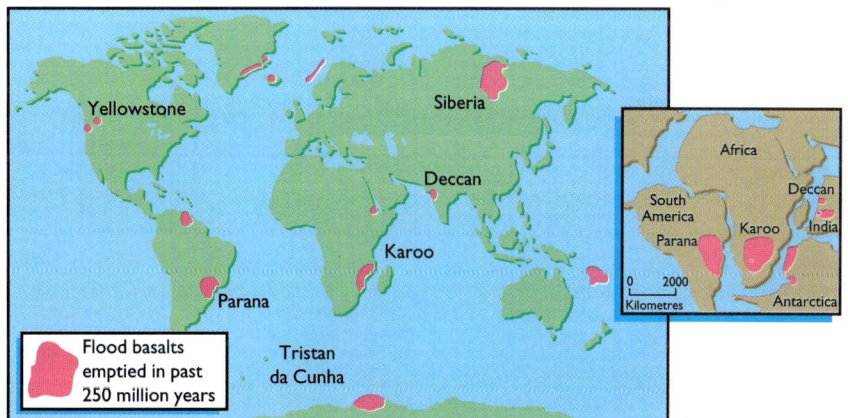

1 Explain why scientists' measurements show the Earth's crust is thickest under land and thinnest under oceans.
2 Explain why it is difficult to get direct evidence of what is happening under the Earth's crust.
3 Use your understanding of waves to explain which types of wave *P* and *S* waves are.
4 *P* and *S* waves speed up in dense rock, and get slower in less dense rock.
   a Describe the pattern linking rock density and wave speed.
   b Use your understanding of particles to explain why this happens.

MAKING MATTER

IN THE MELTING POT

WHY DOES THE EARTH PRODUCE SO MUCH MOLTEN ROCK?

This simple question was one that Professor Dan Mackenzie of Cambridge University set out to answer. We know that molten rock periodically escapes through the Earth's crust. Why it does is something that scientists are still trying to explain. We know that the Earth crust of solid rock. Compared to the size of the planet, the crust is like the skin on an apple. Observations tell us that the parts of the crust have been in different places in the past. A simulation of how the continents seem to have moved is shown on the left. As the 'supercontinent' Pangea, all the continents were still connected 250 million years ago. By 100 million years ago they had started to separate.

Dan Mackenzie tried to link what we can see on the surface of the Earth with what seems to be happening under the crust.

ANSWERS ON A PLATE

During the 1960s observations that the sea floors were spreading and continents moving, gradually led scientists to a grand theory of the Earth's crust. The theory was called **plate tectonics** (tectonics comes from a Greek word meaning builder).

250 million years ago

100 million years ago

0 million years ago

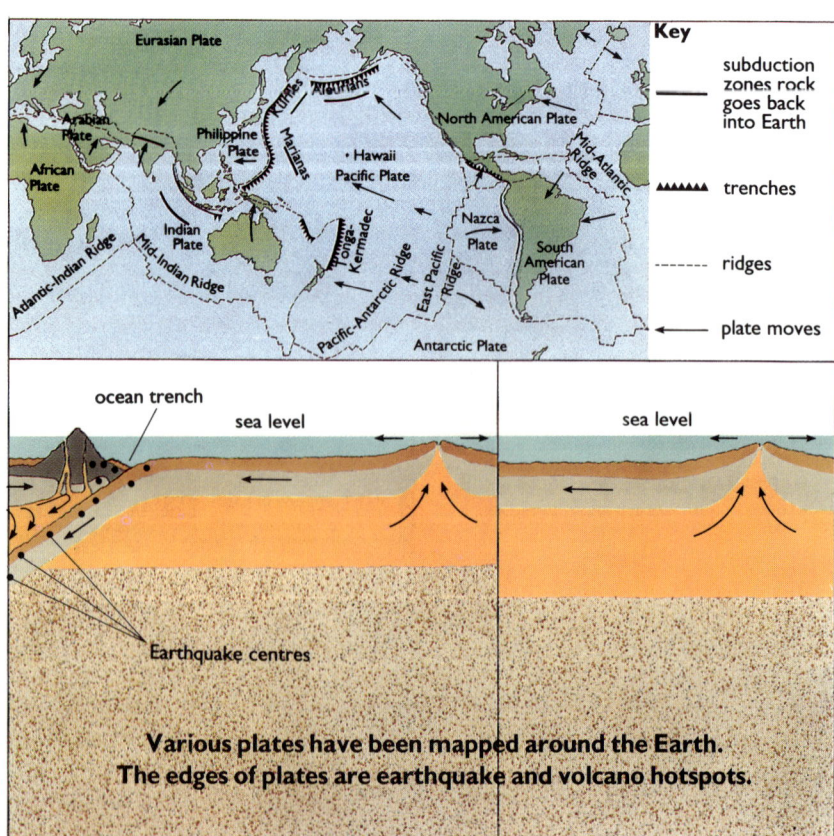

Various plates have been mapped around the Earth.
The edges of plates are earthquake and volcano hotspots.

TAKE ONE PLANET

The plate tectonics theory:
- the Earth's outer layer (lithosphere) is made of 6 or more plates,
- the plates move across the hot mantle,
- the plates bump into each other, move apart, slide past each other,
- as new plates are created, others are returned to the melting pot.

The evidence seems to support plate tectonics as an explanation for what happens on the surface of the Earth.

UNDER THE APPLE SKIN

To answer Dan Mackenzie's question, we need to know what happens in the Earth's mantle. We know that columns of hot, molten rock rise up through the mantle. These columns (or plumes) heat the crust above them. Where the crust is thin along the ocean ridges, the hot rock spills out. Active volcanoes in the Hawaiian islands are just one example of this. Now we know that plumes rise up in the mantle under continents where the crust is thick. The hot springs that bubble in Yellowstone Park in Wyoming show there's a hot spot under the continent.

To work out what was happening under the crust, scientists used some interesting investigations.

The explanation assumes that mantle rock behaves like the golden syrup. Energy from the Earth's core is taken towards the surface by a mantle plume. The plume is sold rock, but it's less dense than the rock around it. A hot, solid plume rises towards the crust. It travels at a speed of about a metre a year.

Energy is transferred from a plume to the crust. If the crust is stretched and thin this can be enough to melt the crust and crack it. If the crust is thick, scientists think that the plume spreads out to make a hot region under the crust. This hot rock pushes the crust up into a broad dome. They may cause the continent to break apart. Scientists think that this may be the cause of the piles of flood basalt in the Deccan Traps.

Syrup rises as it boils.

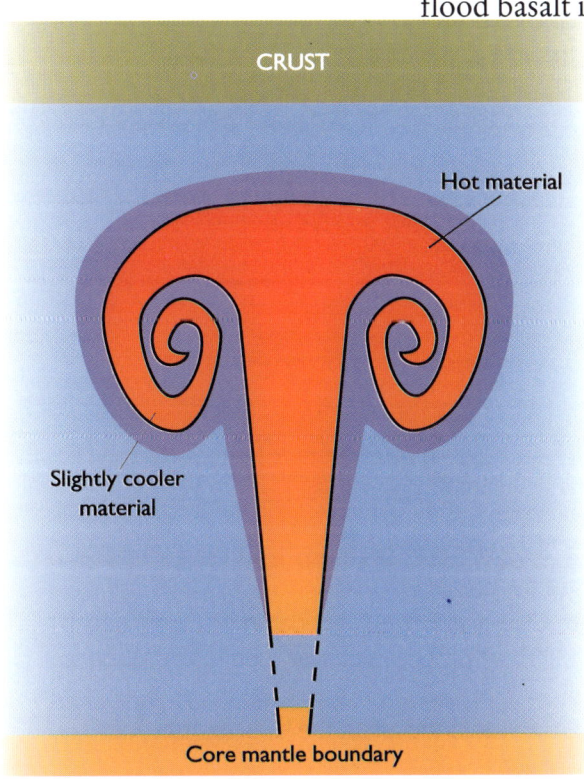

1. What is a convection current? Explain how convection currents could transfer energy from one part of Earth to another.

2. **a** Describe how a plume of molten rock could heat the Earth's crust
   b How long will it take a plume to reach the bottom of the crust? (Use the distances shown on pages 70–71)

3. Use a map showing the plates in the Earth's crust. You may like to work with others to tackle the following tasks.
   a Predict where you think mantle activity will take place in the near future (a few years). Gather evidence to support your predictions
   b Predict where the continents will be in the distant future. Explain the reasons for your suggestions.

MAKING MATTER

QUESTIONS

1. Look again at the photo on page 56. Explain what happens to the energy if the radiation from the Sun falls on surfaces which
   a. are more absorbent
   b. are more reflective
   c. have greater heat capacity
   d. is made of more clouds.
2. Suggest an explanation for the pattern that the least dense planets are farthest away from the Sun.
3. Use the information in this graph to calculate speed of the waves. Describe the pattern you find, and explain what it tells you about the rocks through which the waves are passing.

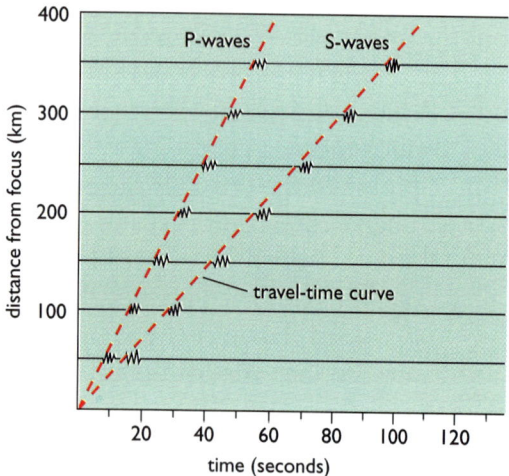

4. Use each of the observations in list 1 on page 64 as a heading. For each item say how it provides evidence of Earth's structure, and say what scientific idea from list 2 is used.
5. Does all the evidence for movement in the Earth's crust come from the rocks? What other evidence could you use? For each suggestion you make, explain the science behind it and outline its advantages and disadvantages.
6. The diagram represents four pollutants in car exhaust fumes.

a. i How can the presence of lead in exhaust fumes be avoided?
   ii Explain why are presence of lead in exhaust fumes is undesirable.
   iii Why are hydrocarbons present in exhaust fumes?
b. When a car is started on a cold morning, drops of water are seen at the end of the exhaust pipe. Explain how this happens.

7. a What evidence is there that most rocks were formed in prehistoric times?
   b The diagram shows a cross section of the Earth. Earthquakes set up shockwaves. Explain the evidence from the study of these shockwaves which supports the belief that the outer core is liquid.

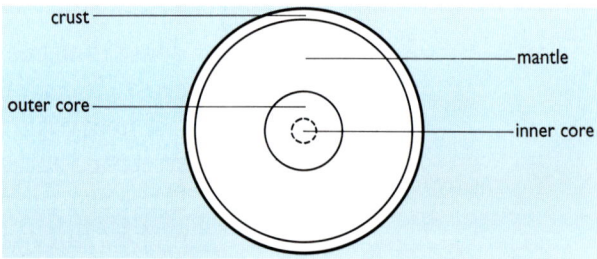

8. The map below shows a large lake which has two rivers draining into it. The size of the lake has not changed much in 1000 years. The rivers run into the lake all the time.

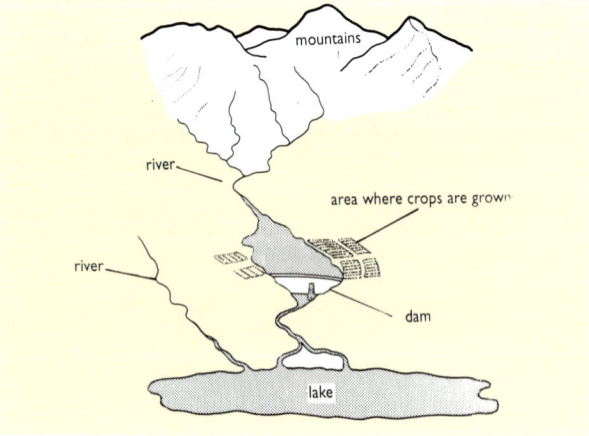

a. Suggest **two** reasons why the lake does not get any bigger.
b. One of the rivers was dammed (see the map) and most of the water was used for irrigation to grow crops.
How would this affect the lake? Explain your answer.

68

5 MAKING UP IS HARD TO DO

Contents
Riches beyond price?
Changing patterns of weather?
The one per cent key
If you go up in the woods today
Where the mountains meet the sea
Questions

As we find out more about the world around us, it makes it easier to find uses for Earth's resources. Sometimes we can recycle what we use, but it's not always possible.

This chapter will enable you to study some of the ways in which humans use the Earth and its resources. You will also learn about some of the ways in which the Earth affects humans.

High above the rainforest canopy an ecologist paints rings to monitor the growth of an oak branch.

MAKING MATTER

RICHES BEYOND PRICE?

Nauru from the air.

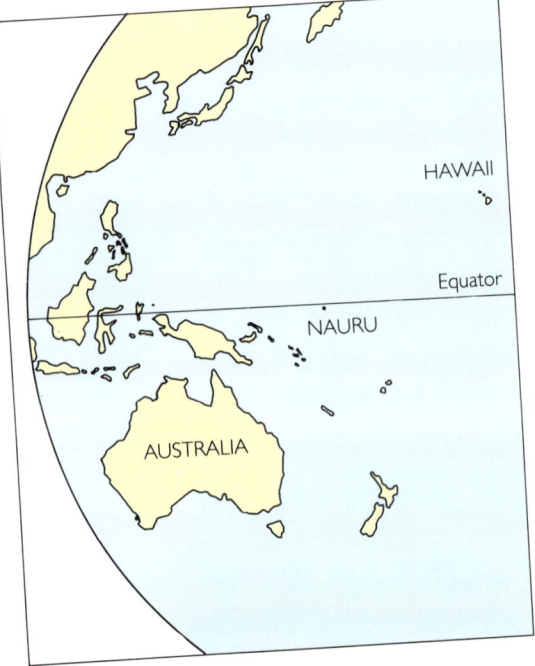

Nauru is the smallest republic in the world, and one of the richest. It is a tiny island half way between Australia and Hawaii. Nauru's riches come from the phosphate deposits found there in 1900. Phosphate mining started on Nauru in 1906. Australia was the main administrator, and most of the phosphate was used in Australia. It looks like the phosphate will have run out by the end of this century.

The phosphate was formed by the decay of marine organisms when the sea covered the island. The phosphate was laid down between the coral. When the coral was raised above sea level bird droppings added to the phosphate deposits. Now most of the island is bare. Taking away the phosphate has left pinnacles of coral up to 8 metres high. Nauruans live in a thin strip of land around the coast.

Phosphate mining on Nauru.

MAKING UP IS HARD TO DO

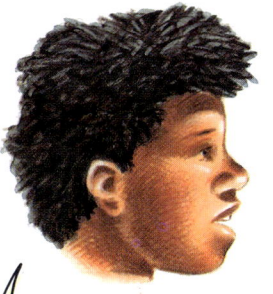
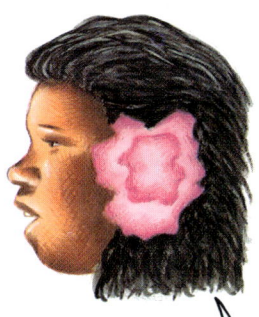

We are one of the richest nations in the world.

We pay no taxes. We have free education, transport, housing, medical care and telephone calls. Most families have several cars... even though a round trip on our only road takes 20 minutes.

The government has invested money abroad. This should bring income when the mining stops.
In the past we had forests of many different trees: wild almond, hibiscus, tomato and palm trees. Mining has removed the soil so no trees grow.

Now hot air rises from the bare landscape and drives away the rain clouds.

The drought stops plants growing and the number of birds has dropped.

Experiments have shown some things we can do: levelling the coral and making a "soil" by mixing crushed phosphate and limestone with humus and nutrients.

We can build fish farms, piggeries and plant trees and grow food hydroponically.

Over many years we were underpaid for the phosphate mined here. Some of that could be paid back by restoring our island's lush tropical growth.

Apart from phosphate, Nauru has no other natural resources.

And the evidence suggests the income from mining hasn't been well spent.

Education and health standards have fallen and about a third of the island's income has been wasted on a national airline.

Nauru never had rich forests of trees. Water passes through the limestone so most of the plants would have been low growing scrub.

The soil would never have been fertile enough to support agriculture.

The best solution is to abandon the island.

Yes it would cost far too much to restore.

And why should we pay? The islanders have wasted much of the profit they gained from the mining.

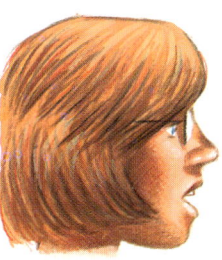

1 Explain each of the following:
  a how the phosphate deposits formed,
  b why coral pinnacles are left after mining,
  c why the supply of phosphate will run out.
2 Phosphate is an important ore used to make fertiliser.
  a What element does phosphate provide?
  b What is the formula for the phosphate ion?
3 Draw labelled diagram to explain the water cycle on Nauru
  a before mining started.
  b now.
4 List the benefits that mining has brought to Nauru. Compare your list with someone else's. Decide which has been the most important benefit and why.
5 List the disadvantages that mining has brought to Nauru. Compare your list with someone else's. Decide which has been the most important and why.

MAKING MATTER

CHANGING PATTERNS OF WEATHER?

COMPUTING THE FUTURE

Whether we are discussing the greenhouse effect or just trying to make accurate weather predictions, we need some idea of the patterns of weather around the Earth. Scientists at the Climatic Research Unit at the University of East Anglia studied the changing patterns in rainfall and temperature between 1925 and 1974. The diagram, below right, shows the pattern they got. They used records of temperature and rainfall kept during that time. One of the problems in looking for weather patterns is getting enough measurements. Another problem is to make sure that measurements are accurate. As you can see you might have to put up with gaps in your patterns.

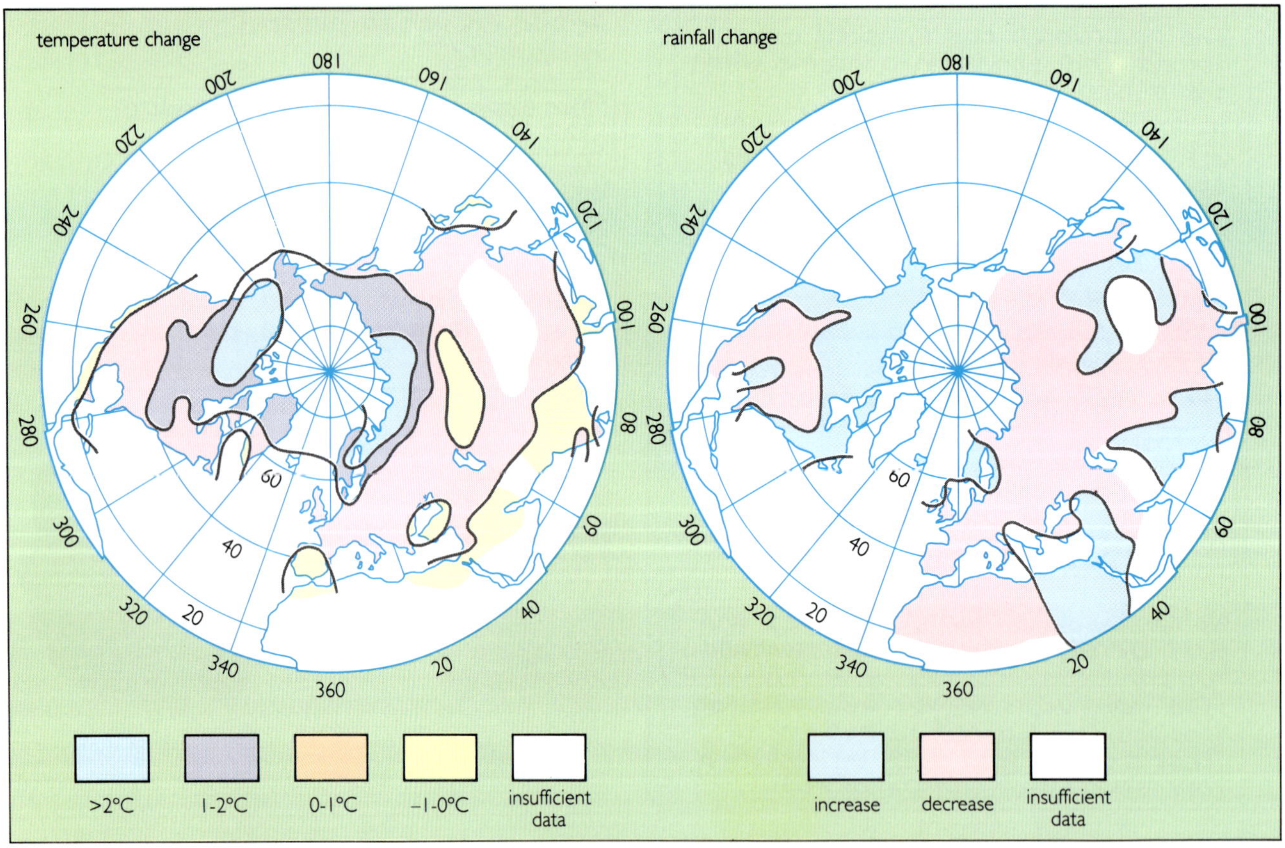

temperature change | rainfall change

>2°C | 1-2°C | 0-1°C | −1-0°C | insufficient data

increase | decrease | insufficient data

GETTING BETTER ALL THE TIME . . .

Scientists do try to get more accurate data. Sometimes they use new technology like more powerful computers and satellites. Sometimes they just try to improve the results from existing equipment.

This type of sunshine recorder is still used to record hours of Sun

72

MAKING UP IS HARD TO DO

For many years, scientists have tried to design better rain collectors. Even the best rain collectors cannot do a perfect job. The rain is the problem. It doesn't fall evenly and it is blown off course by the wind. Rain collectors like the one shown collect more rain and funnel it downwards.

One of the worst problems meteorologists (weather watchers) face is the pattern of weather station sites. Where weather equipment needs people, the weather stations need to be within reach of villages and towns. There are few weather records for areas of the Earth where the human population is low or zero. Weather stations near towns and cities can also give false results. Cities are often warmer than their surroundings. Wind speed and direction and rainfall can be different in cities, too.

SNOW PROBLEM

Snowfall is one of the most difficult things to measure. Snow that settles in one place can contain snow which has drifted from somewhere else. Wind is even more of a problem for snow collectors than for rain collectors. Once the snow is in a collector the usual way to measure it is to melt it. Melting needs a source of energy. Solar panels connected to a collector do not provide the large amount of power needed. Scientists are still trying to build a better snow measurer.

Monsoon!

Weather pattern of the monsoon.

WE HAVE THE TECHNOLOGY

There are instruments which can measure the climate more accurately than old style instruments. They are cheaper to run, too, because they do not need a daily visit from a human. A few of the richer countries have begun to invest in networks of automatic instruments. There is no co-ordinated effort around the Earth.

1 Study the diagram on page 72 and explain why there might have been 'insufficient data' in some places.
2 Explain how the devices on this page record the weather.
3 Give two ways the human population can affect the weather record.
4 Suggest and explain two reasons why cities are warmer than surrounding areas.
5 Cities do not cool much at night. Suggest why.
6 Explain why a city can have different patterns of rainfall and wind than areas around it.
7 Write a 'brief' to weather scientists about where to site instruments to get 'fair' results.
8 Design a snow collector and produce a brochure to advertise it. Wherever possible, test out the ideas, and include data to support your advertising claims.

MAKING MATTER

THE ONE PER CENT KEY

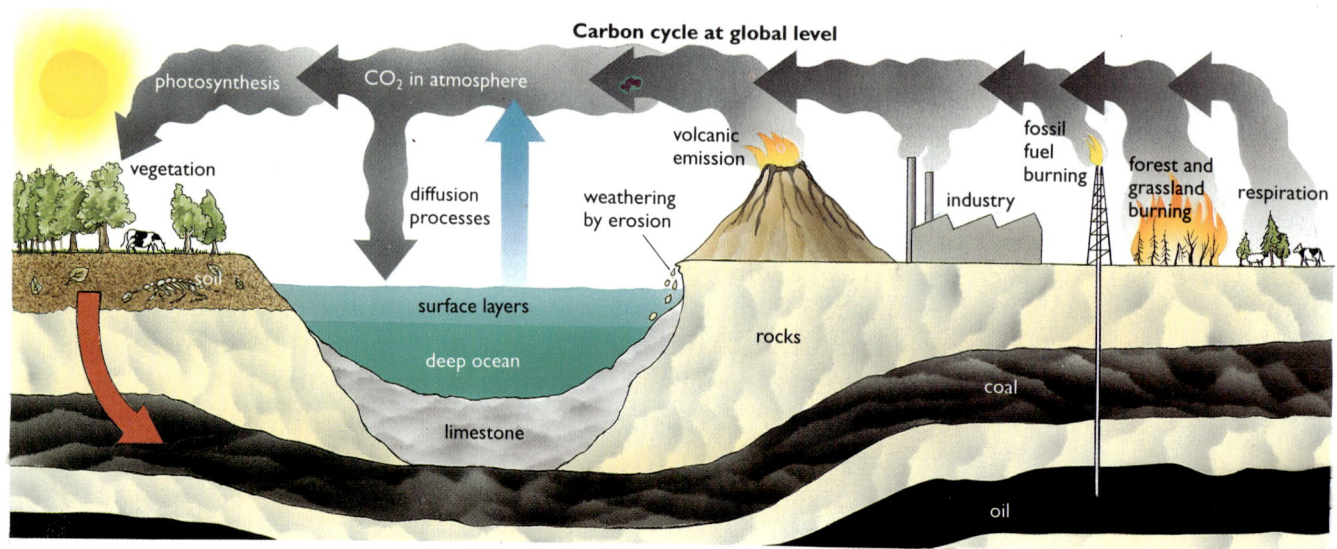

Carbon cycle at global level

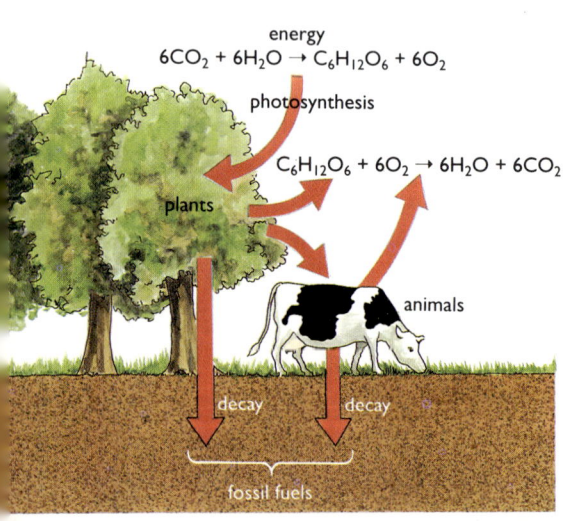

Carbon is the key element for life on Earth. Carbon makes up less than one per cent of the planet. Our bodies, our food and all the organisms on the planet are based on carbon compounds. Having carbon compounds in the atmosphere made the Earth warm enough for life to evolve. The diagram below shows how carbon is used and re-used to keep the planet alive.

As you can see, some parts of the carbon cycle store more carbon than others. Deep ocean water and rocks hold vast amounts of carbon . . . and hold on to it for a long time. Living organisms, the atmosphere and the surface layers of the oceans store much less carbon. The carbon in these stores moves much more quickly, as organisms grow, die and decay.

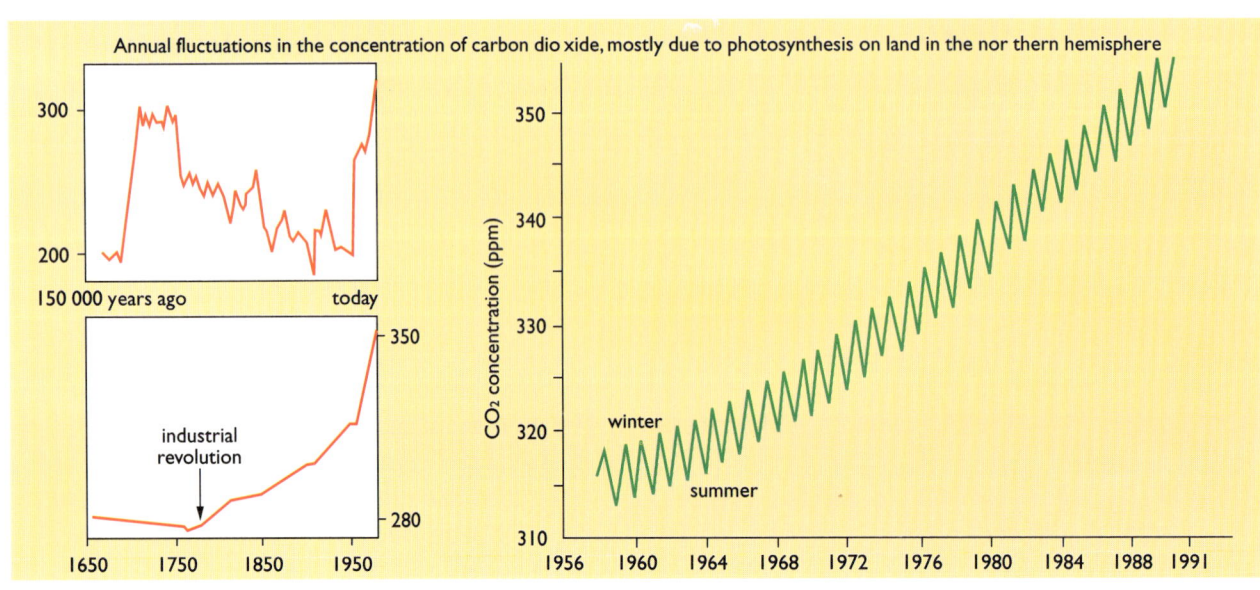

Annual fluctuations in the concentration of carbon dioxide, mostly due to photosynthesis on land in the northern hemisphere

MAKING UP IS HARD TO DO

Plants are the most important part of the global carbon cycle. Through photosynthesis plants convert carbon dioxide into glucose. Plants use it to respire and grow. Animals eat the plants, and the carbon begins its journey through food chains. As living organisms die and decay, their store of carbon is slowly released again.

Scientists have been measuring the amount of carbon dioxide in the atmosphere since 1958. For measurements of carbon dioxide from further back in time, they have studied bubbles of air trapped deep in the Antarctic ice. The diagram at the bottom of the previous page shows these measurement for Earth's Northern Hemisphere. You can see how the level of carbon dioxide in the atmosphere varies with the seasons.

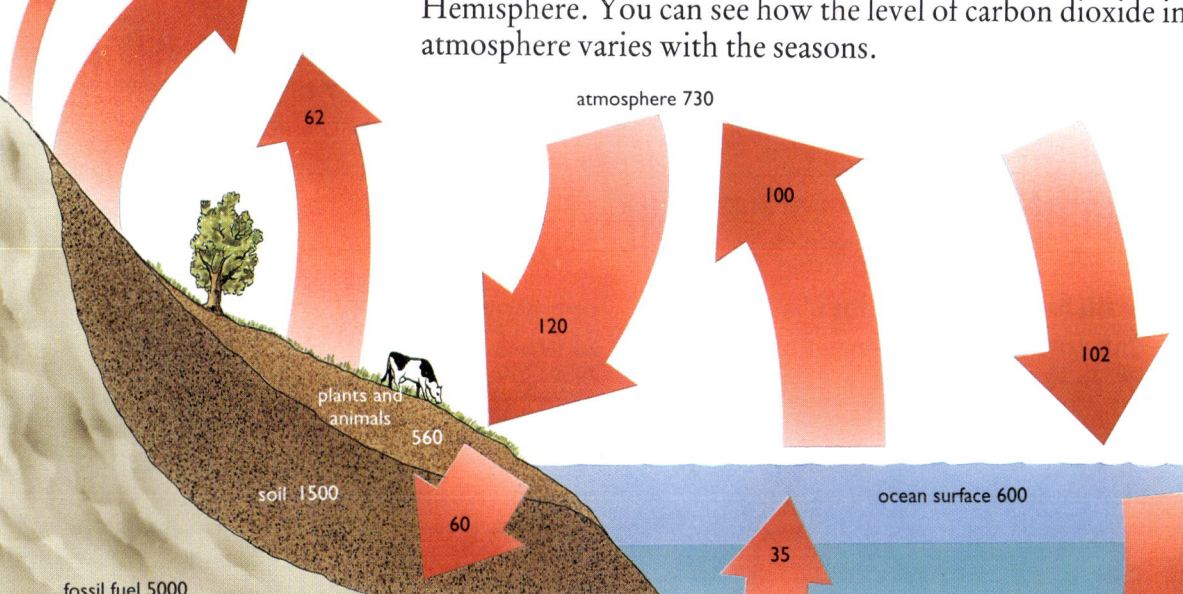

1 Make a list of the various processes which:
  a put carbon into 'store'.
  b release carbon.
2 Explain how carbon dioxide in the atmosphere could make the planet warm enough for life to evolve.
3 Explain how each of the following could affect the level of carbon dioxide in the atmosphere:
  a increase in burning fossil fuels.
  b increased volcanic eruptions.
  c planting more forests.
  d increased weathering and erosion of rocks.
4 Use the information on these pages to describe the pattern of carbon dioxide levels you would expect to find in the atmosphere in the Southern Hemisphere.
5 Imagine you were a tomato grower. How would you investigate whether carbon dioxide affected your tomato harvest? List factors which you would consider and, for each one describe how you would investigate its effect.

Driving the drivers: tomato growers make their crop grow faster by increasing carbon dioxide levels.

75

MAKING MATTER

IF YOU GO UP IN THE WOODS TODAY...

Monday 15th

It was a world of shadows, broken by beams of greenish sunlight. The ground was a patchwork of light and dark. The soil was covered with plants and animals.

30 metres above me was a rich garden, alive with animals and plants. Brilliant sunshine at the tops of the trees, means that 90 per cent of the photosynthesis takes place there. The tree tops provide food for the animals in the canopy. Dead material dropping to the forest floor brings nitrogen, phosphorus and other nutrients to the organisms living there. Decaying material on the forest floor is taken up by the plant roots and used to support life at the canopy.

Ahead, I could see the foot of the 40 metre tower.

LIFE IN THE FOREST

Tropical rain forests cover about 6% of the land surface, but contain **half** the growing wood on the Earth. They are in tropical areas where the climate is fairly stable. In the forests, the temperature is almost constant. Scientists think this is one reason why there are so many different species in the forests. A species in the rain forest has evolved to survive in a small area. In other parts of the Earth, there are changes in temperature and other weather conditions. Plants and animals which have evolved to survive in climates like this can put up with changes in their environment. This means that you can find the same species thousands of miles apart.

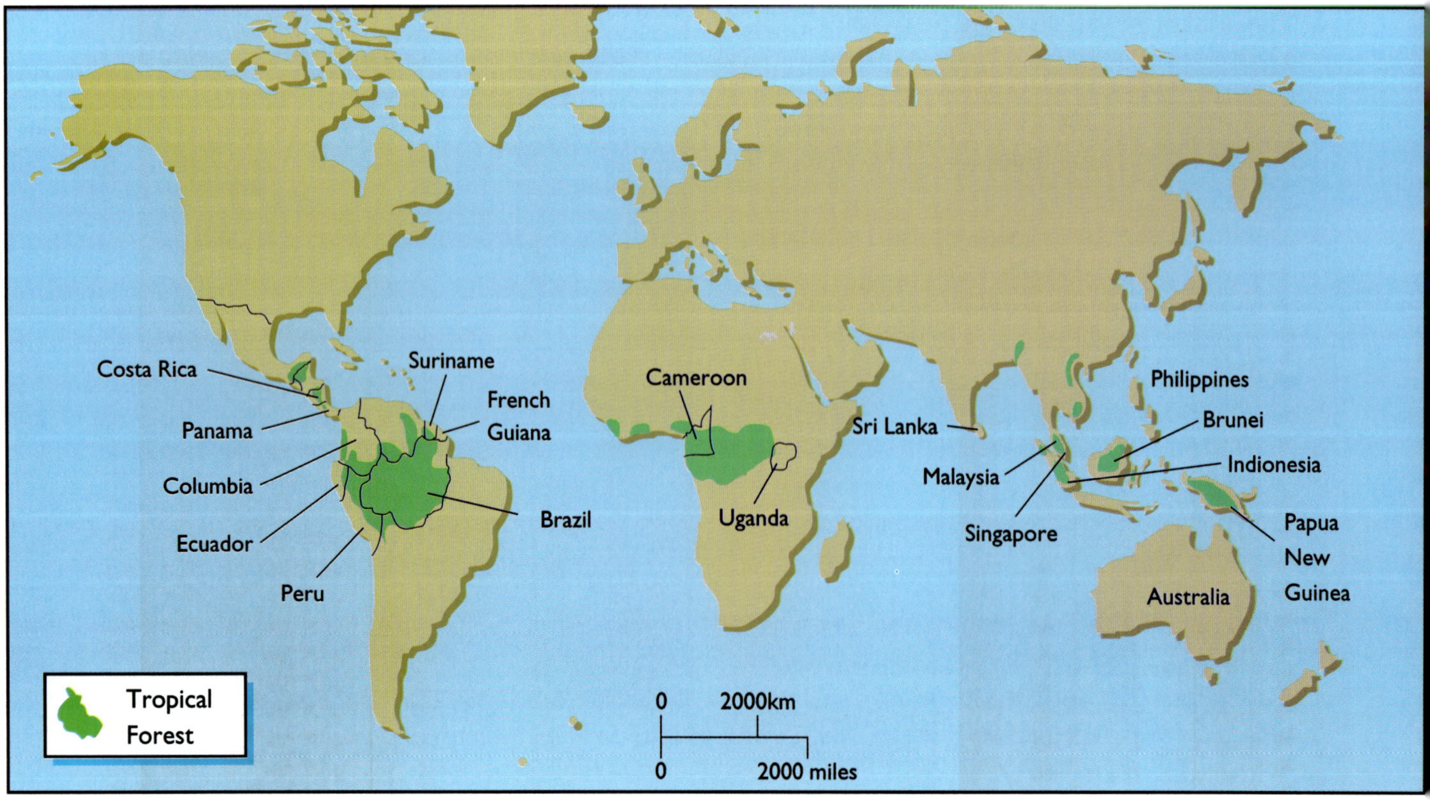

76

MAKING UP IS HARD TO DO

HOW MANY SPECIES LIVE ON PLANET EARTH?

No one really knows how many species exist on the Earth. About 1.4 million species have been found and named . . . so far. Scientists think tropical rain forests are home to most of the species still to be found. One tree in the Amazon rain forest contained more species of ants than the British Isles. New species of organisms are being found faster than we can give them scientific names!

YOU'LL WONDER WHERE THE GOODNESS WENT

Tropical forests grow in very poor soil. Tropical forests store and recycle the substances they depend on. When leaves fall, or a tree crashes down, they will decay within a few weeks and the nutrients will be returned to the forest. This is much faster than an ordinary forest. If organisms are taken out of the forest, then the nutrients are not returned.

Very little of the rain falling on the forest hits the soil. The soil is protected by the layers of the forest vegetation. Where the forest has been cut down, the soil is washed away by tropical rain.

The canopy vegetation has spiny and saw-tooth edges: there are stinging wasps and ants . . .

Products from the rain forest. On the left rubber, mangoes, bananas, avocados, coffee, derris and below, curara, which relaxes muscles.

1. Explain how each of the following processes help to move substances through the forests: photosynthesis, respiration, transpiration, osmosis.
2. How does the climate in the tropics differ from the other parts of the Earth? Use your own understanding, other sections of this book and any other sources of information, to help you give as much detail as you can.
3. Study the methods of exploring the forest shown in the photographs. For each one explain its advantages and disadvantages.
4. Read the diary extract and pick out the energy transfers which are taking place in the forest. Use diagrams to describe these energy transfers.
5. List some of the important products of the tropical rain forests. Explain some of the advantages and the disadvantages of taking them from the forests.

MAKING MATTER

WHERE THE MOUNTAINS MEET THE SEA

Human Spoils

Over a tenth of the world's soil is much less fertile than it was. A 15 year United Nations programme has published its first results. Soils described as of 'serious concern' need major work to make them fertile again. Some are beyond repair. Soils in arid areas are degraded by over grazing. About a third of the trouble is caused by cutting down forests. Poor farming practices count for another third. These human activities leave land exposed to erosion by rain and wind.

1992

FACT OR THEORY?

When forests are cut down, the soil is exposed to the force of the falling rain. In the rain forests the poor soil is washed away. On mountains the rain washes soil down the slopes. Many people think that this combination kills people. In 1954 when the Yangtze flooded 30 000 people died. In recent years we have heard more about floods in Bangladesh. In Bangladesh the Ganges and the Brahmaputra rivers cause great floods. To prevent floods, many trees have been planted in the Himalayas. The idea is that soil is washed down from the mountains by the heavy rains of the monsoon. The rains make the rivers flow faster and the rivers carry more soil and this clogs the river channels.

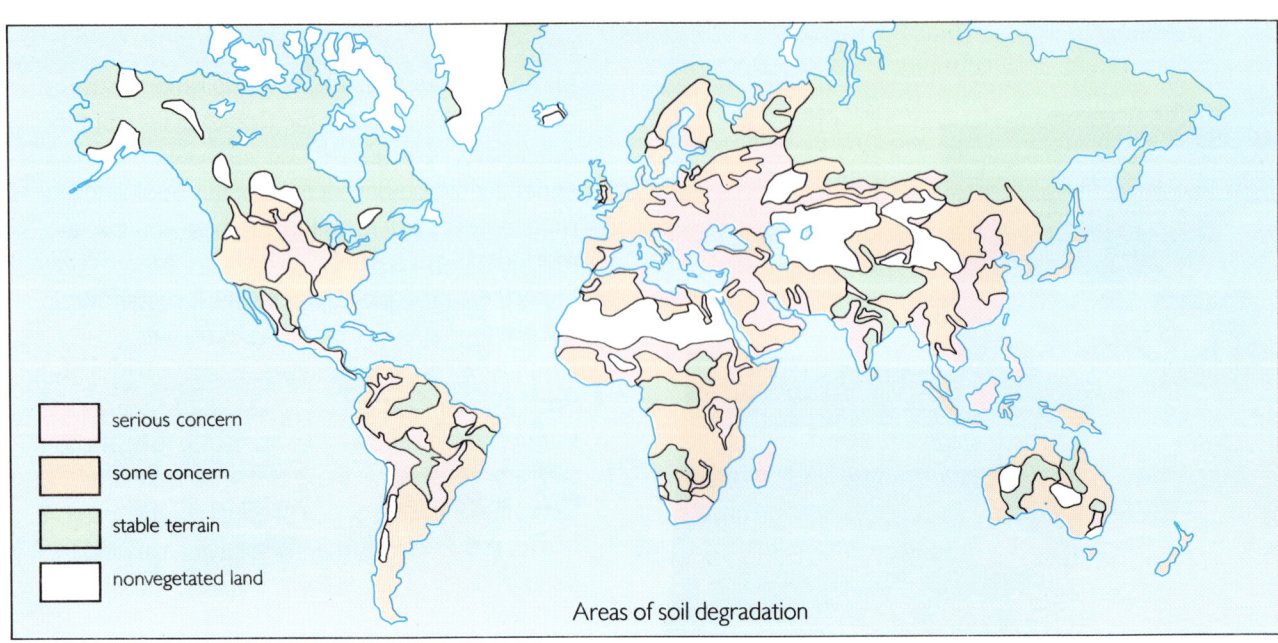

Areas of soil degradation

MAKING UP IS HARD TO DO

All this increases the flooding across the flood plain. The theory is that trees stop the soil being washed away and make water flow downhill more gently.

Floods in Bangladesh are getting worse. Most people say this is because farmers in the Himalayas have cut down so many trees.

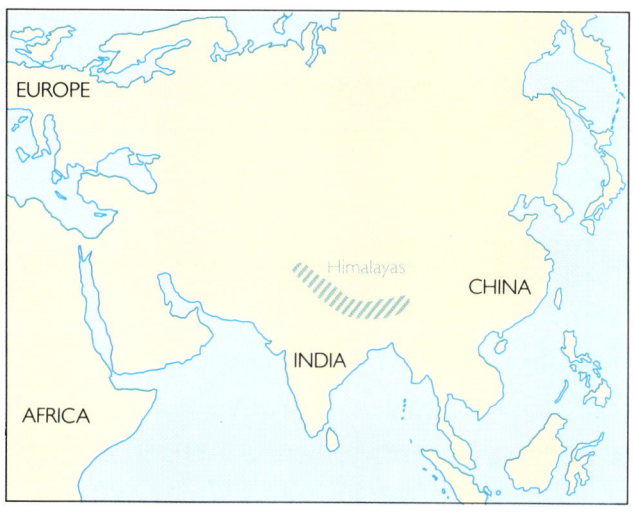

HAVE WE GOT THE RIGHT EXPLANATION?

1 More and more tourists visit Mount Everest, in the Himalayas. Trees are cut down to make fires to keep them warm at night. Many people think that there have been more trees cut down in the last 20 years than in the last two centuries. However up-to-date photographs compared with the ones taken of same views in the 1950s show that the loss of trees may not be as bad as we thought.

2 Some scientists say that tree cover protects the soil from the force of rain drops hitting them. However, the force of raindrops hitting bare soil under the trees over 10 m tall is greater than if they hit bare soil out in the open. Other scientists explain this by saying that drops falling off trees are larger than normal, and so do more damage. They say that low growing plants give more protection than trees.

The Yangtze (yellow) river is so called because of the colour of the silt, brought down from the mountains, turns the water yellow.

3 Soil washed down in the rivers, usually doesn't get all the way down in one trip. The sediment is dropped, and picked up again, many times. In a large river like the Ganges it might take hundreds of years to reach the flood plains. Soil eroded in the Himalayas during this century might not have been in any floods . . . yet.

1 Make a summary to explain how cutting down trees is thought to cause soil erosion. Explain why erosion is worse on slopes.
2 Plan investigations to test out the claims made about:
   a the force of rain drops.
   b the effect of slopes on erosion.
   c the flow of sediments down the river.
3 Imagine you have to help the people affected by flooding. Some possible solutions are:

a plant more trees higher up.
b limit the amount of tourism.
c build channels and banks on flood plains.
d move people from the flood plain.
e do more investigations or try out different things on a small scale.

Discuss the advantages and disadvantages of each one (you could divide the work between several people). Produce a report which says what you'd recommend, and why.

MAKING MATTER

QUESTIONS

1 a Imagine you are Nauruan (see pages 70–71). Explain how you would answer the Australian's arguments.
  b Imagine you are Australian, answer the Nauraun's arguments.

2 Using solar powered instruments to gather weather data has some disadvantages. Explain why.

3 Explain why measuring snowfall is difficult.

4 a Draw a food chain to show how carbon passes from plants to humans.
  b Explain how the carbon stored in humans is returned to the atmosphere.
  c Explain how the industrial revolution affected the atmosphere.

5 Explain why plants are said to 'drive' the carbon cycle.

6 Describe and explain what the atmosphere above the rain forests would be like.

7 Suggest and explain some of the adaptations to the environment(s) you might expect to find in organisms that live
  a at bottom of the rain forest.
  b at top of the rain forest.

8 Study the pattern of soil degradation on page 78. Describe and explain any link with the patterns in Earth's.

9 The information in this question has been adapted from *A deal to save the world*, by Richard Heller, 'The Mail on Sunday', 26th July 1987.

> THE massive burden of debt that is crippling the world's poorest countries could destroy natural resources essential to our survival. It makes people destroy animals and plants around them. People burn down 5000 years of forest to gain two years of grain or a few tonnes of minerals.
> Every three years the world loses – forever – an area of tropical rain forest the size of Germany. At this rate of destruction NONE will be left in fifty years' time.
> Tropical forests have been called the lungs of the world. They remove the excess carbon dioxide from the Earth's atmosphere. Carbon dioxide absorbs heat from the Sun.
> Forests do another vital job by absorbing, and then evaporating, a huge proportion of the world's rainfall which falls on the land.
> Plants from the tropical forests supply 40 per cent of current medicines, and they store the genes of plants which we would need to restart our food crops if any were hit by disease.
> One of Britain's leading ecologists has warned, "This destruction poses a greater threat than nuclear weapons."

a i Explain how tropical forests use *the excess carbon dioxide from the Earth's atmosphere*.
  ii Suggest **two** methods by which carbon dioxide is returned into the atmosphere.
b The article says
Every three years the world loses – forever – an area of rain forest the size of Germany. At this rate of destruction NONE will be left in fifty years' time.
Suggest and explain the effect that this could have on the Earth's atmosphere.
c Write a letter to 'The Mail on Sunday' explaining the advantages and disadvantages of destroying tropical forests. You should make up to **five** points. Finish your letter by explaining whether you agree with the view of the ecologist.

10 There are two major methods of mining coal, underground mining and open-cast mining.

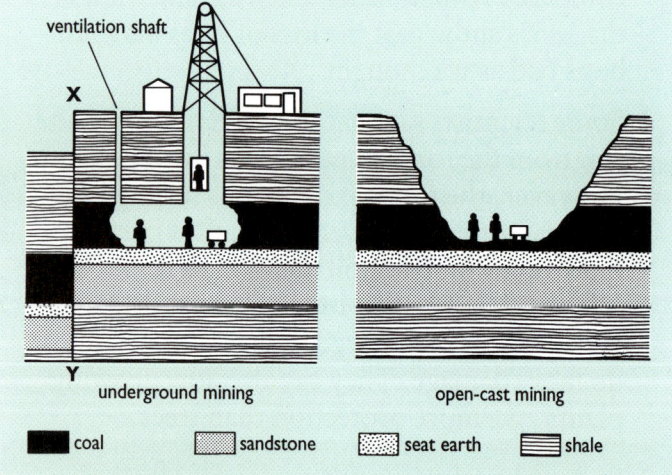

a Suggest reasons why it is sometimes more appropriate to open-cast mine than to mine underground.
b **XY** is a fault in the rocks. Suggest what effects this might have on the future operation of the mine.
c Discuss the effects of each type of mine on the local community and environment.

11 Draw a simple diagram of the nitrogen cycle and then answer the following questions.
  a What type or organism converts nitrogen in the soil into nitrate in the soil?
  b How are the nitrogen containing compounds in dead plants released into the soil?
  c How do some plants, e.g. clover, manage to use nitrogen from the air?

6 ELEMENTS INCORPORATED

Understanding the properties of materials is important. Apart from anything else, it helps us to make the materials we need, in the quantities we want and at a reasonable price!

In this chapter you will learn more about materials, elements and compounds, the patterns in their properties and how they are extracted from the Earth. You will see how factors like the speed of a reaction are important – especially in industry.

Contents
Planet Earth – the factory
Metals or not?
Elementary patterns
Getting to know you
Periodic patterns
Building matter
Reacting speeds matter
The path to success
Questions

Stromboli, Italy, erupting.

MAKING MATTER

PLANET EARTH – THE FACTORY

Cassiterite crystals (SnO_2) from Cornwall.

Ores are rocks which we mine to extract metals and important, useful minerals. Ores can be made by processes inside the Earth, or ones which happen on the surface. The diagrams on these pages show a few of the ways the Earth produces ores. You learned in Book 1 that ores contain minerals. Minerals are compounds of metals: carbonates, sulphides or oxides usually.

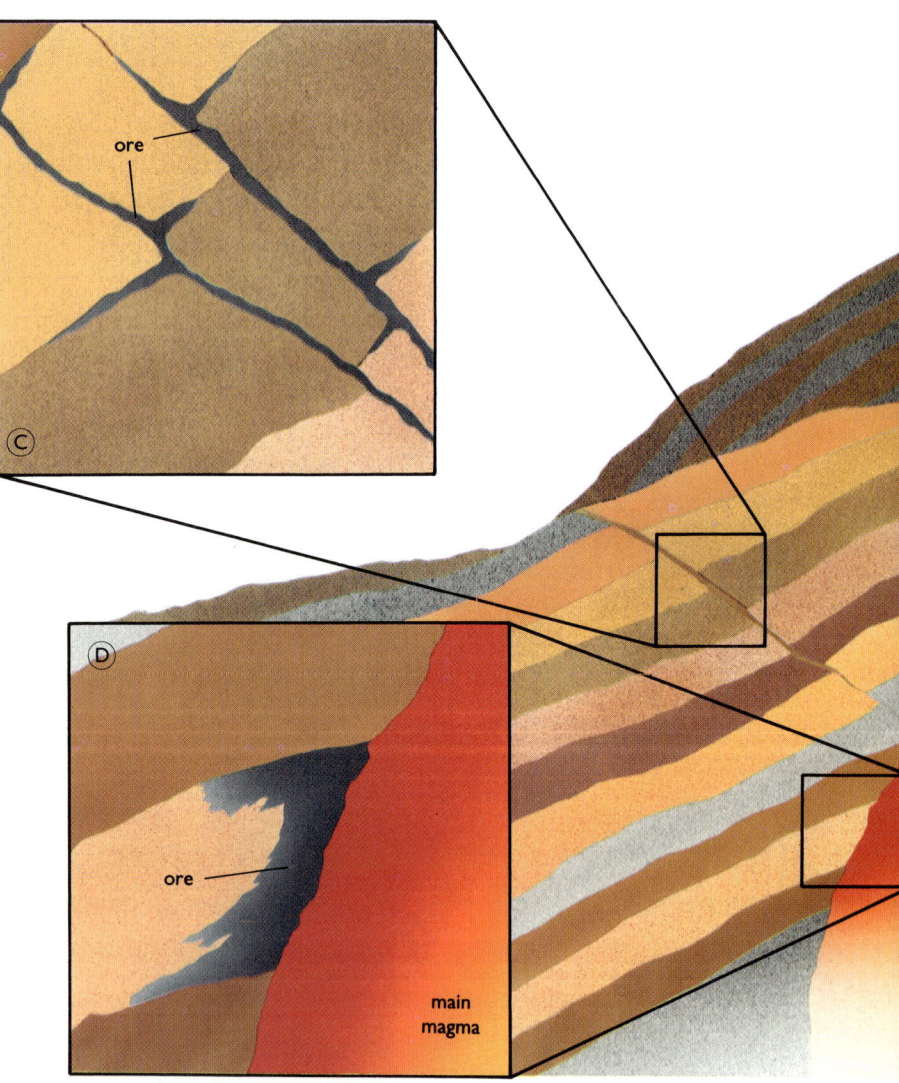

A sample of bauxite – hydrated aluminium oxide. It is a sedimentary material. Its reddish colour comes from iron oxide impurities.

PROCESSES INSIDE THE EARTH

Under the Earth's surface molten rock (**magma**) is a mixture of different substances. Just like any solution, ore minerals in the magma form crystals. Some ores crystallize sooner than others. If they are more dense then they settle to the bottom. Others are dissolved in hot water and are left behind in faults. Some magmas give off water rich in chlorides and fluorides. These react with surrounding rock, and replace the minerals in them.

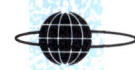

PROCESSES AT THE SURFACE OF THE EARTH

Minerals that dissolve in water will be carried away when a rock is weathered. Minerals that don't dissolve in water will be left behind.

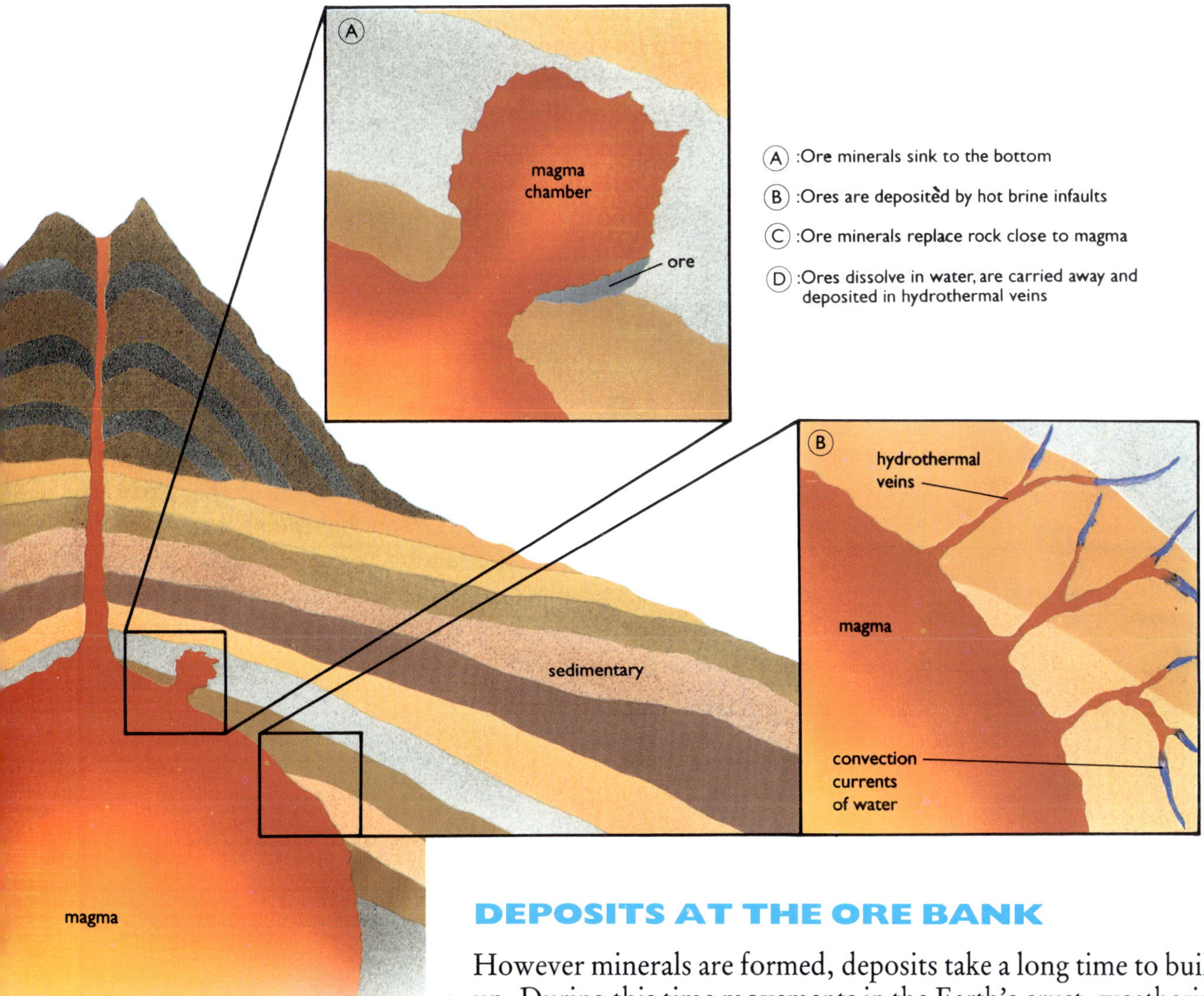
A
magma chamber
ore
A :Ore minerals sink to the bottom
B :Ores are deposited by hot brine infaults
C :Ore minerals replace rock close to magma
D :Ores dissolve in water, are carried away and deposited in hydrothermal veins
B
hydrothermal veins
magma
convection currents of water
sedimentary
magma

DEPOSITS AT THE ORE BANK

However minerals are formed, deposits take a long time to build up. During this time movements in the Earth's crust, weathering and erosion can move them to different places. When humans find an ore deposit it may be a long distance from where it formed.

1 Pick out the processes shown on these pages. For each one explain what's happening to the particles (for example, why some ores crystallize sooner than others.)
2 How certain can we be that the processes described are the ones which happen? To help you, you may need to look at your earlier work, or Chapter 5.
3 List any other processes in the Earth's crust which might affect the way ores are produced. Explain the effects these may have.

MAKING MATTER

METALS OR NOT?

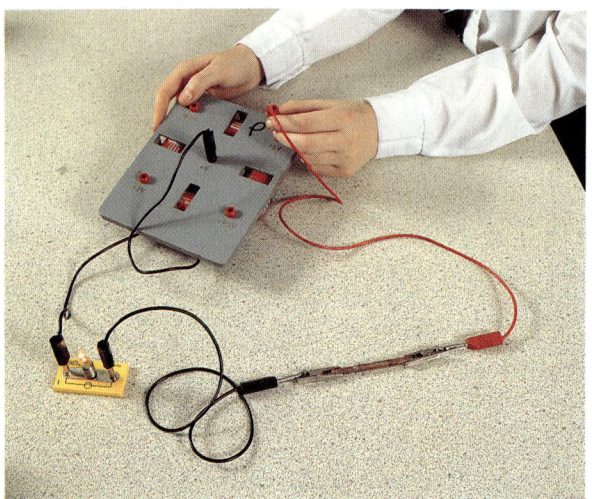

Copper makes the connection

Silver can be worked without breaking it.

Non-metal carbon is brittle.

These photos and Table 1 should remind you of some of the main differences between metals and non-metals. Table 1 shows the patterns in their properties. By now you will know that a pattern gives you an overall description. To say that metals react with air or oxygen is generally true. If you look at Table 2, you can see that some metals are better at reacting with air. Some metals don't seem to react with air or oxygen at all. The following pages go into more detail about the reasons why.

Table 1 Properties

Property	Metal	Non-metal
Physical		
looks	shiny	dull
conducts?	heat and electricity	doesn't conduct
working it	bends without breaking	brittle
	can be hammered into shape	
	can be pulled into a wire	
strength	yes	no
melting temperature	high	low
boiling temperature	high	low
density	high	low
when hit	ringing sound	no ringing sound
Chemical		
with dilute acid	many react and give hydrogen	do not react
oxides	make a basic solution or don't dissolve	make an acidic solution
compounds with hydrogen (hydrides)	break down easily (unstable)	stable
chlorides	unreactive e.g. NaCl	very reactive e.g. HCl

1 For the properties shown in Table 1
   a choose another example relating to that property (for example, name a metal that can be beaten).
   b find some exceptions to the patterns in the table and explain why you feel they do not fit the pattern.
2 Explain what is meant by the terms 'physical properties' and 'chemical properties' (Table 1 may help you answer).

ELEMENTS INCORPORATED

3 On the right is a copy of Jo's table of results.

a Copy the table and fill in the blanks.

b Hydrogen burns with a blue flame to give an oxide (steam): and the oxide turns pH paper green.

Explain where you place hydrogen if including it in this table.

4 Write equations for the reactions in Table 2. If you are stuck see pages 86–7.

Element	burning it	oxide made	oxide solution and pH paper
Metals:			
magnesium	bright flash	white powder magnesium oxide	blue
calcium	–	–	–
sodium	–	white sodium oxide	–
iron	–	–	–
Non-metals:			
carbon	glows red	–	–
phosphorus	yellow flame	white smoke phosphorus oxide	red
sulphur	blue flame	–	–

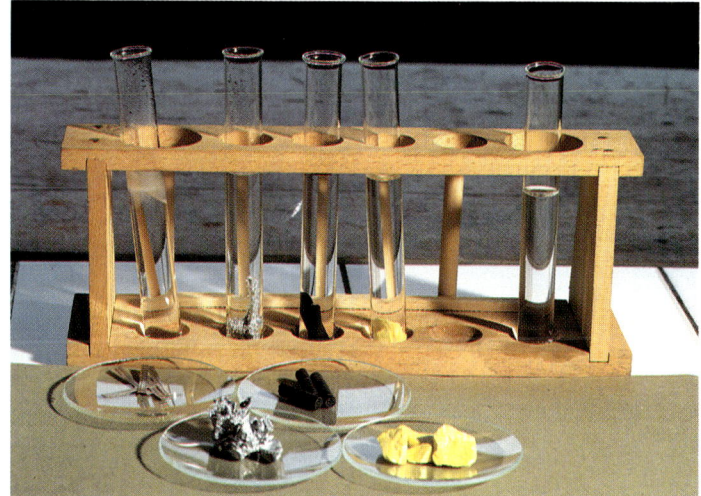

Testing substances with dilute hydrochloric acid. From left to right: magnesium strip, zinc, carbon, sulphur and a control.

Table 2 How metals react

Metal	with air (O$_2$)	with cold water	with steam	with acids
K Na	burns brightly	Hydrogen produced reaction gets slower K → Mg	Hydrogen produces reaction slower as go down K → Fe	Hydrogen from dilute acids slower reaction going down K → Pb
Ca Mg	burns giving oxides, slower reaction going down Ca → Fe			
Al Zn Fe				
Pb	slow reaction to a layer of oxide on the surface of the metal	no reaction with cold water	no reaction with steam	no reaction with dilute acids
Cu Hg				
Ag Au Pt				

MAKING MATTER

ELEMENTARY PATTERNS

K (potassium)
Na (sodium)
Ca (calcium)
Mg (magnesium)
Al (aluminium)
Zn (zinc)
Fe (iron)
Pb (lead)
Cu (copper)
Hg (mercury)
Ag (silver)
Au (gold)
Pt (platinum)

Reactivity decreases as you go down the reactivity series

REACTIVITY SERIES OF THE METALS

If you look at the diagram (left) you should see that it lists the metals in the same order that they appear in Table 2 p85. This list is called the **reactivity series**. You might have met it before. You might even know a rhyme to help you remember the metals in order.

You can use the reactivity series to help you write equations for the reactions in Table 2 p85. Using the pattern for one reaction, the metals which react like it have the same sort of equation. Here are some examples:

$$\text{sodium} + \text{oxygen} \rightarrow \text{sodium oxide}$$
$$2\,Na + O_2 \rightarrow 2\,Na_2O$$

$$\text{magnesium} + \text{water} \rightarrow \text{magnesium hydroxide} + \text{hydrogen}$$
$$Mg + 2H_2O \rightarrow Mg(OH)_2 + H_2$$

$$\text{zinc} + \text{hydrochloric acid} \rightarrow \text{zinc chloride} + \text{hydrogen}$$
$$Zn + 2HCl \rightarrow ZnCl_2 + H_2$$

If you count the atoms involved in each equation, you'll see none are lost on the way. There's more about reactions and equations in Chapter 7.

A FAMILY LIKENESS?

Since 1830 the number of elements we know about has doubled. Keeping track of the elements and their properties is quite a task. Luckily, there are a number of patterns in the way elements behave. For many years scientists tried to come up with one

ELEMENTS INCORPORATED

pattern they could use for all the elements. The most useful pattern is the one we use today. It's called the Periodic Table. Dimitri Mendeléev, a Russian, set out the Periodic Table in 1860. He succeeded where others had failed, because he thought that some elements might not have been discovered. He left spaces for them. Recently, in 1994, elements 106 Seaborgium, and 107 Nielsbohrium have been added to the list.

A simplified version of the Periodic Table. A fuller version can be found on p88.

FAMILIES IN THE PERIODIC TABLE

There are three large families of elements. The Periodic Table groups them together. The smallest family is the **noble (or inert) gases.** For a long time scientists thought they didn't react with anything. Noble gases *have* been made to react, but it's not easy.

The non-metal family has a variety of members. Some are very reactive (like chlorine); others like nitrogen are not so reactive.

There are three branches of the metal family. Out on the left hand side of the table is the family of reactive metals. Over towards the right, close to the non-metals, are a family of metals that have some properties like non-metals. This family is described as poor metals, some books call them metalloids (or semi-metals). In between the other two metal families is the transition metal family.

1. Use the information here (and on pages 84–5) to help you explain why
   a. gold and silver are used to make jewellery.
   b. iron gets covered in rust (iron oxide).
   c. copper is used to make hot water pipes.
   d. aluminium is expensive to extract from its ore.
2. Find out above Mendeléev's organisation of elements and about the other suggestions which have been made for organising the elements.
3. Find data about one or more of the element families. You could try the library, or a database. Does the data you have show that the elements in one family are related to each other? Explain your answer.

MAKING MATTER

GETTING TO KNOW YOU

Iron

Fe fi fo fum
As hard as nails
As tough as they come

I'm the most important
Metal known to man
(though aluminium
is more common
do we need another can?)

Five per cent of the earth's crust
I am also the stone at its centre
Iron fist in iron glove
Adding weight to the system
I am the firma in the terra

Fe fi fo
Don't drop me on your toe

My hobbies are space travel
And changing the course of history
(they even named an Age after me
– eat your heart out Gold)

And changing shape of course
From axe heads and plough share
To masks maidens and missiles
I am malleable
I bend to your will
I am both the sword and the shield
The bullet and the forceps

I am all around you
And much more
You are all round me 2, 3, 4 ...

You've got me
Under your skin
I'm in your blood
What a spin I'm in
Haemoglobin
You've got me
Under your skin

So strike while I'm hot
For if I'm not there
What are you?
Anaemic that's what

Fe fi
High and mighty
Iron

Gregarious and fancy free
Easy going that's me
No hidden depths
I'm not elusive
To be conclusive
You get what you see
fe Fe

Group ▶ Period ▼	I Alkali metals	II Alkaline earth metals						
1	H Hydrogen 1							
2	Li Lithium 3	Be Beryllium 4						
3	Na Sodium 11	Mg Magnesium 12	← Transition elements →					
4	K Potassium 19	Ca Calcium 20	Sc 21	Ti 22	V 23	Cr Chromium 24	Mn Manganese 25	Fe Iron 26
5	Rb 37	Sr 38	Y 39	Zr 40	Nb 41	Mo 42	Tc 43	Ru 44
6	Cs 55	Ba 56	57-71 See Below	Hf 72	Ta 73	W 74	Re 75	Os 76
7	Fr 87	Ra 88	89-103 See Below	Ku 104	Ha 105			

KEY: H Hydrogen 1 ← symbol, name, atomic number

Lanthanides	La Lanthanum 57	Ce 58	Pr 59	Nd 60	Pm 61	Sm 62
Actinides	Ac Actinium 89	Th 90	Pa 91	U Uranium 92	Np 93	Pu 94

The diagram above shows a modern version of the Periodic Table. The elements are arranged in order of their atomic number. The rows of the table are called **periods.** The columns in the table are called **groups.** Apart from the transition family in the middle of the table, the groups are given a number. As you can see, the group numbers are often shown as Roman numbers.

- Group I (or Group 1) contains the **alkali metals**
- Group II contains the **alkaline earth metals**
- Group VII (or Group 7) contains the **halogens**
- Group 0 contains the **noble gases**

ELEMENTS INCORPORATED

Carbon

I am an atom of carbon
And carbon is the key
I am the element of life
And you owe yours to me

I am the glue of the Universe
The fixative
used by the Great Model-maker
I play a waiting game
Lie low that's my secret
Take a breath every millenium

But though I'm set in my ways
Don't be misled . . . I'm not inert
I will go down in cosmic history
as an adventurer
For when I do make a move
Things happen fast

I am an atom of carbon
And carbon is the key
I am the element of life
And you owe yours to me

When the tune is called
I carry the message
to the piper
Take the lead
in the decorous dance
of life and death

Patient, single minded and stable
I keep my talents hidden
Bide my time
Until by time I am bidden.

Poems from An A–Z of Elements by Roger McGough, Channel 4 Publications. Reprinted by permission of the Peters, Fraser and Dunlop Group Ltd.

1. Explain what the atomic number of an element is, and what information it gives you.
2. Suggest why Group 1 and 0 are given the names they have.
3. What's the difference in atomic number between an atom in period 2 and
   a its neighbours to the left and right.
   b in the period below it.
4. Roger McGough has used poetry to summarise information about elements. Study his poems about iron and carbon.

   Explain what he means by each of the following
   a 'the firma in the terra'.
   b 'I am malleable, I bend to your will'.
   c 'I'm in your blood'.
   d 'I am the glue of the Universe'.
   e 'I am the element of life'.
5. Choose some elements and way to 'demonstrate' their properties. Roger McGough chose poems: you could choose poetry, advertisements, plays. Whatever you choose, the science must be right. You may need to do some research first. You could work with others.

MAKING MATTER

PERIODIC PATTERNS

Look at the information in the tables. They show some information about the elements in the Periodic Table. You can see that there are patterns in the groups of the Periodic Table. There are patterns as you go across a period.

Elements in the same group have the same sort of reactions. As you move down the group, there is a change. Groups on the left of the Periodic Table get more active as you move down the group. On the right of the table elements get less reactive as you move down it (except for group 0, the noble gases).

Table 1

	with cold water	oxide	symbol of ion	compounds
Lithium	! reacts to give H_2 and LiOH	Li_2O basic	Li^+	carbonates, nitrates, chlorides all white solids, soluble in water
Sodium	!! reacts to give H_2 and NaOH	Na_2O basic	Na^+	
Potassium	!! reacts to give H_2 and KOH	K_2O basic	K^+	

! = a fast reaction   !! a very fast reaction   !!!! explodes

Potassium reacts with water, and burns with a lilac flame. **CAUTION** Do not try this yourself.

Table 2

	appearance	with hydrogen	with hot iron	symbol of ion
Chlorine	green-yellow gas	!!!! explodes in sunlight, to give HCl	!! very easily forms $FeCl_3$	Cl^-
Bromine	red-brown liquid	! when heated reacts easily to give HBr	reacts to give $FeBr_3$	Br^-
Iodine	purple-black solid	very slow reaction to give HI	very little reaction	I^-

very unreactive ⟶

I																VII	0
						H											He
Li	Be											B	C	N	O	F	Ne
Na	Mg											Al	Si	P	S	Cl	Ar
K	Ca	Sc	Ti	V	Cr	Mn	Fe	Co	Ni	Cu	Zn	Ga	Ge	As	Se	Br	Kr
Rb	Sr	Y	Zr	Nb	Mo	Tc	Ru	Rh	Pd	Ag	Cd	In	Sn	Sb	Te	I	Xe
Cs	Ba	La	Hf	Ta	W	Re	Os	Ir	Pt	Au	Hg	Tl	Pb	Bi	Po	At	Rn
Fr	Ra	Ac	Ku	Ha													

⎣ form positive ions e.g. Na^+

form negative ions e.g. Cl^-

ELEMENTS INCORPORATED

Table 3 picks out period 3. If you look at the compounds, you can see an important pattern. Oxides to the left of the Periodic Table are bases. When they dissolve in water, the solution turns pH paper blue. Oxides from the right of the table will turn pH paper red. Oxides on the right are acidic. In group 3 the oxides can behave as acids *and* as bases. As you move across a period from one element to the next, the atoms have one more electron with every step. You can see that atoms in the same group, have the same number of electrons in the outer shell of the atom. Pages 92–3 goes into more detail. If you want to check your understanding of an atom's structure, use pages 128–9 to help you.

Table 3

	Na	Mg	Al	Si	P	S	Cl	Ar
at room temp	solid	solid	solid	solid	solid	solid	gas	gas
boils at (°C)	892	1110	2450	2680	280	444	−34	−186
formula of oxide	Na_2O	MgO	Al_2O_3	SiO_2	P_4O_{10} (P_2O_5)	SO_2	Cl_2O_7	–
formula of chloride	$NaCl$	$MgCl_2$	$AlCl_4$	$SiCl_4$	PCl_5	S_2Cl_2	–	–
number of electrons in outer shell	1	2	3	4	5	6	7	8

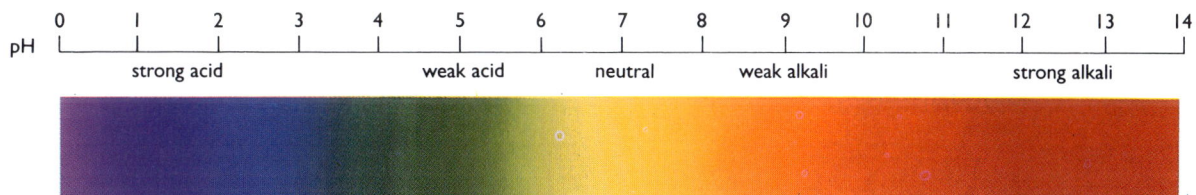

A pH scale

1. Describe some of the periodic patterns shown in the tables. For each pattern, point out any exceptions to the pattern.

2. Write equations for the reactions of the elements
   a in group 1.
   b in group 7.

3. Make some predictions about the reactions of the next elements in the group 1 and 7. Explain your reasons and write equations where you can.

4. Choose one group or a period. Plan an investigation into the trends in the properties of the elements. You could do some research to help you. Explain anything which may be difficult to do in a school laboratory.

MAKING MATTER

BUILDING MATTER

Imagine you were able to see particles being built into the different forms of matter. The illustration above shows what you might see. You might not see the factory workers, but you would see how the particles are arranged. You can see that the main building blocks are atoms and ions (see pages 128–9). Atoms can be arranged to make three different structures, ions are only built into one type of structure.

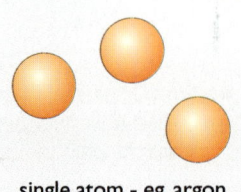

single atom - eg. argon

molecule of water (found in steam)

Structure			Examples
Molecules	small molecules	gases, many liquids, some solids	steam, sulphur, nitrogen
	large molecules	organic solids	starch, polymers
Giant structure	ions	ionic crystals	sodium chloride, copper sulphate
	atoms	metals, some other solids	copper, sodium, diamond

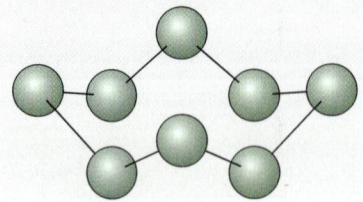

molecule of sulpher S_8

WHAT'S THE LINK BETWEEN STRUCTURE AND PROPERTIES?

From your study of particles you should be able to answer this question. You know that the temperature at which a substance boils depends on the amount of energy it takes to make its particles move fast enough to escape from the others. Where the particles are large, or held together tightly, it will take a lot of energy to get them moving fast enough to break free. It's no surprise that giant structures have very high boiling points.

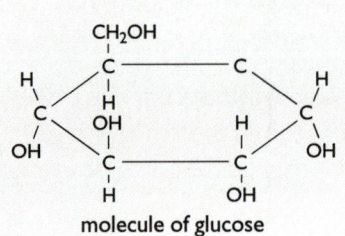

molecule of glucose

92

ELEMENTS INCORPORATED

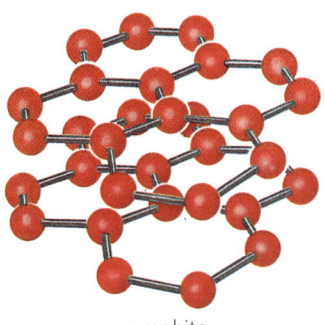

graphite

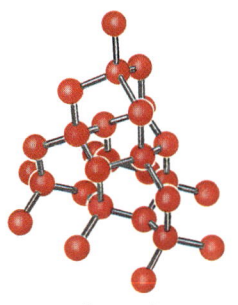

diamond

The world's largest uncut diamond.

A model of sodium chloride, next to a sample of the compound.

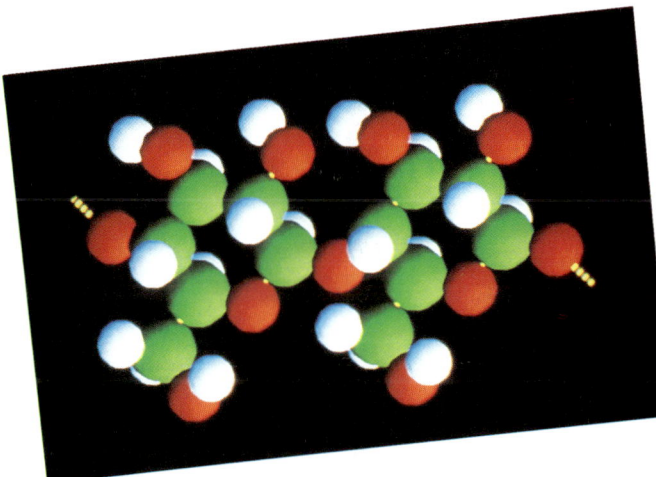

Some properties of structures are:
- giant structures have high melting and boiling temperatures
- molecular structures have lower boiling points and melting points
- giant ionic structures only conduct electricity when they are molten or in solution
- metals conduct electricity

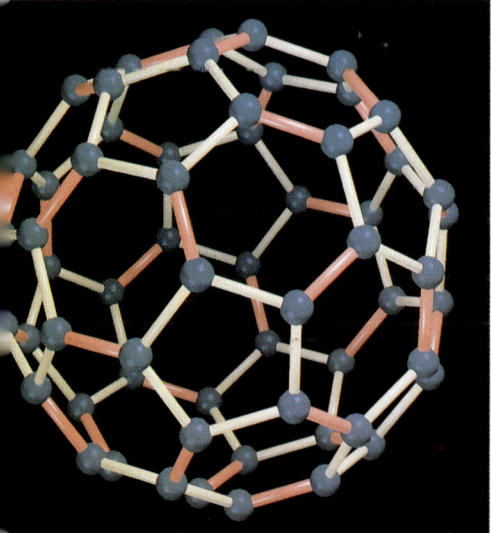

1. Which types of structure could you have for
   a elements.
   b compounds.
2. Use your understanding of particles to explain properties as shown in the tinted box above.
3. Make a copy of the Periodic Table and mark on it where you would expect to find the different types of structures.
4. The picture (left) shows a form of carbon called buckminsterfullerine. This one has formula C_{60}. The formula tells you how many carbon atoms are in one molecule. Your task is to make some decisions about which structure it forms. You can work alone or with others.
   a What information do you need to use?
   b Make a decision about its structure. Give reasons for your decision.

MAKING MATTER

REACTING SPEEDS MATTER

PUSHY METALS?

The pupils in the picture on the left investigated how different metals reacted. They used solutions of the compounds of the metals. They added pure metal, as a powder. Their results are shown (left).

Where a reaction occurred, this is the sort of thing that happened:

magnesium + copper nitrate → magnesium nitrate + copper
Mg $Cu(NO_3)_2$ $Mg(NO_3)_2$ Cu

Look back at the reactivity series to see if you can explain the pattern they found in their results.

The patterns they found showed that some of the metals were more reactive than others. Where there was a reaction, one metal displaced the other. As the equation and the table illustrated below shows the magnesium displaced copper. They found that some of the reactions happened faster than others.

ions in solution	metal added	
	X	Y
magnesium	yes	no
calcium	yes	no
copper	yes	no
iron	yes	no
zinc	yes	no

Table 1

time (in seconds)	volume of gas (in cm³)
0	0
20	25
40	50
60	60
80	70
100	75
120	80
140	80

ions in solution	metal sample added				
	Ca	Mg	Zn	Fe	Cu
magnesium	yes	no	no	no	no
calcium	no	no	no	no	no
copper	yes	yes	yes	yes	no
iron	yes	yes	yes	no	no
zinc	yes	yes	no	no	no

94

ELEMENTS INCORPORATED

Table 2

	time taken to collect first 25 cm³(s)
large chips	60
medium chips	20
small chips	10

MAKING BETTER CHIPS

These pupils then investigated the factors that affect the speed of reactions. They used calcium carbonate. Calcium carbonate reacts with hydrochloric acid like this:

calcium carbonate + hydrochloric acid → calcium chloride + water + carbon dioxide

$CaCO_3$ $2HCl$ $CaCl_2$ H_2O CO_2

They decided to follow the reaction by measuring the volume of carbon dioxide gas produced. They tried the reaction with different sized particles of calcium carbonate. They used different sized chips of marble (calcium carbonate). Table 1 shows their results for one run of the investigations. Table 2 compares the three investigations they did.

As you can see from the illustration, the acid can only react with the marble it can touch. Big chips of marble leave just a small surface area for the acid to attack. Making the chips smaller, increases the available surface area so the acid can attack more carbonate in the same time. The reaction is much faster.

All reactions follow this pattern:

	temperature	concentration	surface area	particle size
reaction faster when	↑	↑	↑	↓
reaction slower when	↓	↓	↓	↑

1. Take each investigation in turn and explain the measures which were taken to make the investigation fair.
2. Write equations for the rest of the reactions mentioned.
3. Using the pupils' results, place the metals in order of activity. Add X and Y to your list. Look back at the reactivity series and suggest what X and Y might be.
4. The results in the student's table are for chips of calcium carbonate. Explain what pattern of results you would expect if the experiment were repeated using powdered calcium carbonate.

MAKING MATTER

THE PATH TO SUCCESS

CLUES: HOT AND COLD

Lime (calcium oxide) when reacted with water, causes lots of energy to be released.

Coal is a form of carbon. When we burn coal, carbon is reacting with oxygen.

Reactions like these give us a clue what's happening to the particles. Burning carbon as a coal fire releases enough energy to keep us warm. Many reactions end with energy to 'spare'. Just like the coal fire, the energy is released to the surroundings. Sometimes reactions don't have much energy to spare, or they release it slowly. We don't always notice the energy then.

Some reactions don't have any energy to spare, and may take some energy from their surroundings. You can get an idea of what that's like if you dissolve some ammonium nitrate in water in a test tube. Hold onto the tube: you can feel your hand getting colder. The mixture in the test tube takes energy from your hand.

WHEN SUBSTANCES REACT

Atoms move around at random, occasionally colliding with other atoms.

Breaking bands need energy!

ELEMENTS INCORPORATED

The following graphs are one way of summarising what happens to the energy during reactions.

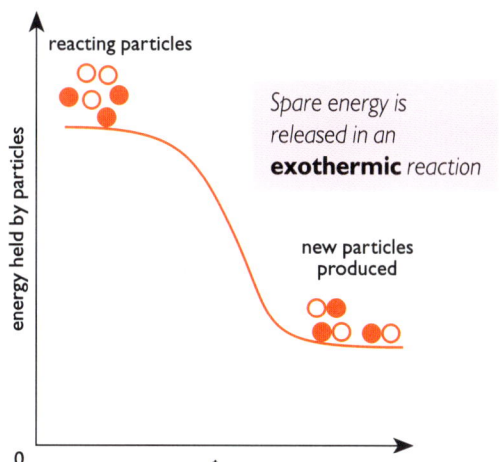

Spare energy is released in an **exothermic** *reaction*

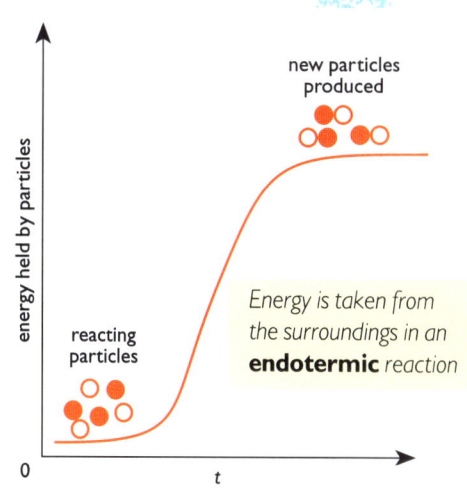

Energy is taken from the surroundings in an **endotermic** *reaction*

DON'T GET INVOLVED

The photo (left) shows pupils investigating hydrogen peroxide. Hydrogen peroxide comes in brown bottles. If you have any at home (it has antiseptic properties) you'll know that it 'goes off' easily. When hydrogen peroxide goes off, this is what happens:

hydrogen peroxide → water + oxygen
$2H_2O_2$ $2H_2O$ O_2

Light can make this reaction happen, so that's why the bottle is brown. The same reaction happens in the pupil's flask. The manganese dioxide isn't involved in the equation, but it is being a **catalyst** during this investigation.

CROSSING THE ENERGY BARRIER

Catalysts are very important. Most catalysts work by making it easier for a reaction to happen. That means catalysts usually speed up reactions. Without catalysts, life would be much slower, or might not happen at all! Nature's catalysts are the enzymes – think of the many processes which involve enzymes in your body.

With catalysts many industrial processes are cheaper and harmful exhaust gases can be changed to less harmful ones.

1 a Explain the meaning of the terms exothermic and endothermic.
  b Look at the photos and explain which reaction you think is most exothermic. Give some other examples of exothermic reactions.
2 Write equations for the reactions shown in the photographs.
3 Do some research to find out some of the ways in which enzymes are used. You may know some already, particularly if you have studied breadmaking, or brewing.
4 Catalysts help reactions happen more easily. Why will this help industry?

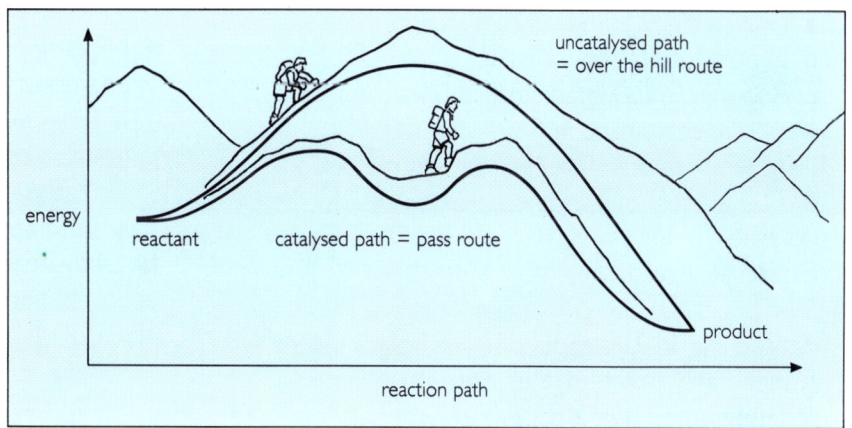

QUESTIONS

1. Describe and explain how the size of crystals would vary depending on the rate at which they cooled from molten rock.
2. What causes faults in the Earth's crust?
3. Look back to Table 2 on page 85, and pick out the exceptions to the patterns in the table. For each exception, explain what could be done to make it fit the pattern.
4. Explain the meaning of the terms atom and molecule.
5. What is different in atomic number between an atom in period 3 and
   a its neighbours to left and right.
   b in the period below it.
6. Choose one of Roger McGough's poems and use some extra information about the elements to adapt the poem, or compose a new one.
7. The results below came from a run of the experiment shown below:

time (seconds)	volume of gas (cm³)
0	0
20	5
40	15
60	25
80	35
100	35

   a Draw a graph to show these results.
   b Explain pattern shown in your graph.
   c Add lines to your graph to show what you would expect to happen if
   i the temperature of the reaction was increased,
   ii if the amount of manganese dioxide was doubled.
   Explain your reasoning.
8. Two pupils had baked potatoes for lunch. They noticed that the large potato stayed hot for longer than the small potatoes (they were all at the same temperature to start with). Explain why.

9. Yorvik Drug Company's research department investigated whether antibiotics would be better as solid tablets or as gelatin-coated capsules containing the antibiotic as a powder. Sodium hydrogencarbonate was investigated as a substitute for the antibiotic. They investigated whether tablets or capsules reacted faster with hydrochloric acid. (Hydrochloric acid occurs in the stomach.)
   a Draw a labelled diagram of suitable laboratory apparatus to measure how quickly carbon dioxide is given off when sodium hydrogencarbonate reacts with hydrochloric acid.
   b Write a balanced chemical equation using symbols for this reaction.
10. The equation for the reaction between calcium carbonate and hydrochloric acid is

    $CaCO_3(s) + 2HCl(aq) \rightarrow CaCl_2(aq) + CO_2(g) + H_2O(l)$

    Two different 10.0 g samples of calcium carbonate were reacted with excess hydrochloric acid for 6 minutes. One sample was large lumps and the other small lumps. The table shows the results.

	mass of flask and contents	
time/min	large lumps/g	small lumps/g
0	112.4	111.6
½	111.6	109.2
1	111.1	108.3
2	110.2	107.4
3	109.6	107.2
4	109.1	107.2
5	108.7	107.2
6	108.5	107.2

   a i Explain why the mass of each flask and contents decreases.
   ii Draw **two** graphs on the same axes to show how the **total loss of mass** changes with time for each sample. Label the lines 'large lumps' and 'small lumps'.
   b Calculate the volume of hydrochloric acid, of concentration 1 mol/dm³, which would react with 10.0 g of calcium carbonate.

7 PURE MAGIC

Contents
Reactions? No problem!
Electrifying reactions
Industry makes matter
Oiling the wheels of industry
You can't always get what you want
Questions

Which came first – the industry or the reaction? Sometimes it's hard to tell. Some industries have grown up because our investigations discovered some useful reactions. In other cases, industries produced materials before we knew in detail what was happening in the reactions.

This chapter deals with some of the most important reactions used in industry. Some of these involve separating mixtures of molecules (as with crude oil), while others involve making new molecules.

MAKING MATTER

REACTIONS? NO PROBLEM!

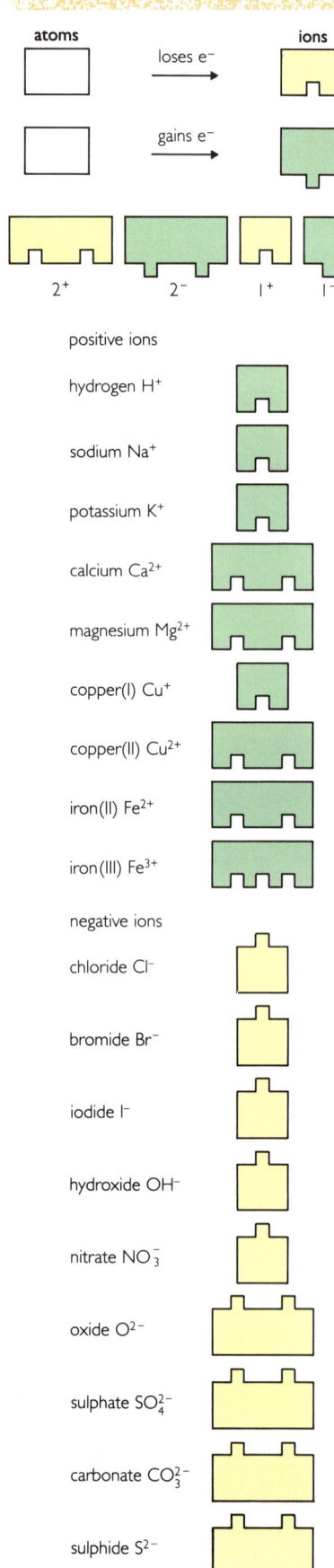

REACTIONS MATTER

Atoms, or groups of atoms, are called **ions** when they have a charge. The diagrams above show this happening in a simple way. You can see that there are bits *added* to show a negative ion. The bits represent **electrons**. Bits are *missing* to show a positive ion. The diagram shows many of the ions that you will meet during your science studies.

Look at the diagram below which shows the equations for some reactions. The equations are set out using the words and symbols as well as the coloured blocks.

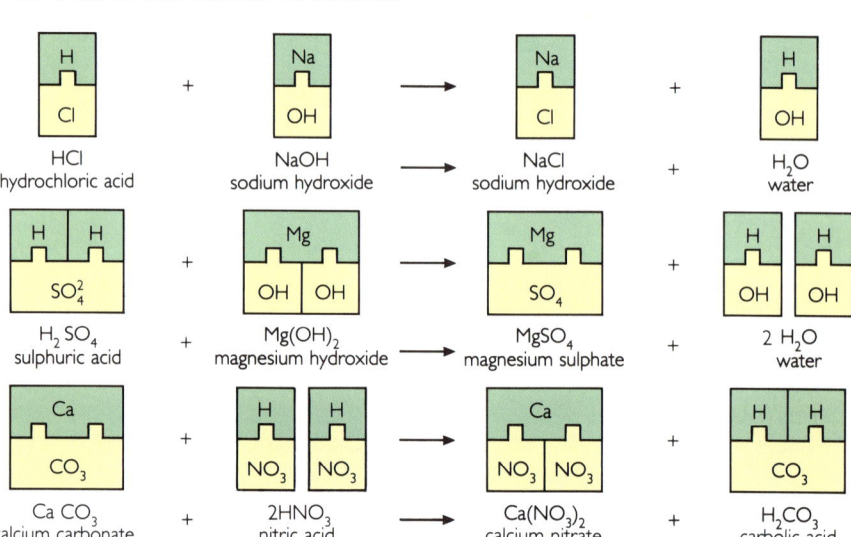

The total number of atoms at the start of a reaction is the same as the total number at the end.

In a matter reaction nothing gets lost along the way. Look carefully at the blocks and follow one reaction through. You can get a clue to why nothing is lost. All that's happening during the reaction is that the blocks are breaking apart, and building new molecules. In other words the ions are swapping around and charges are balanced.

EXPLORING AN IMPORTANT PATTERN

Table 1 above right shows some acids and bases. They are usually dissolved in water. The last column in the table shows the ions that each one makes in solution. You could check what's happening by drawing yourself some blocks like you see on this page.

PURE MAGIC

Table 1 Acids and bases

	Formula	dilute solution is like	ions produced	
hydrochloric acid	HCl	water	H^+	Cl^-
nitric acid	HNO_3	water	H^+	NO_3^-
sulphuric acid	H_2SO_4	water	H^+	SO_4^{2-}
ethanoic (acetic) acid	CH_3COOH	water, vinegar smell	H^+	CH_3COO^-
sodium hydroxide	NaOH	water	Na^+	OH^-
potassium hydroxide	KOH	water	K^+	OH^-
ammonium hydroxide	NH_4OH	water, ammonia smell	NH_4^+	OH^-
calcium hydroxide	$Ca(OH)_2$	water, often cloudy	Ca^{2+}	OH^-

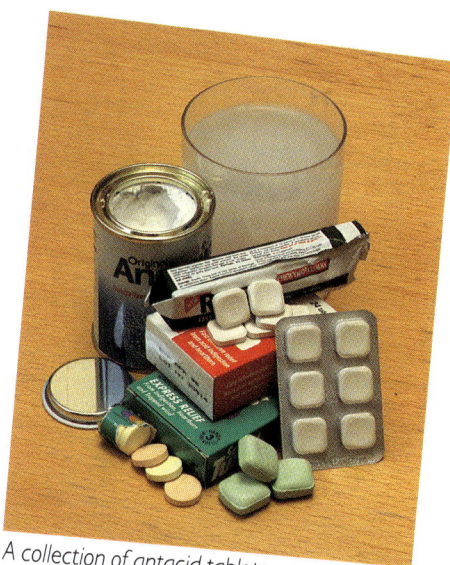

A collection of antacid tablets.

The table shows a very important pattern. When they dissolve in water
- the acids produce H^+ (hydrogen ions)
- the bases produce OH^- (hydroxide ions).

It is the H^+ ions that makes a substance acidic. The pH scale gives an indication of the concentration of H^+ ions. The more H^+ in a solution, the redder the pH paper. Bases that dissolve in water (alkalis) produce OH^- ions. This is why the solution is basic (or alkaline), and makes pH paper go blue. The bluer the pH paper, the more OH^- there is.

WHY NEUTRAL?

Two everyday examples of reactions between acids and bases are shown left. The reaction is described as **neutralisation.** Let's see why. Look at these neutralisation reactions:

hydrochloric acid + sodium hydroxide → sodium chloride + water
$$HCl \quad\quad NaOH \quad\quad NaCl \quad\quad H_2O$$
$$H^+Cl^- \quad\quad Na^+OH^- \quad\quad Na^+Cl^- \quad\quad H_2O$$

nitric acid + ammonium hydroxide → sodium chloride + water
$$HNO_3 \quad\quad NH_4OH \quad\quad NH_4Cl \quad\quad H_2O$$
$$H^+NO_3^- \quad\quad NH_4^+OH^- \quad\quad NH_4^+Cl^- \quad\quad H_2O$$

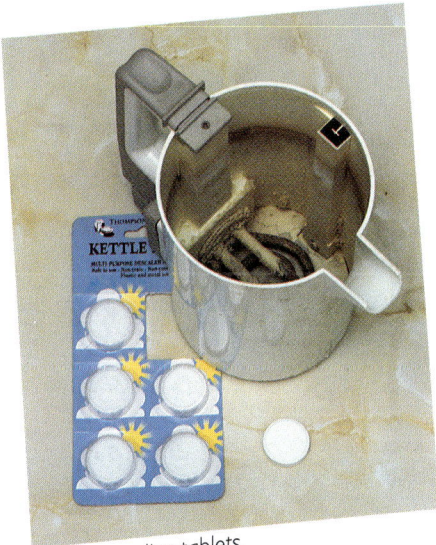

Kettle descaling tablets.

sulphuric acid + potassium hydroxide → potassium sulphate + water
$$H_2SO_4 \quad\quad 2KOH \quad\quad K_2SO_4 \quad\quad 2H_2O$$
$$2H^+SO_4^{2-} \quad\quad 2K^+OH^- \quad\quad 2K^+SO_4^{2-} \quad\quad 2H_2O$$

All these reactions have something in common. In each one this is happening:

$$H^+ + OH^- \rightarrow H_2O$$

This is an **ionic equation.** It picks out the ions that react and shows what happens. This ionic equation shows that pairs of hydrogen ions and hydroxide ions react together to make water molecules. The charges are balanced. The ions are able to affect pH paper. When an acid and a base neutralise each other, the pH of the solution is 7. The solution is neutral.

1. Write the equations for the reactions which take place when you
   a. take an antacid.
   b. use kettle descaler.
2. Explain why the ions below have the charge shown. (You might find it helps to look at the Periodic Table.) Na^+, Ca^{2+}, Cl^-, Br^-, O^{2-} and H^+.
3. Write the formula for ions not shown which have charges 1^+, 2^+, 1^-, 2^-, 3^+, 3^-.

MAKING MATTER

ELECTRIFYING REACTIONS

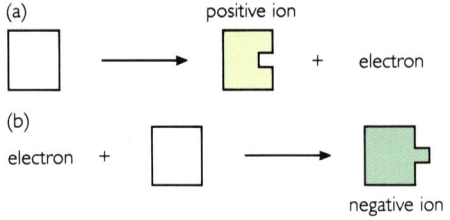
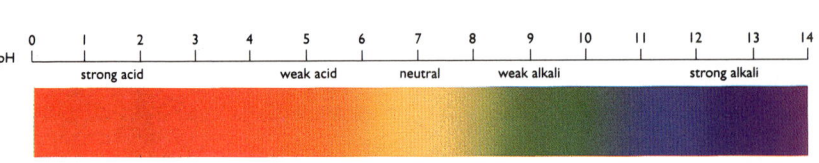
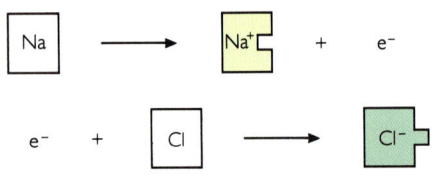
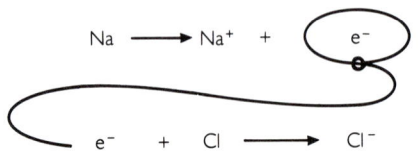

YOU'LL WONDER WHERE THE ELECTRONS WENT

Atoms can lose electrons (e^-), or pick them up. The electrons can move from a 'losing' atom to a 'gaining' atom. The diagram shows how the ions sodium and chloride ions will arrange themselves in solid sodium chloride. An atom can only lose an electron if there is somewhere for the electron to go. An atom can only pick up an electron if there is one to pick up!

ELECTROLYSIS

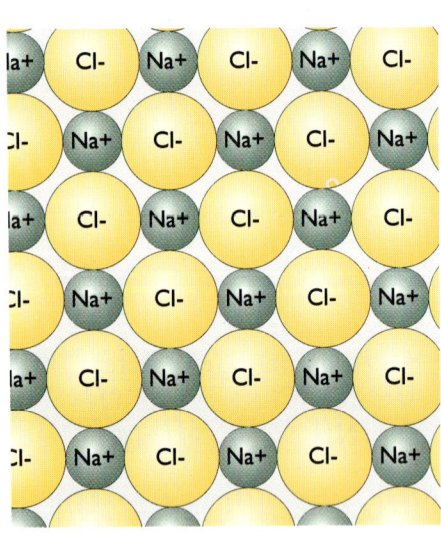
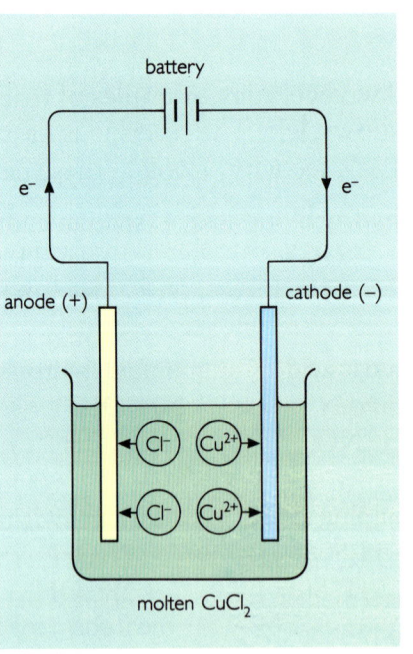
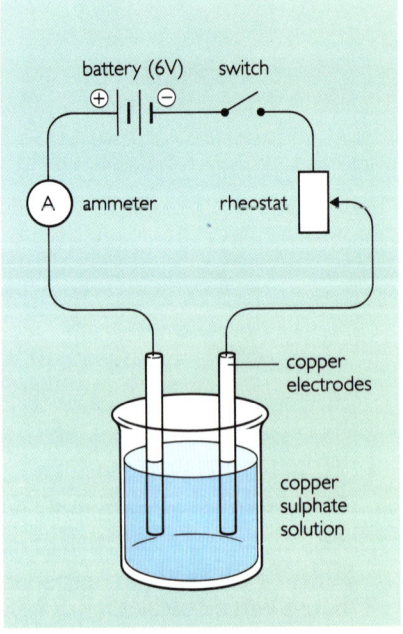

The set of equipment shown above is used to persuade electrons to move from copper to chlorine, taking the long way round. Solid copper chloride is made of chloride ions (Cl^-) and copper ions (Cu^{2+}). When the solid is melted, the ions are free to move.

The battery pumps electrons around the circuit. Electrons arrive at one electrode so the negative charge builds up. That's the negative electrode. Electrons keep moving around the circuit to the negative electrode. The other electrode loses electrons, and their negative charge. This is the positive electrode.

An open battery

PURE MAGIC

Now look at the copper chloride (left picture p102). As the ions are free to move, the negative ions move towards the electrode with a positive charge. The positive ions move to the electrode with a negative charge.

At the positive electrode:

Negative chloride ions lose electrons like this:
$$Cl^- \rightarrow Cl + e^-$$

The electrons pass to the electrode and on around the circuit. The chlorine atoms pair up to make molecules of chlorine gas:
$$Cl + Cl \rightarrow Cl_{2(g)}$$

At the negative electrode:
$$2e^- + Cu^{2+} \rightarrow Cu_{(s)}$$

Each copper atom picks up two electrons. Its charges are balanced and an uncharged copper atom collects on the electrode.

> $Cl^-_{(s)}$ and $Cu^{2+}_{(s)}$ means the ions in the solid state.
>
> $Cl^-_{(aq)}$ and $Cu^{2+}_{(aq)}$ means the ions are dissolved in water.

Zinc balls being placed in an electroplating tank.

LOOKING FOR PATTERNS IN ELECTROLYSIS

The copper collects on the negative electrode. One way of setting up an electrolysis reaction so that the amount of copper can be measured can be seen (p.102). Copper collects on the negative electrode, and the other one dissolves. If you weigh the electrodes before and after you can work out how much copper has been moved. You can also work out how much electricity has been used to move the copper. Table 1 shows the results of a series of investigations like this.

Table 1

element	ions	units of charge to move the same number of atoms
sodium	Na^+	1
silver	Ag^+	1
copper	Cu^{2+}	2
lead	Pb^{2+}	2
aluminium	Al^{3+}	3

You can see that there is a pattern. There's a link between the charge on the atoms and the amount of electricity to move them.

---

1 Study the copper chloride electrolysis and use your understanding of the reactivity series and the Periodic Table to predict an electrolysis reaction which might be
   a quicker and easier to carry out.
   b slower and more difficult. Explain your reasoning.
2 Give an example of another electrolysis (by words or diagram) and explain what happens.
3 Suggest and explain some of the precautions you would need to take if you were carrying out the investigations for which Table 1 shows results.

MAKING MATTER

INDUSTRY MAKES MATTER

Many of the things we use every day are made from fairly simple compounds. Industry depends on many of the reactions you have learned about. Here are just two examples of the way industry works with matter on a very large scale.

SODIUM HYDROXIDE BY THE TONNE

Sodium hydroxide is made by the electrolysis of sodium chloride solution (brine). There are two designs of cell for the electrolysis. One is the mercury cathode cell (see below left). The other is the diaphragm cell (see below right).

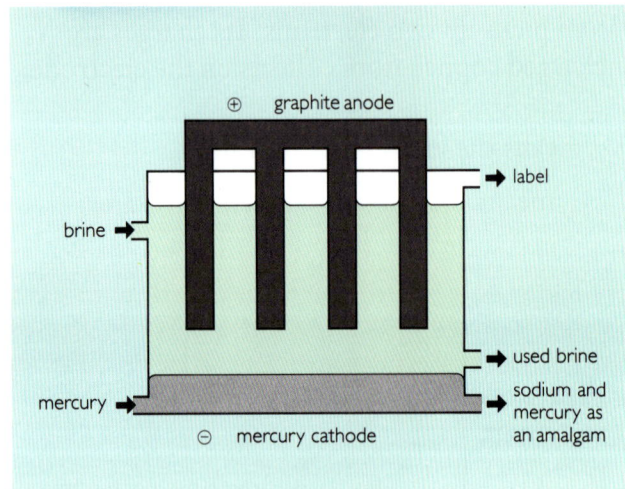
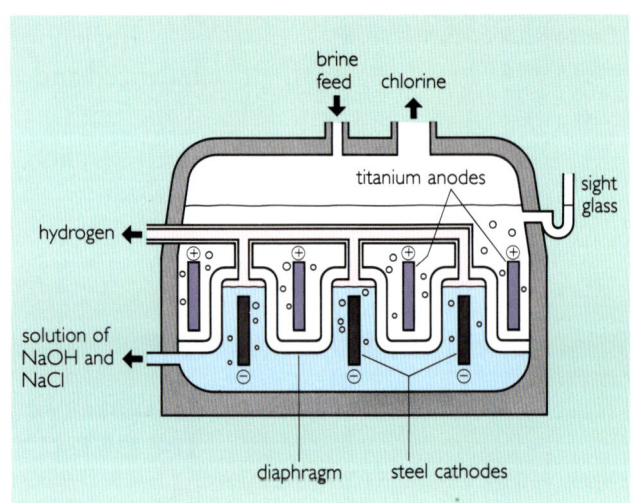

Solvent reactor towers at an ICI Castner Kellner plant.

Both cells use concentrated brine. This contains sodium ions and chloride ions. The same reaction happens at the positive electrode in both cells.

1 Chloride ions lose electrons, and pair up to make chlorine molecules:

$$2Cl \rightarrow Cl_{2(g)} + e^-$$

2 At the negative electrode sodium ions pick up electrons:

$$Na^+ + e^- \rightarrow Na_{(s)}$$

Sodium atoms collect on the cathode. When the cathode is mercury, the liquid metal keeps flowing through the cell carrying the sodium with it. It flows into water where the sodium reacts with water to produce sodium hydroxide:

$$2Na/Hg_{(l)} + 2H_2O_{(l)} \rightarrow 2NaOH_{(aq)} + H_{2(g)} + Hg_{(l)}$$

The mercury can be used again.

At the negative electrode water molecules pick up electrons to make hydroxide ions:

$$2H_2O_{(l)} + 2e^- \rightarrow 2OH^- + H_{2(g)}$$

The mixture that comes out of the cell contains ions of sodium hydroxide and some chloride. This mixture needs some work to produce pure sodium hydroxide and pure sodium chloride.

SODA TOWERS

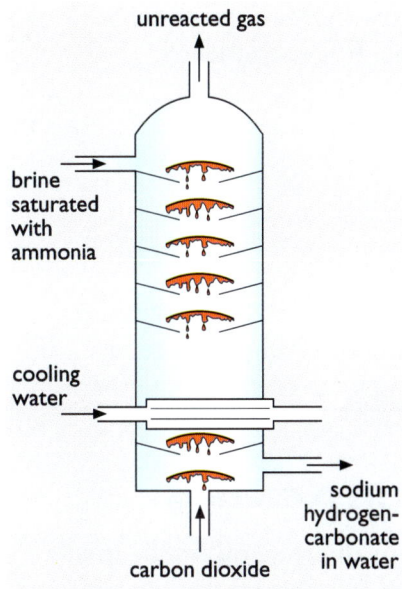

Most sodium carbonate made in the UK is made in a Solvay Tower. Carbon dioxide is pumped in at the bottom of the tower. Brine, saturated with ammonia is pumped in at the top.

The brine-ammonia mixture trickles down the tower. It meets the carbon dioxide coming up and reacts.

$$NaCl_{(aq)} + CO_{2(g)} + NH_{3(g)} + H_2O_{(l)} \rightarrow NaHCO_{3(s)} + NH_4Cl_{(aq)}$$

This reaction is exothermic, so the tower needs cooling.

The $NaHCO_{3(s)}$ and $NH_4Cl_{(aq)}$ mixture is a white sludge. It is taken out at the bottom of the tower. $NaHCO_3$ (sodium hydrogen carbonate) is separated from the mixture and heated:

$$2NaHCO_{3(s)} \rightarrow Na_2CO_{3(s)} + H_2O_{(l)} + CO_{2(g)}$$

$NH_4Cl_{(aq)}$ is reacted to produce ammonia again.

RAW MATERIALS

To make one tonne of sodium carbonate it takes:

- 1.5 tonnes of brine
- 1.5 tonnes of limestone
- 2 kg of ammonia
- 50.0 tonnes of water (mostly for cooling)

The limestone is used to make the carbon dioxide and recycle the ammonia. Apart from the ammonia, the raw materials are fairly cheap. The ammonia is recycled, and very little is used up.

1. Find out, and explain, some of the uses of
   a. sodium hydroxide.
   b. sodium carbonate.
2. List the advantages of each cell for producing sodium hydroxide.
   What are the disadvantages of each cell?
3. a. Describe and explain some of the design features of a Solvay tower.
   b. Discuss the advantages and disadvantages of producing sodium carbonate in this way. (Remember to consider siting and costs.)
4. Although ammonia is recycled in the Solvay process, 'very little is used up'. Explain how this could happen.

MAKING MATTER

OILING THE WHEELS OF LIVING

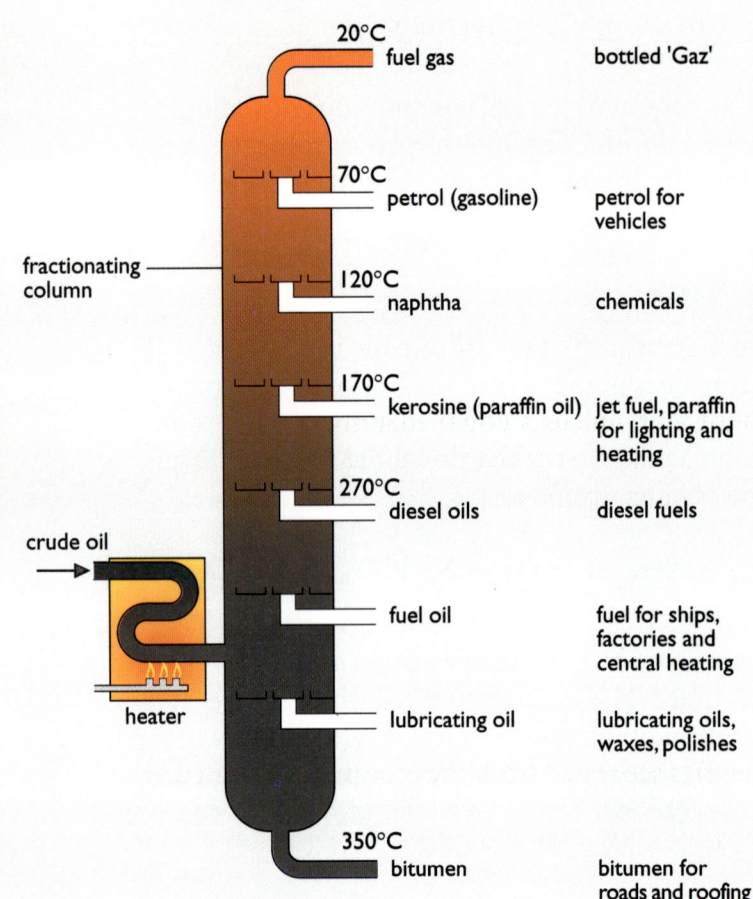

NOT SO CRUDE

Crude oil is a mixture of thousands of different compounds. Most of the compounds are made from hydrogen and carbon: they are called **hydrocarbons.** The molecules are different sizes. The bigger the molecules, the higher their boiling points. This is used as a way of separating the oil mixture into fractions.

We can show how big molecules are built by drawing structures. For example:

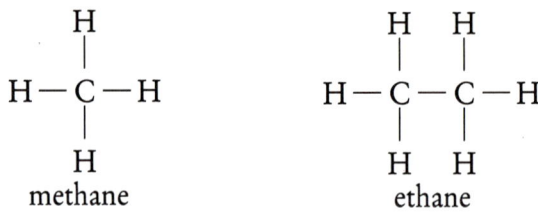

Each line represents one bond between a carbon atom and a hydrogen atom, or another carbon atom.

LET'S GET CRACKING

The heavy fractions of crude oil can be made more useful. Big molecules are broken into smaller ones by catalytic cracking. Cracking large alkane molecules produces a mixture of **alkanes** and **alkenes.**

Here is one example of cracking a large molecule:

Calor gas and margarine are both derived from hydrocarbons.

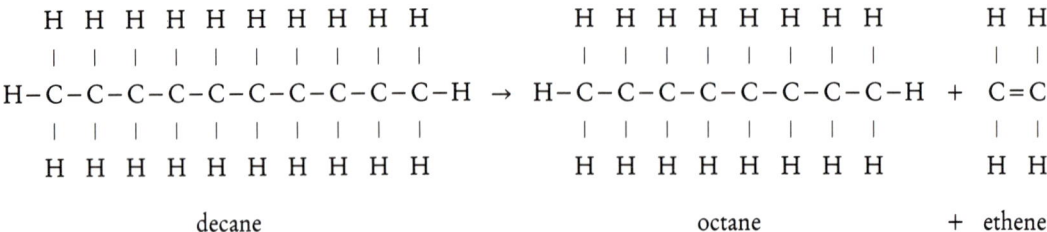

HYDROCARBON FAMILIES

There are families of hydrocarbon compounds. Carbon and hydrogen atoms are joined together with slightly different ways in each family. Two of the families are the alkanes and the alkenes.

PURE MAGIC

> Alkanes are **saturated**: all the bonds are used up.

> Alkenes are **unsaturated**: they have space for two more atoms to join.

A cat-cracking plant.

1 Work out the name and formula for
   a alkanes
   b alkenes
   which have 10, 12 and 20 carbon atoms.

2 Another family is the **alkynes**, as shown in Table 2.
   Use your understanding of hydrocarbon patterns to work out what **a** to **f** should be.

Table 2

Alkynes	
name	formula
ethyne	C_2H_2
propyne	C_3H_4
butyne	**a**
b	C_5H_8
c	C_6H_{10}
heptyne	**d**
e	**f**

3 Why isn't there an alkene with just one C?

Table 1

Alkanes		Alkenes	
name	formula	name	formula
methane	CH_4	—	—
ethane	C_2H_6	ethene	C_2H_4
propane	C_3H_8	propene	C_3H_6
butane	C_4H_{10}	butene	C_4H_8
pentane	C_5H_{12}	pentene	C_5H_{10}
hexane	C_6H_{14}	hexene	C_6H_{12}
heptane	C_7H_{16}	heptene	C_7H_{14}
octane	C_8H_{18}	octene	C_8H_{16}

- The first half of the name tells you how many carbon atoms there is in the molecule.
- The second half of the name tells you the family it belongs to.
- In a family, all the compounds behave in the same way.

REACTING HYDROCARBONS

Alkanes are not very reactive. However, they do burn like this:

$$CH_{4(g)} + O_{2(g)} \rightarrow CO_{2(g)} + 2H_2O_{(g)}$$

Reactions like this produce a great deal of energy. They also make carbon dioxide and steam, and no ash. Alkanes make 'clean' fuels. The other alkanes will follow this pattern of reaction.

Alkenes burn too.

$$C_2H_{4(g)} + 3O_{2(g)} \rightarrow 2CO_{2(g)} + 2H_2O_{(g)}$$

However, they are not used as fuels. They are much more useful for making other compounds. Alkenes have unsaturated molecules, so other atoms can add on.

Some of ethene's addition reactions:

$$C_2H_{4(g)} + Br_{2(aq)} \rightarrow C_2H_4Br_{2(g)} \text{ dibromoethane}$$

$$C_2H_{4(g)} + H_{2(g)} \rightarrow C_2H_{6(g)} \quad \text{ethane}$$

$$C_2H_{4(g)} + H_2O_{(g)} \rightarrow C_2H_5OH \quad \text{ethanol}$$

Ethene molecules can add on to each other to make large molecules like polyethene:

```
H H H H H H              H H H H H H
| | | | | |              | | | | | |
C=C+C=C+C=C... → (...C-C-C-C-C-C...)
| | | | | |              | | | | | |
H H+H H H H              H H H H H H
   ethene monomers        poly(ethene) polymer
```

In polyethene up to 1500 ethene molecules join together. Addition reactions like this can produce all sorts of large molecules (polymers).

MAKING MATTER

YOU CAN'T ALWAYS GET WHAT YOU WANT

SOMETIMES YOU CAN'T WIN

Have you ever been in a situation like the cartoon? As fast as you do something it's undone. You might have tried things like going faster. You might have got rid of the action that was competing with you. In the cartoon you could do that by getting rid of the dog.

There are some reactions that suffer like this: one that produces ammonia is a typical example:

$$\text{nitrogen} + \text{hydrogen} \rightarrow \text{ammonia}$$
$$N_{2(g)} + 3H_{2(g)} \rightarrow 2NH_{3(g)}$$

This reaction takes 1 molecule of nitrogen gas and 3 molecules of hydrogen gas and makes 2 molecules of ammonia gas releasing 'spare' energy to the surroundings. As it releases 'spare' energy we call this an **exothermic** reaction.

Unfortunately, the good work is undone by this reaction:

$$2NH_{3(g)} \rightarrow N_{2(g)} + 3H_{2(g)}$$

This reaction takes 2 molecules of ammonia gas and makes 1 molecule of nitrogen gas and 3 of hydrogen gas taking in energy from the surroundings. This is an **endothermic** reaction.

So what happens? Just like the dog as fast as one reaction makes ammonia, the other one turns it back into nitrogen and hydrogen!

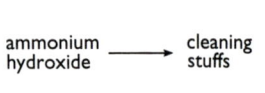

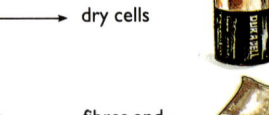

Ammonia converted to	used to make
liquid ammonia	refrigerants
concentrated nitric acid	explosives
ammonium hydroxide	cleaning stuffs
ammonium chloride	dry cells
nylon, rayon, polyurethane	fibres and other polymers
azo-compounds	dyes
ammonium, urea, ammonium sulphate, ammonium nitrate	fertilisers

Scientists use an arrow like this ⇌ to show that this pair of reactions will keep undoing each other's good work. So these equations:

$$N_{2(g)} + 3H_{2(g)} \rightarrow 2NH_{3(g)}$$
$$2NH_{3(g)} \rightarrow N_{2(g)} + 3H_{2(g)}$$

are written like this:

$$N_{2(g)} + 3H_{2(3)} \rightleftharpoons 2NH_{3(g)}$$

A reaction like this is called an **equilibrium** reaction. The two reactions go at the same speed, so you end up with the same amount of ammonia, just like the gardener you have the same number of plants.

PURE MAGIC

PROBLEMS FOR PRODUCERS

Ammonia is an important product to us all (85% is used to make fertiliser, 15% to make nylon). Getting the better of the problem pair of reactions is important. Studying the reaction gives the sort of pattern you can see in the graph. The yield of ammonia is better at low temperatures and high pressures.

Problem 1: low temperatures = slower reactions so it takes a longer time to get the yield.

Problem 2: high pressure costs money (equipment that stands up to high pressure is expensive).

The solution is to go for a reasonable yield of ammonia, in a reasonable time, and to use fairly high pressure. Using a catalyst helps speed up the ammonia producing reaction too.

nitrogen + hydrogen $\xrightarrow[\text{catalyst}]{\text{high temperature and pressure}}$ ammonia

$$N_{2(g)} + 3H_{2(g)} \xrightarrow[\text{catalyst}]{\text{high temperature and pressure}} 2NH_{3(g)}$$

This sort of solution was developed by Fritz Haber in 1904. The production process is named after him.

- The nitrogen comes from air.
- The hydrogen is made from methane or naphtha processed from crude oil.

methane + steam $\xrightarrow[\text{catalyst}]{\text{high temperature and pressure}}$ carbon dioxide + hydrogen

$$CH_{4(g)} + 2H_2O_{(g)} \xrightarrow[\text{catalyst}]{\text{high temperature and pressure}} CO_{2(g)} + 4H_{2(g)}$$

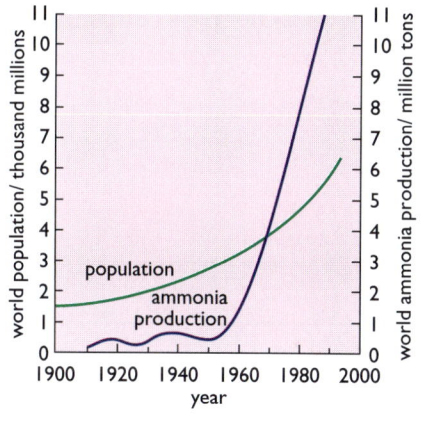

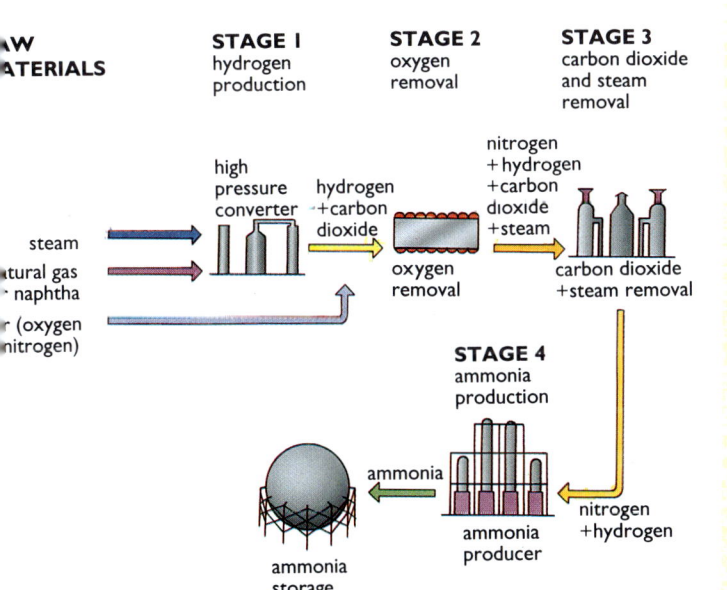

1 Look at the cartoon. Suggest what the gardener should do in order to 'win'.
2 Design an advertisement for ammonia which points out why it is useful.
3 It's been said that one of the most useful things that could be done to help a developing country would be to give it a Haber plant.
 a Explain it could be useful.
 b What other actions might be important to help a developing country?
4 Look at reactions involved in producing ammonia. Explain why
 a why increasing the pressure will help the forward reaction. (Explain what's happening to the particles, and how this helps to drive the forward reaction.)
 b increasing the temperature will favour the reverse reaction. (Use the energy transfers involved to help you explain.)

MAKING MATTER

QUESTIONS

1. Write equations using words and symbols for the reactions between solutions of:
   a. nitric acid and sodium hydroxide.
   b. sulphuric acid and calcium hydroxide.
   c. ethanoic acid and potassium hydroxide.
   d. hydrochloric acid and calcium hydroxide.
   e. copper sulphate and magnesium.
   f. lead nitrate and silver chloride.

2. Write ionic equations for the reactions in question 1.

3. a. What is a hydrocarbon?
   b. Why are hydrocarbons important?

4. Draw a flow chart to summarise how crude oil is processed to produce useful materials.

5. Write down the formula for:
   a. alcohols
   b. alkynes
   which have 10, 15, 20 carbon atoms.

6. Explain each of the following terms, and give an example in each case.
   a. Exothermic.
   b. Equilibrium reaction.
   c. Electrolysis.
   d. Fractional distillation.

7. Explain why oil is described as a fossil fuel.

8. Write equations (including the names of the products) for the reactions between:
   a. ethane and bromine.
   b. ethyne and oxygen.
   c. ethene and water.
   e. butene and hydrogen.
   e. propane and chlorine.

9. What catalyst is used in the production of ammonia? Explain why it helps.

10. The nitrogen used to make ammonia in the Haber process is produced from the air. Liquid air is distilled and the nitrogen fraction is collected. Explain what this means.

11. The diagram on the right, above shows some of the ions in a solution of copper chloride. Explain carefully what would happen to the copper ions after the switch is closed.

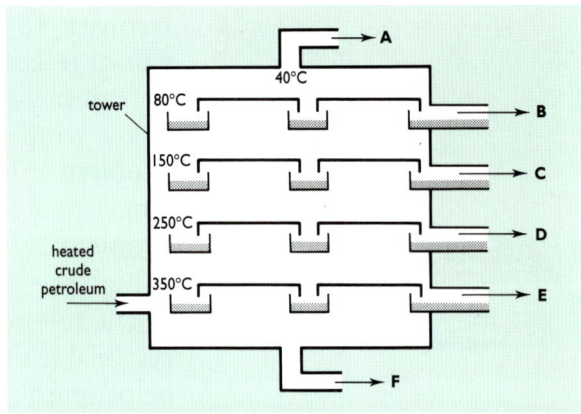

12. The diagram below shows a section through the chemical plant used to separate crude petroleum fractions.

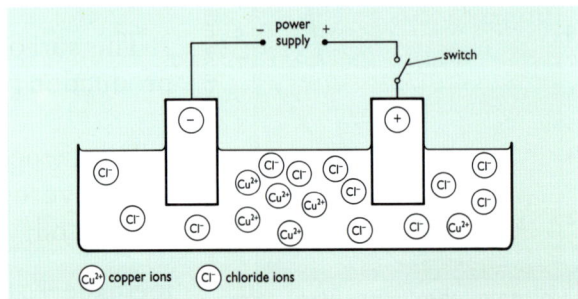

As the crude petroleum is heated many of the substances in it change into gases. These gases are fed into the inlet at the bottom of the tower. Hot gases rise up the tower and condense into liquids at different heights according to their boiling points.
a. Name this method of separating crude petroleum into fractions.
b. At which of the outlets, A to F, would you expect the fractions below to leave the tower?
   i. Gases   ii. Bitumen residue   iii. Naphtha
c. Copy and complete this table shows three of the substances which can be obtained from crude petroleum.

substance	Formula	Structural formula	Use
Methane	CH_4	H–C–H (with H above and below)	fuel
	C_3H_8		
Ethene	C_2H_4		

SECTION 3

USING ENERGY

USING ENERGY

ENERGY TRANSFERS

Here are some examples of energy transfer that you studied in Book 1.

Ready for harvest.

Feeding time.

Portable power.

Going places.

Energy store.

The transport system.

1 Each photograph shows energy being transferred.
 a For each photograph explain what useful job is being done by the energy transfer.
 b Say where the energy is transferred from and where it goes to. You might be able to describe more than one energy transfer in some photographs.

Remember, remember, the fifth of November...

In orbit.

Music to my ears.

Strip lights.

Faster than sound.

Using hot air.

USING ENERGY

QUESTIONS

1 Power stations are designed to produce large quantities of electrical energy. The diagram below shows a coal-fired power station.

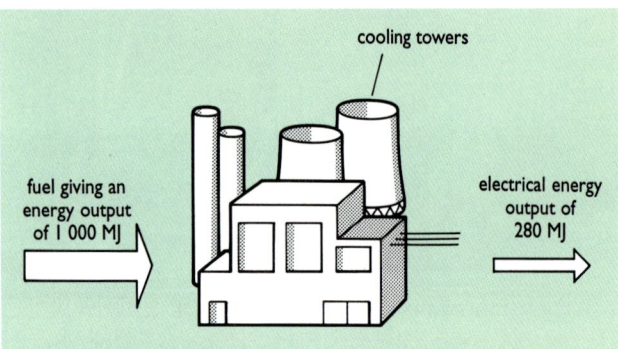

a Choose the words from the list in the box below which will complete the sentences which follow.

chemical	electrical	gravitational
potential	heat	light
nuclear	sound	kinetic

In the power station .... energy in the coal is changed into .... energy. This energy turns water into steam. The steam turns turbines and these turn generators. Generators change .... energy into electrical energy.

b Explain where the energy in coal originally came from.

c i Calculate how efficient the power station is at changing the energy in the coal into electrical energy.
 ii In what form is most energy lost from this power station?
 iii What eventually happens to this 'lost' energy?

2 The diagram below shows a microwave oven.

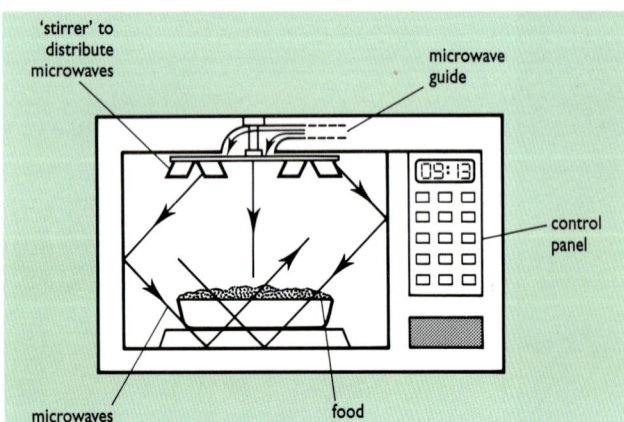

Microwaves are absorbed by the water in the food. The specific heat capacity of water is 4.2 kJ per °C.

a A plastic jug containing 500 g of water at 20 °C was placed in the microwave oven. The oven was switched on at full power. After two minutes in the oven the temperature of the water had risen to 44 °C. Calculate how much energy had been transferred to the water in two minutes.

b The output power of the oven is rated at 650 W. How much energy does the cooker transfer from the electricity supply in two minutes?

c Compare the amounts of energy you have calculated in (a) and (b). Account for any difference.

d The microwaves produced by the oven have a frequency of 2450 MHz and a velocity of 300 000 km per second. Calculate their wavelength.

3 The pie chart shows five sources of energy used by a country.

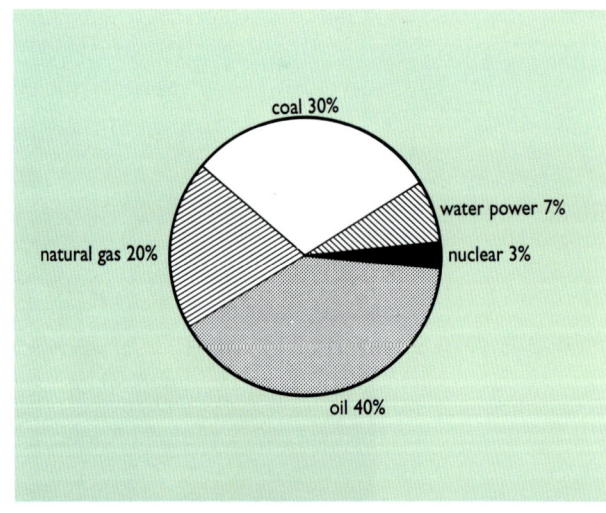

The table shows the proportional use and estimated reserves of coal, oil and natural gas.

	Relative estimated reserves	Relative quantity used/year
Coal	500	1.25
Oil	100	3
Natural Gas	90	1.5

a Explain why it is always difficult to make accurate predictions of how long reserves will last.
b Why will the pie chart be likely to be different in about 20 years' time?
c Explain the economic, environmental and social benefits of using nuclear energy as the main source of providing electrical power.

8 ELECTRO-MAGNETIC RADIATION

Contents
Bouncing and bending
Forming images
Colour
Electromagnetic spectrum
Bigger images
Questions

The transfer of energy by electromagnetic radiation is essential for our survival. Electromagnetic waves carry energy from the Sun to Earth. It keeps us warm, grows our food and gives us light. By studying how light behaves, we learn how other invisible electromagnetic waves also behave. In this chapter you will learn about reflection and refraction and how images are formed. The position of visible light in the electromagnetic spectrum is compared to other waves. Finally you will find out how microscopes and telescopes help us to see more easily.

By focusing your eyes at different distances you may be able to see a three dimensional image in this picture.

How to see the image: a) Stare at the 2 dots on the white strip. b) Cross your eyes so you see double, making four dots. c) Continue to do this until two of the dots overlap, making three dots. d) Slowly bring the centre dot into clearer focus, then gradually glide your eyes downwards. e) Your Alpha brain waves ought to be stimulated and a 3D image should miraculously appear.

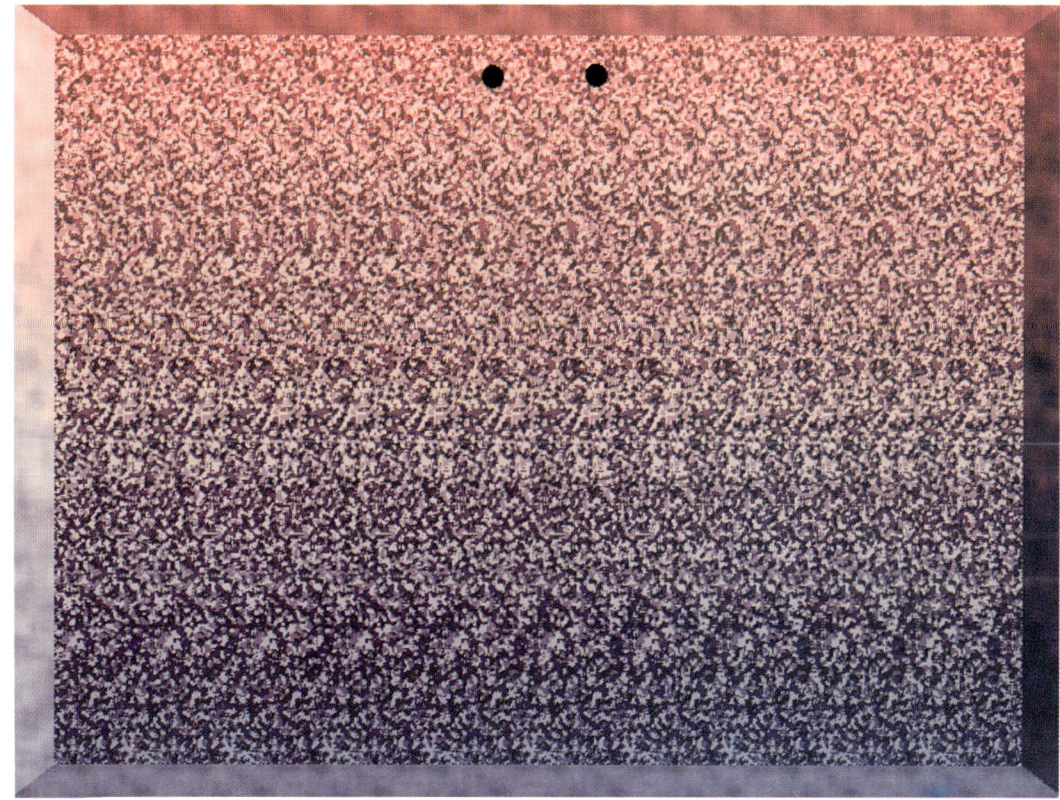

USING ENERGY

BOUNCING AND BENDING

IS IT A BIRD? IS IT A PLANE? NO, IT'S . . . DONE BY MIRRORS

In the film *Superman* mirrors were used to create the illusion that Superman could fly. The actor, Christopher Reeve, was supported in front of a screen by a hydraulic arm which was concealed by his cloak. A background scene was projected from a film projector in front of the screen by bouncing the image off mirrors. The image on the screen gave the impression that Superman was moving but really it was the image behind him that moved. A camera in front of the screen filmed Superman, against the moving background, by shooting through a two-way mirror. The picture (left) is a still from the film and shows what the camera filmed.

The illustration below shows how the camera was set up to film Superman in flight. Light from a lamp bulb in the projector passes through a film and the projection lens. The light from the projector will form an enlarged image on a screen of the picture on film. Instead of shining straight onto the screen, the light from the projector is turned through 90° by the first mirror and then turned again by the second mirror, which is a two-way mirror. The image is formed on a special screen behind the actor.

The two-way mirror allows the camera to film the stationary actor in front of a moving image. This creates the illusion that Superman is moving against a stationary background.

The actor Christopher Reeve appeared to fly in the film Superman *through a technique called 'front projection'. This technique relies on the scientific laws of reflection and the fact that light travels in straight lines.*

1 Copy the diagram showing the projector, mirrors, screen and camera.
  a Mark arrows on the edges of the light beam to show how the light travels from the projector to the camera.
  b Look at the light beam which is reflected at the first mirror and draw dotted lines behind the mirror to show where the beam appeared to be coming from. Where is this point in relation to the projector?
  c In your own words, say what laws of reflection the light obeys.
  d What is the angle between each mirror and the beam of light?
2 What would be the difference on the screen if the first mirror was removed and the projector was placed at 90° to the screen. Draw a diagram to help you explain the difference.

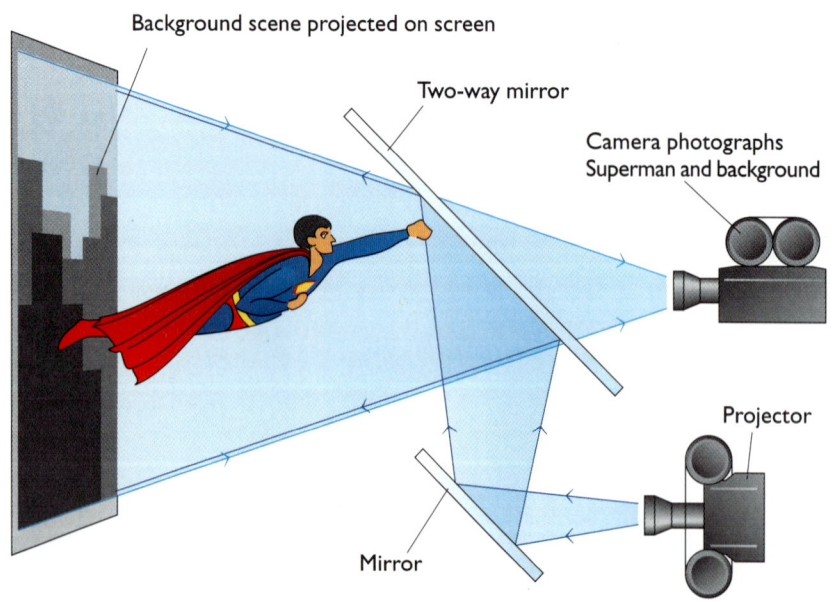

How Superman was able to 'fly' without really moving

ELECTROMAGNETIC RADIATION

CHANGING DIRECTION

An optical illusion makes water in a swimming pool appear to be shallower than it really is. It is caused by the refraction of light.

The apparent bending of the pencil is caused by refraction

You might have noticed that the bottom of a swimming pool appears to be closer than it actually is. If you put part of a pencil into a glass of water the pencil appears to be bent, just at the point where it enters the water. These effects can be explained if you understand that light changes speed when it changes medium e.g. when moves from air into water or glass or vice-versa. The change in speed bends the light along another straight line. The word **refraction** is used to describe this change of direction, the illustrations below will help you to understand how it happens.

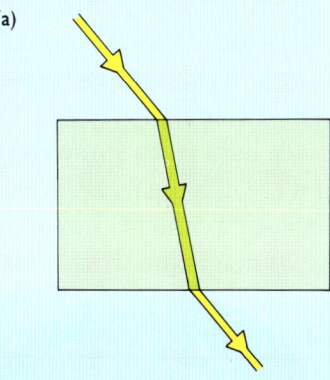

Refraction of a beam of light through the glass block.

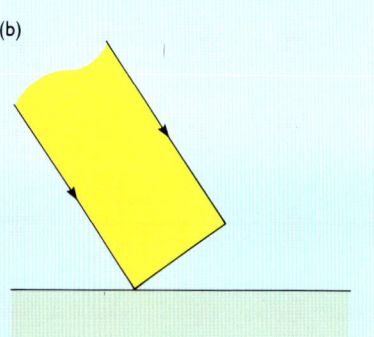

This enlarged diagram shows a beam of light in air, just arriving at the glass surface.

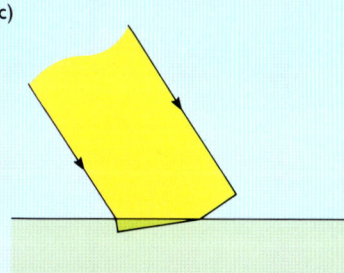

A split second later, the part of the light beam in the glass has slowed down. The rest of the light beam is still travelling at a faster speed in air. This causes the part of the beam in the glass to change direction.

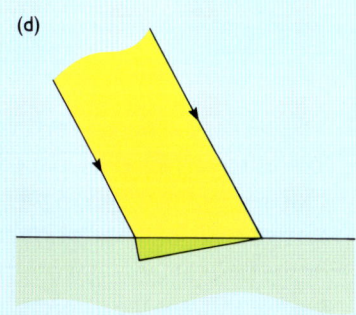

By the time the full width of the beam has reached the glass, all the light has slowed down. This change of speed has caused the beam to change its direction.

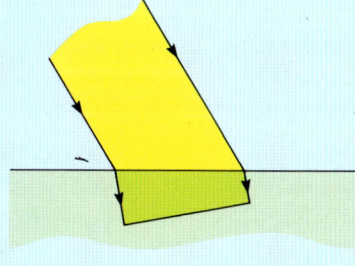

Once the whole beam has entered the glass, it moves forward in a straight line.

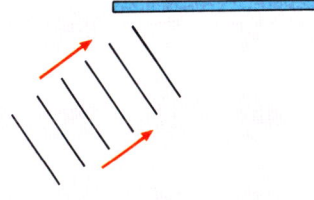

3 The diagram above shows water waves moving towards a barrier. Copy the diagram and show on your diagram how the water waves will be reflected by the barrier.

4 Water waves change their speeds as they move from deep water to shallow water. What other differences would you expect to see on the water at different depths?

5 Plan an investigation to find out if water waves speed up or slow down when they move from deep water to shallow water.

USING ENERGY

FORMING IMAGES

Your eyes respond to light and help you to see the world. The way that your eyes work is similar to the way a camera works. Both have a small opening which lets light in; this is called the aperture in a camera and the pupil in your eye. With some cameras you can change the size of the aperture according to how bright the light is. Your eye controls the size of your pupil automatically with the iris. Eyes and cameras have lenses which focus an image. In a camera the image is formed on a special film whilst in your eye it is formed on a light sensitive layer called the retina.

Whilst some things may be similar, there are differences in the way that your eyes and a camera work. One of these is the way that they both change to focus light from objects which are different distances away.

Rays of light from something far away, for example other traffic if you were driving a car, are parallel when they reach the lens in your eye, or a camera. Rays from something close up, for example a book or magazine when you are reading, are **diverging**. This means that the lens has to bend the light rays through different angles, depending on how far away the object is. The diagram shows how the lens in a camera and your eye do this differently.

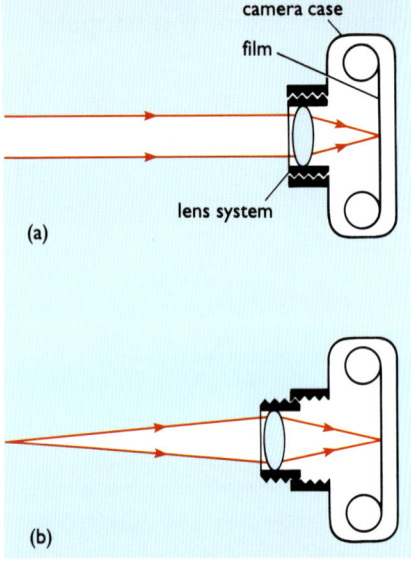

In a camera the lens is moved in front of the film. For a close up photograph, the distance needed for the lens to focus an image on the film is greater than that needed to focus an image of an object far away.

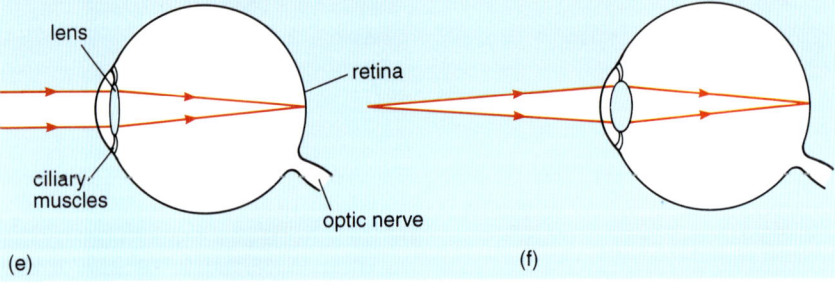

1. You will need a friend to do this. Ask your friend to look at something in a subdued light and then suddenly look at something very bright. You should study the size of the pupil in your friend's eye as he or she looks at the bright object. Draw diagrams of the eye showing the difference you observed.
2. Sit at one end of a room and focus your sight on some large writing at the other end of the room. Keeping your eyes in focus on the end of the room, bring your hand up in front of your face. How many fingers can you see? When you focus on your hand, what happens to the writing you could see at the end of the room? Explain why this happens.
3. Hold a book, or a sheet of paper with writing on it, at arms length and close one eye. Slowly bring the page closer to your open eye and adjust your vision so that you can still see it in focus. Find the nearest point to your eye that you can hold the page with the print still in focus. This is called your **near point**. Repeat it to find the near point of your other eye. Is this the same distance for both eyes?
4. Plan an investigation to find out:
   a if there is any connection between the length of someone's near point and the colour of their iris,
   b if there is any connection between the length of someone's near point and their age.
   When you have made your own plan, talk about it with a small group and plan how you can collect data between you. Carry out your plan with the rest of your group and write a report about your investigation.

ELECTROMAGNETIC RADIATION

In your eye the lens changes shape. Muscles around the edge of the lens will stretch it to make it thinner. A thin lens is needed to focus parallel rays from distant objects. When you are reading, the lens needs to be fatter to bend the rays through a bigger angle. Because the lens is flexible, it becomes fatter when the muscles relax.

OUT OF SIGHT

Many people need the aid of additional lenses to be able to see clearly. Jane is shortsighted (myopic) and needs to wear spectacles at all times. Andrew is longsighted (presbyopic) and needs to wear spectacles for reading. The following illustration explains why they cannot focus properly.

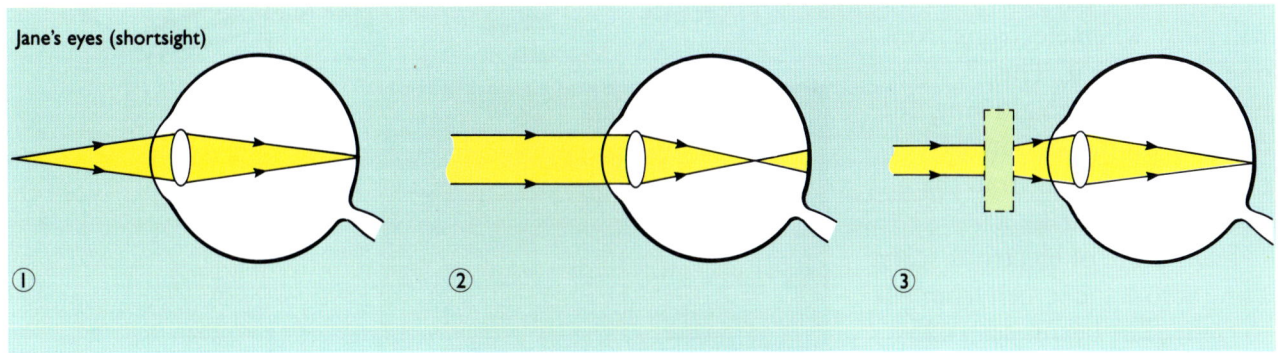

Jane's eyes (shortsight)

① Jane can read and see close up objects clearly because the lens in her eye is fat enough to bend the rays so that they focus on the retina.

② When Jane looks at something far away, the lens in her eye bends the parallel rays too much and the rays are focused before they reach the retina. Jane can still see things but they are blurred.

③ Jane needs a spectacle or contact lens which will diverge the parallel rays from a distant object so that the lens in her eye can focus the image on the retina. Jane should wear these lenses at all times.

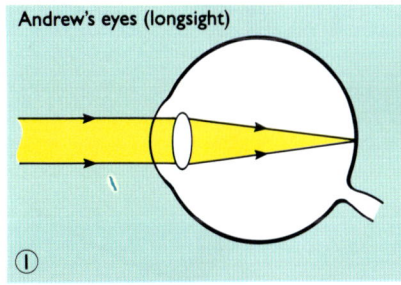

Andrew's eyes (longsight)

① Andrew can see distant objects clearly because the muscles around the lens in his eye can stretch the lens and make it thinner. A thin lens is needed to bend the parallel rays through a small angle and focus them on the retina.

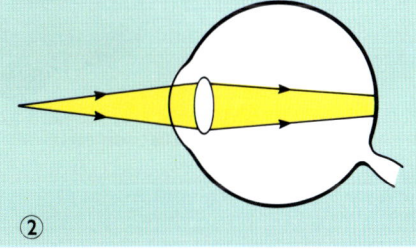

② When Andrew tries to read, the lens in his eye does not go fat enough to bend the diverging rays through the angle need to bring them to focus on the retina. Instead the rays do not quite focus properly.

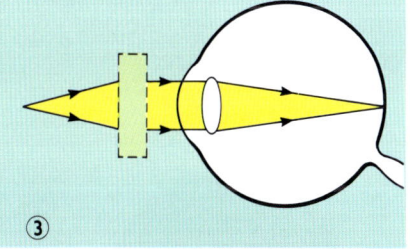

③ Andrew needs spectacles that will converge the diverging rays so that they are parallel when they enter his eyes. The lens in his eye can then focus these rays on the retina. Andrew only needs to wear these lenses when he is reading.

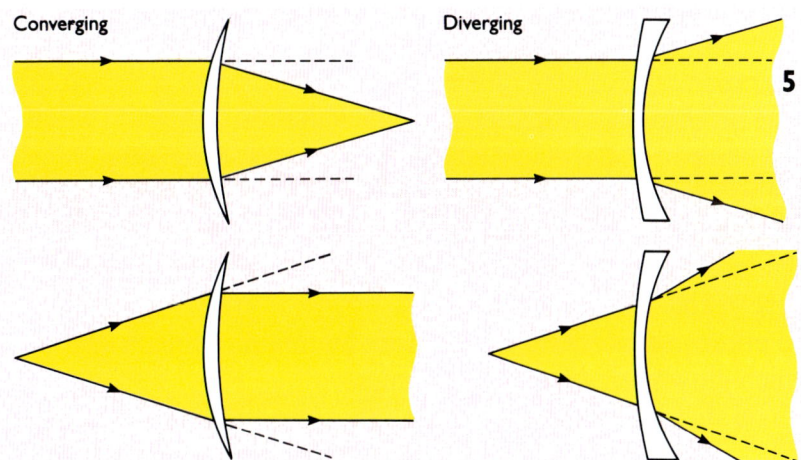

Converging

Diverging

5 Some lenses will converge rays of light and others will diverge rays.

Copy the diagrams that show how spectacles can correct long sight and short sight. Draw the lens you think is needed.

119

USING ENERGY

COLOUR

The coloured image that appears on a television screen is made from the three **primary colours** of light: red, blue and green. Three different beams of electrons are fired down the cathode ray tube from three separate electron guns. The screen at the end of the tube contains a pattern of tiny dots of three different **phosphors.** Each phosphor will glow when electrons from one gun strike it. The brightness of each glowing dot depends on the amount of energy transferred from the electrons that strike it.

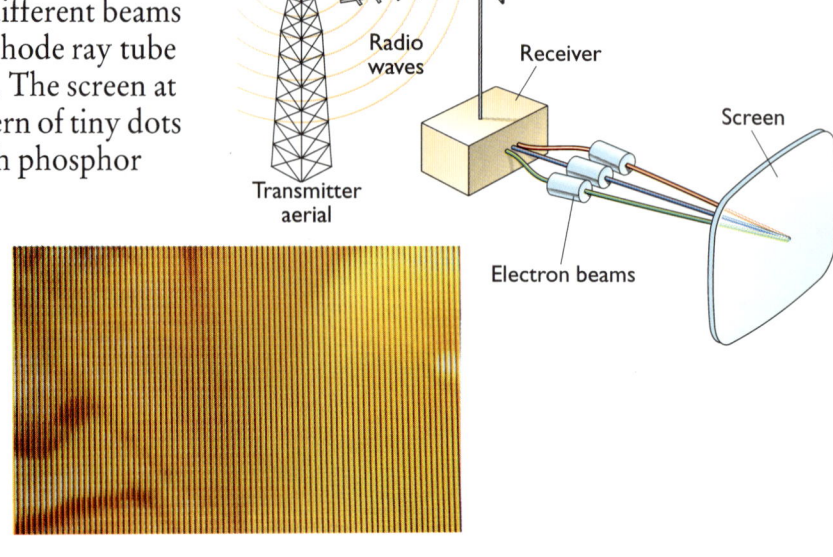

Each beam of electrons scans a line across the screen from left to right. The beams scan 625 lines across the screen from top to bottom and form a still picture every twenty-fifth of a second. Human eyes retain an image for a twenty-fifth of a second so we see a series of images that looks like one continuous picture.

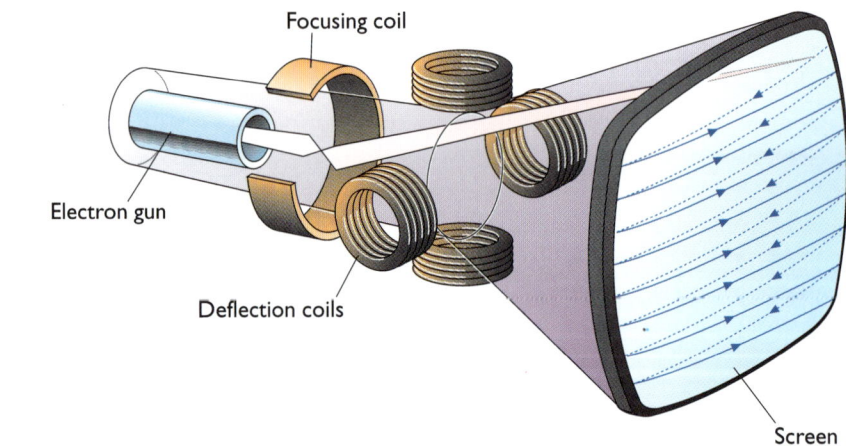

COLOUR MIXING

The different colours on the screen are produced by mixing the glowing red, blue and green dots. The whole screen appears blue when only the blue dots are glowing. The same happens for the other primary colours. When all three sets of dots glow with the same brightness, the screen appears white.

When pairs of primary coloured dots glow with equal brightness, **secondary colours** are produced as follows:
- red and blue make magenta
- blue and green make cyan
- green and red make yellow.

All other shades of colour are made by mixing primary colours which glow with different brightness.

You should note that coloured lights mix differently to coloured paints.

ELECTROMAGNETIC RADIATION

THE VISIBLE SPECTRUM

Sunlight, sometimes called white light, is a mixture of different colours. You can see the different colours in a rainbow. A rainbow is formed when sunlight bends as it passes through raindrops. The series of colours seen is known as the **visible spectrum.** Each colour has a different wavelength, and each light wave will be bent by a different amount, according to its wavelength. You can produce your own spectrum by shining white light through a triangular glass block called a **prism.**

The visible spectrum can be seen by shining white light through a glass prism.

SEEING COLOURS

Your eyes are sensitive to different wavelengths of light. You recognise one wavelength as red light, another as blue, and so on. When you look at a green leaf in sunlight, only green light comes from the leaf to your eye. Because it is in sunlight, you know that light from all colours in the spectrum shines on the leaf. The coloured pigment in the leaf absorbs light from all wavelengths other than green. Only the wavelength that you recognise as green light is reflected into your eyes.

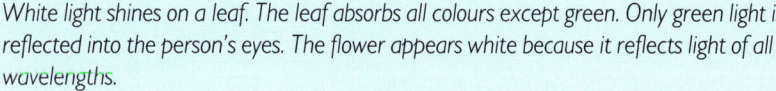

White light shines on a leaf. The leaf absorbs all colours except green. Only green light is reflected into the person's eyes. The flower appears white because it reflects light of all wavelengths.

1 What coloured light is produced when you mix each of the following?
   a red light and green light
   b green light and blue light
   c blue light and red light
   d red light and cyan light
   e blue light and yellow light
   f green light and magenta light
2 Set up a 60° glass prism and a light source to produce a visible spectrum. Which colour is refracted most and which is refracted least?
3 Carmel and Christopher have produced a coloured spectrum of light using a triangular prism. Carmel says that there must be something in the prism which produces the colours. Christopher says that the colours are already in the light and the prism just separates them.
   Plan an investigation to test Carmel's and Christopher's ideas.
4 Coloured filters only allow certain wavelengths of light to pass through. What would you expect to see in each of the following?
   a White light is shone through a red filter?
   b White light is shone through a red filter and then a blue one?
   c White light is shone through a yellow filter and then a green one?
   When you have predicted what you would expect, collect the equipment you need and find out if you were correct.
5 What colour will each of the following snooker balls appear in different coloured light?
   a a red ball in white light
   b a green ball in red light
   c a white ball in blue light
   d a black ball in green light
   e a red ball in yellow light
   f a yellow ball in green light
   When you have predicted what you would expect, collect the equipment you need and find out if you were correct.

USING ENERGY

ELECTROMAGNETIC SPECTRUM

radio waves | television waves | radar waves | microwaves

Visible light covers one small band of wavelengths in the whole electromagnetic spectrum. All electromagnetic waves consist of fluctuating electric and magnetic signals and they all share two properties:
- they can travel through a vacuum,
- they move at a speed of 300 million metres per second.

COMMUNICATION

The longest electromagnetic waves are used for communicating. Radio and television transmitters are huge aerials which send **radio** waves out in all directions. Your television or radio receiver detects all these waves and a special tuning circuit picks out one particular wavelength, or frequency. The rest of the receiver changes the radio signal into sound and vision. Live television pictures have been transmitted from the moon. Today you can see live broadcasts from around the world via satellites.

Very short radio saves, called **radar,** are used to help aircraft pilots to navigate. Radar waves are sent out by a transmitter on the aircraft and they are reflected by other objects around, including the ground. This information is shown on a radar screen.

IN THE HOME

Microwave ovens use electromagnetic waves to cook food quickly. 'Microwaves' are produced in a tube called a magnetron and the waves have a wavelength of about 12 cm. They are absorbed by water and cause molecules in food to vibrate. Rapidly vibrating molecules heat the food and cook it quickly.

Infra-red waves are close to the visible spectrum but we cannot see them with our eyes. All objects emit infra-red waves, depending on how hot they are. Special photographic film can detect these waves and we can produce images which show how much infra-red radiation is given off by different parts of a body. Infra-red rays are also used in burglar alarms to detect intruders and switch on the alarm. Although you cannot see infra-red rays, your skin is sensitive to this radiation which you can feel as heat on your skin.

Your skin is also sensitive to **ultra-violet** rays which are found just beyond the other end of the visible spectrum. They cause chemical changes in your skin that makes it appear tanned. Sunbeds produced ultra-violet rays to give you a suntan. Certain wavelengths of ultra-violet rays are harmful as they are known to cause skin cancer.

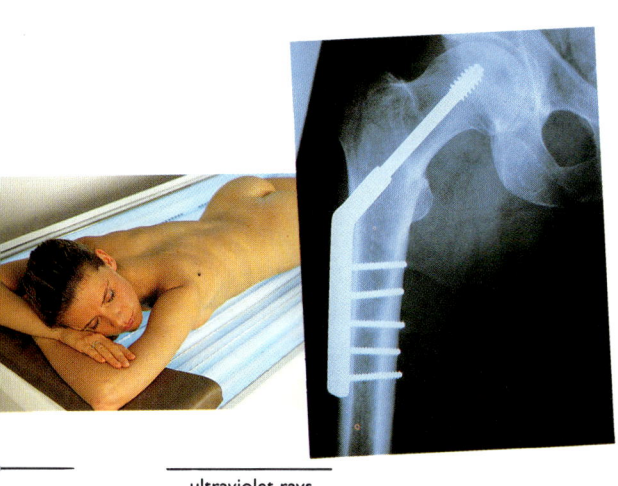
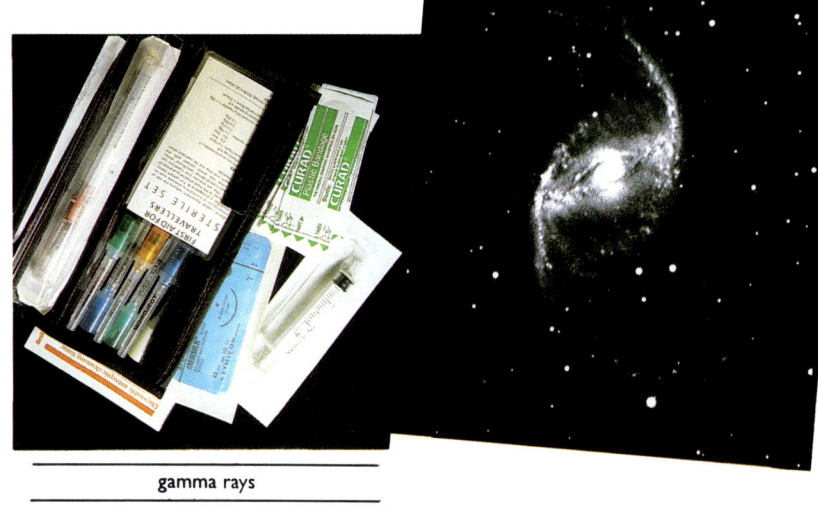

ultraviolet rays | gamma rays
visible light | X-rays | cosmic rays

MEDICINE

As electromagnetic rays get shorter they become more harmful to our bodies. Prolonged exposure to energetic **X-rays** will produce cancer but small doses, or short exposure, to low energy X-rays will not damage your body. In fact X-rays are used to help doctors because they penetrate the fleshy parts of your body but are absorbed by bones. Even shorter rays, known as **gamma rays**, are used to irradiate bandages, needles and other surgical instruments. This kills all the living bacteria which may be present and ensures that the equipment is sterile. It will protect patients from the danger of infection.

1 What do all electromagnetic waves have in common?

2 Copy and complete this table. Decide what should be written in place of A-N

3 **a** Write down everything you can remember about how light is reflected at a flat mirror.

b If you were given sheets of three different materials: glass, hardboard, aluminium, plan how you could investigate whether light, radio waves, infra-red and gamma rays are reflected by these materials. Your teacher will show you generators and detectors for 3 cm radio waves, infra-red and gamma rays.

c When you have planned the investigation, ask your teacher to carry it out. Write an account of your results.

d What happens to the radiation when it is not reflected?

Electromagnetic spectrum

Radiation	Typical wavelength (m)	Frequency (Hz)	How it is produced?	How it is used
radio	1000	300 00	Electric circuits	communication
television	1	A	Electric circuits	B
microwaves	0.1	C	D	cooking
infra-red	0.000003	E	any hot object	F
light	G	6×10^{14}	H	visual communication
I	3×10^{-8}	J	mercury vapour lamp	suntanning
X-rays	3×10^{-10}	K	metal surfaces hit by fast moving electrons	L
gamma rays	M	3×10^{20}	radioactive substances	N

USING ENERGY

BIGGER IMAGES

Microscopes and telescopes are designed to help you to see objects in greater detail. Whilst they may have a similar purpose, the instruments are made differently because they are used to look at different objects. A microscope is used to look at very small objects which are held close to the instrument. A telescope is used to look at much larger objects which appear small because they are far away.

MAGNIFYING LENS

A single convex lens may be used to magnify small print or to look at small objects. It is sometimes called simple microscope. When you use a lens in this way you must make sure that the lens is close to the object you want to look at. In fact, the object must be nearer to the lens than its **focal length**. You can find the focal length of a convex lens by focussing the image from a distant object, like a window or even the Sun, onto a piece of paper. The focal length is the distance from the paper to the lens. When the object is nearer than the focal length of the lens, you will see a magnified image when you look through the lens.

COMPOUND MICROSCOPE

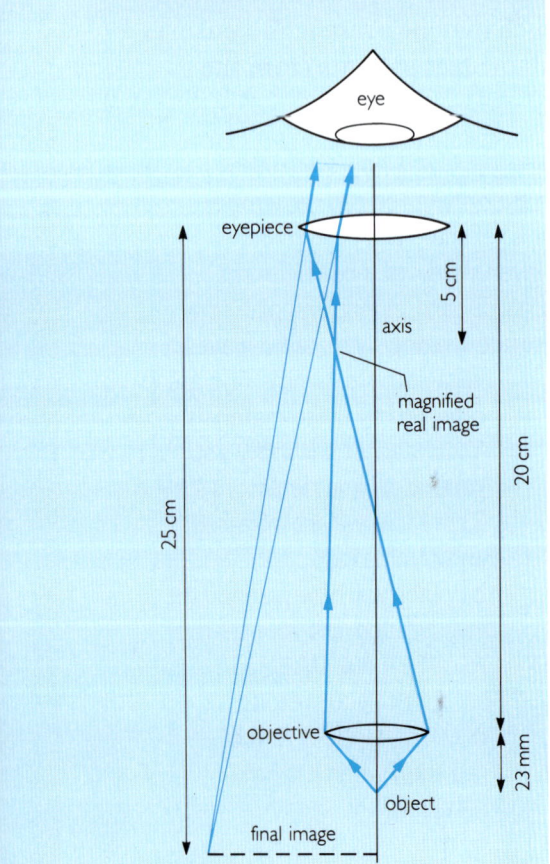

How a compound microscope works

A microscope magnifies in two stages. The specimen is held on the platform and illuminated from below using a mirror or light. The lens system nearest to the specimen is called the objective and this produces the first magnification. A magnified, real image is formed inside the microscope tube. This real image is then magnified a second time by the eyepiece. The eyepiece works in the same way as a magnifying glass. This means that the first magnified image, produced by the objective, must be nearer to the eyepiece than its focal length. The final image, which you see when you look through the eyepiece, is a bigger version of the first magnified image.

TELESCOPE

A lens telescope works in two stages like a compound microscope but there is a very important difference. A microscope is used to look at very small things that you cannot possibly see in detail with your own eyes. A telescope is used to look at things which can be very large. The only reason they appear small is because they are far away. You can hold a coin in front of your eyes and cover the moon with it. Although it appears to you to be bigger than the moon, you know that is not the case.

The objective lens system in a telescope is used to produce an image of the distant object. This real image is formed inside the telescope tube and it is then magnified by the eyepiece.

ELECTROMAGNETIC RADIATION

Two views of the 4.2 m William Herschel Telescope at Roque de los Muchachos Observatory at Las Palmas, in the Canary Islands. Left: the open dome; right a view of the telescope.

Just like the microscope, the eyepiece in the telescope works like a magnifying glass. You see the final magnified image by looking through the eyepiece. A telescope with an objective lens system is called a refracting telescope. There is a limit to the size of the objective lens before its weight distorts its shape.

REFLECTING TELESCOPES

Large astronominal telescopes use a mirror instead of a lens to produce the first real image. A large diameter mirror will focus light from distant stars and galaxies that cannot be seen with your own eyes. The largest single mirror used in a telescope has a diameter of 6 m. The Very Large Telescope being built in Chile has four mirrors, each with a diameter of 8 m which can be worked together to produce a single image.

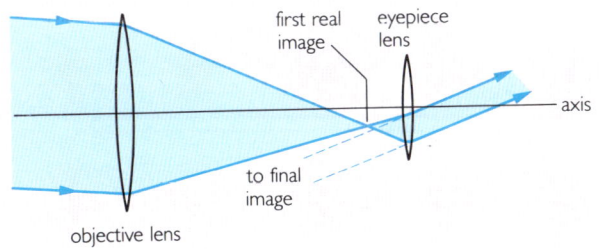

1 You will need two convex lenses, one with a long focal length, say 50 cm, and another with a short focal length, say 5 cm.
  a Fix the lens with the long focal length in a holder and point it at a distant brightly lit object.
  b Use a piece of tracing paper to find the image that the lens produces.
  c Hold the paper with the image on it and use the lens with the short focal length to magnify this image.
  d Remove the paper and look through the lenses. You have made a telescope.

QUESTIONS

1 a Complete the table to show the electromagnetic spectrum by writing the names of the waves in the correct boxes. Use the names from this list:

X-RAYS, ULTRA-VIOLET WAVES, MICROWAVES, INFRA-RED WAVES

Low frequency						High frequency
RADIO WAVES			VISIBLE LIGHT			GAMMA RAYS

b State a use for each of these waves.
  i Infra-red waves
  ii Ultra-violet waves
  iii X-rays
  iv Microwaves

2 The police can check a vehicle's speed using radar waves. They have special radar guns which consist of a radar transmitter and receiver. The transmitter sends out a radar wave to a vehicle. The wave hits the vehicle and is bounded back to the receiver. When a vehicle is approaching, the reflected waves gets squashed up. A microprocessor in the gun compares the patterns of the two waves and calculates the vehicle's speed.

The figure below shows the gun in action on a parked car.

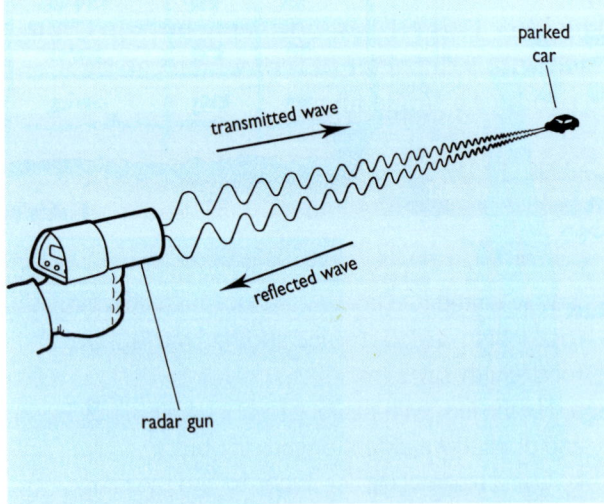

a Apart from their direction, in what way are the two wave patterns different?
b The next figure shows the wave patterns when the radar gun is used on an approaching car.

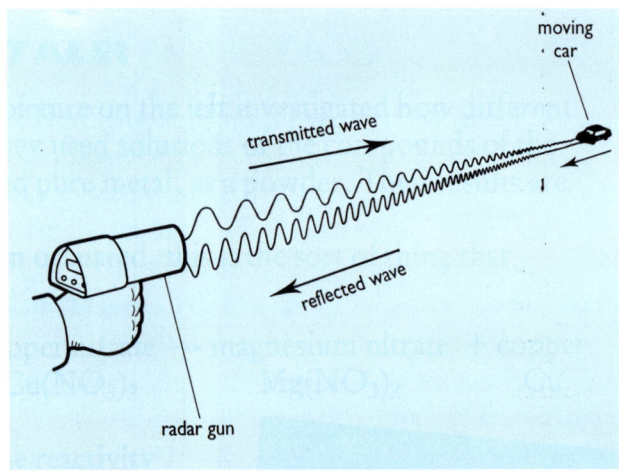

  i What change has taken place to the **wavelength** of the **reflected wave**?
  ii What change has taken place to the **frequency** of the **reflected wave**?

3 Below is a diagram of the inside of a microscope. The lenses change the direction of (bend) the light rays from the specimen on the slide so that they focus in the eye.

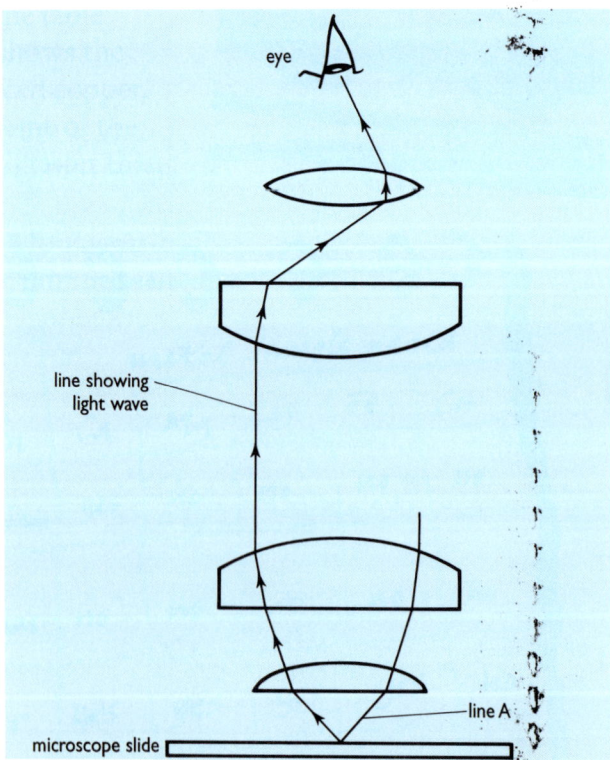

a What name is given to the bending of light?
b Why does the light bend when it enters and when it leaves a lens?
c Copy the diagram and complete the path of light shown by line A.

126

9 RADIOACTIVITY

Contents
Breaking up
Serendipity
Detective work
Absorbing activities
Hazards and benefits
Questions

The accidental discovery of radioactivity is described in this chapter. You will learn more about radioactive decay and the different types of radiation. After looking at the different ways of detecting radiation, you will find out about their penetrating powers. This chapter also describes some of the potential benefits and hazards of radioactivity.

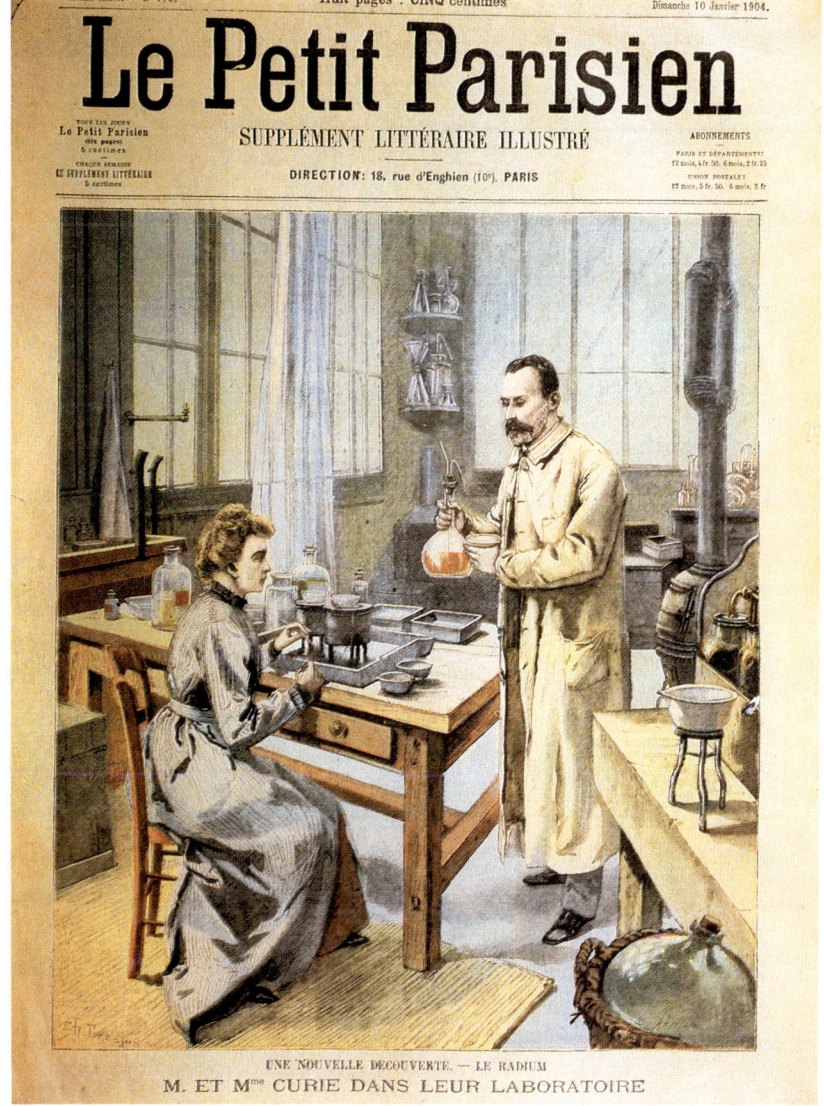

In 1898 Marie Curie gave the name 'radioactivity' to the invisible radiation given off by certain types of uranium. She was awarded the Nobel prize for physics in 1903 for her work on radioactivity.

USING ENERGY

BREAKING UP

After reminding you about the structure of atoms, this page describes what happens to a nucleus during radioactive decay.

Atoms are too small to see even with the most powerful microscope. But a model like this one can help us to understand how they behave.

Every atom contains a cloud of fast-moving electrons. The electrons move around a tiny nucleus at the centre of the atom.

Each electron is a small bundle of energy that has hardly any mass. Electrons carry negative charges.

The moving electrons are arranged in shell around the nucleus. Each shell can only contain a certain number of electrons. The first shell may contain two electrons. The second shell can hold up to eight. When that is full electrons must go into the next shell.

The large nucleus contains protons and neutrons. Each of these particles has a large mass compared to an electron. Each proton has a positive charge which is equal but opposite to the charge on an electron. There are always the same number of protons and electrons in an atom.

A neutron has the same mass as a proton but it does not carry any charge. This means that an atom has no overall charge because the positive charges on the protons are balanced by the negative charges on the number of electrons.

You can work out the structure of an atom from the atomic number and the mass number. They are shown with the symbol of an element like this:

E = Element.
A = Mass number.
Z = Atomic number.

$_{Z}^{A}E$

Na
A = 23
Z = 11

$_{11}^{23}Na$

These symbols are the atomic number and the mass number. The atomic number is the number of protons in the nucleus. The mass number is the total number of protons and electrons.

Here is the symbol for sodium. The atomic number for sodium is 11 and the mass number is 23. This means that there must be 11 protons and 12 neutrons in the nucleus of a sodium atom. There will also be 11 electrons in orbit around the nucleus.

Element	Symbol	No. Protons	No. of electrons in each shell			
			shell 1	shell 2	shell 3	shell 4
hydrogen	H	1	1			
helium	He	2	2			
lithium	Li	3	2	1		
berylium	Be	4	2	2		
boron	B	5	2	3		
carbon	C	2	6	4		
nitrogen	N	7	2	5		
oxygen	O	8	2	6		
fluorine	F	9	2	7		
neon	Ne	10	2	8		
sodium	Na	11	2	8	1	
magnesium	Ma	12	2	8	2	
aluminium	Al	13	2	8	3	
silicon	Si	14	2	8	4	
phosphorus	P	15	2	8	5	
sodium	S	16	2	8	6	
chlorine	Cl	17	2	8	7	
argon	Ar	18	2	8	8	
potassium	K	19	2	8	8	1
calcium	Ca	20	2	8	8	2

This chart chows the arrangement of the electrons in the atoms in the first 20 elements.

After the first 20 elements the arrangement gets more complicated.

RADIOACTIVITY

Some elements have different isotopes. These are atoms with the same number of protons but different numbers of neutrons.

Chlorine isotopes
$^{35}_{17}Cl$ $^{37}_{17}Cl$

Carbon isotopes
$^{12}_{6}C$ $^{14}_{6}C$

Because they have the same number of protons and electrons in each atom, the isotopes of the same element all have the same chemical properties.

Here are two isotopes of chlorine. They are called chlorine-35 and chlorine-37, according to their mass numbers. Both have 17 protons in each nucleus but one has 18 neutrons while the other has 20 neutrons.

Here are two isotopes of carbon. Most natural carbon is carbon-12 but there is also a small percentage of carbon-14 which is radioactive.

$$^{238}_{92}U \rightarrow {}^{234}_{90}Th + {}^{4}_{2}\alpha$$

$$^{234}_{90}Th \rightarrow {}^{234}_{91}Pa + {}^{0}_{-1}\beta$$

Radioactive decay can be shown in equations like these. This top one shows how a radioactive uranium-238 atom changes to thorium-234 when its nucleus looses an alpha particle.

Thorium-234 is still radioactive. The equation shows how proactinuium-234 is produced when the nucleus of a thorium atom emits a beta particle.

THREE TYPES OF RADIOACTIVE DECAY FROM A NUCLEUS.
1. An alpha particle = 2 protons + 2 neutrons.
2. A beta particle = 1 fast moving electron released by a neutron.
3. A gamma ray = energy released by the nucleus.

Radioactive elements are unstable. The nucleus of a radioactive atom will decay by emitting one or more of these forms of radiation.

After an alpha particle is released, both the mass number and the atomic number of the remaining part of the nucleus will be reduced.

When a beta particle leaves a neutron the neutron is converted to a proton and the additional positive charge increases the atomic number of the remaining nucleus.

If the atomic number of a nucleus increases or decreases the original atom changes into a different element after decay.

A gamma ray is an electromagnetic wave that transfers energy from the nucleus. There is no change to the mass number or atomic number of the nucleus.

---

1. Name the three particles in an atom. Say what charge each particle carries and describe their mass compared to each other.
2. The arrangement of electrons in a sodium atom is sometimes shown like this: Na 2, 8, 1. Write down the symbol followed by the arrangement of electrons, for: oxygen, silicon, potassium and iron.
3. How many protons, neutrons and electrons are there in the following atoms:

   $^{19}_{9}F$, $^{35}_{15}P$, $^{238}_{92}U$, $^{242}_{94}Pu$,

4. **a** Explain what is meant by the term *isotope*.
   b Draw diagrams to show the arrangement of protons, neutrons and electrons in the atoms of neon-20 and neon-22.
   c In natural chlorine there are three chlorine-35 atoms for every chlorine-37 atom. Calculate the average atomic mass of chlorine.
5. Name the three types of radioactive decay. Describe each type and say what effect it has on a nucleus when it is released.
6. Use a copy of the periodic table to help you to write equations to show the following examples of radioactive decay.
   a Protoactinium-234 emits a beta particle
   b Uranium-234 emits an alpha particle
   c Carbon-14 emits a beta particle
   d Radium-226 emits an alpha particle

USING ENERGY

SERENDIPITY

In 1896 a Frenchman called Henri Becquerel was investigating some fluorescent materials to see if they produced X-rays. A few months earlier Wilhelm Röntgen, a German scientist, had accidentally discovered X-rays whilst experimenting with cathode rays. Becquerel thought that a uranium compound, which glowed in sunlight, might be giving off X-rays. In order to test this idea, he decided to keep a photographic plate wrapped in black paper and bring it close to the uranium compound when the Sun was shining on it. He had already noticed that some other fluorescent materials produced a faint image on a photographic plate.

During his investigations the weather was cloudy for several days. Consequently he could not expose the uranium compound to sunlight and make it glow. While he waited for the weather to improve, Becquerel put the uranium compound and the photographic plate, still wrapped in black paper, into a drawer. After a few days the cloudy weather still continued so he decided to develop the plate anyway, hoping to find a faint image from the short time that the uranium had been glowing. He was amazed to find that the plate was completely fogged. Becquerel soon realised that some form of invisible radiation was being emitted by the uranium compound while it was in the dark drawer of his desk, without any sunlight. It was not X-rays, nor anything else that scientists knew about at the time. Becquerel had accidentally discovered a new form of radiation which we now call **radioactivity.**

Both Röntgen and Becquerel made important discoveries partly by accident. **Serendipity** is a word that is used to describe the accidental discovery of something which gives great pleasure.

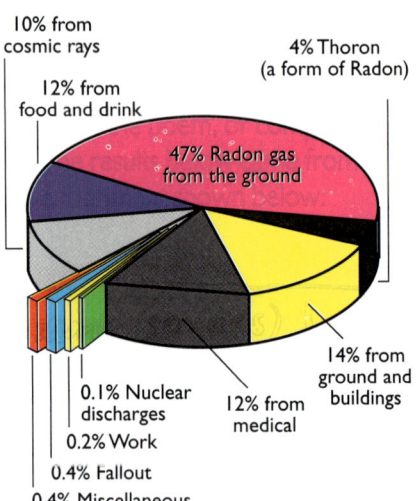

BACKGROUND RADIATION

Radioactivity is all around us. It is in the air that you breathe, the food you eat and drink and the ground you stand on. It is harmless and most of it (87%) is natural. The pie chart shows you the different sources of background radiation in the UK

Natural sources

Radon is a radioactive gas released by natural uranium deposits in the ground. Radon is quickly dispersed in the open air, but indoors it can build up and may be harmful. The map shows where the highest doses of radon gas have been recorded.

Gamma rays are also released by rocks and other radioactive materials in the Earth. Some buildings, that use materials extracted from the Earth, also release gamma rays. The food you eat contains radioactive materials. Potassium-40 is a major source of radiation in food, but remember that all the background radiation you receive does little harm and is unavoidable. Cosmic radiation,

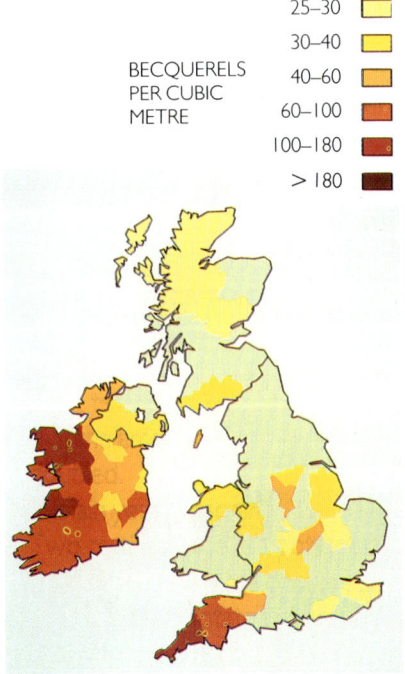

RADIOACTIVITY

1 The name radioactivity was given by Marie Curie, a French scientist, who is famous for her work with radioactive elements. Find out more about Marie Curie and prepare a short article for a school magazine.

2 This chart shows how the average dose of radiation received from fall-out in the UK changed from 1951 to 1988.

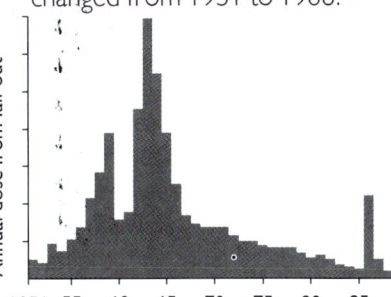

  a Why do you think there were higher readings in the early 1960s than in the early 1980s?
  b What happened in 1986 which could account for the sudden rise in fall-out?

3 Explain why commercial aircrews receive the same average annual radiation dose as workers in the nuclear industry.

4 What is the biggest
  a natural,
  b artificial,
  source of background radiation in the UK?

5 Use a polythene strip to give a negative charge to a gold leaf electroscope. Remove the glass front.
  a Bring a burning splint near to the charged leaf. What happens? Explain why.
  b Earth the electroscope and charge it again with a negative charge. What happens when a radium-226 source is brought close to the charged leaf? Explain why.
  c Repeat a and b with a positively charged electroscope.

from outer space, penetrates the Earth's atmosphere. At sea level the dose you receive is very low, but when you fly in an aircraft you will receive higher doses of cosmic radiation. You will find more about the effects of radioactive doses on page 136.

Artificial sources

X-rays and radioactive materials used for medical purposes form nearly all the background radiation that has been made by humans. Radiation is used to kill cancer cells and the doses are carefully controlled by doctors. The remaining 1% of background radiation comes from:
- fall-out after nuclear weapons testing and reactor leakage
- waste products from nuclear power stations
- radiation used in some industries
- smoke detectors in the home
- luminous watches

IONISATION

On page 128 you will find a description of the model that scientists use to explain how atoms behave. You will find that atoms have no overall charge because there are the same number of positive charges (protons) as negative charges (electrons).

When atoms gain or lose electrons the charge they carry is no longer balanced. This process is called **ionisation** because the atom changes into an ion. A positive ion is formed when an atom loses one or more electrons. Negative ions are made by adding electrons to atoms.

Radiation from radioactive materials creates ions in the air around the source. As a result it is also called **ionising radiation.**

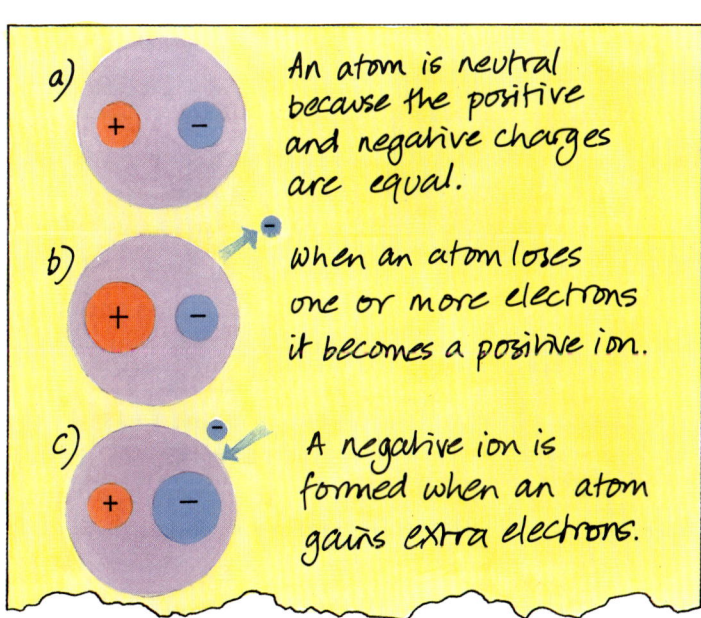

USING ENERGY

DETECTIVE WORK

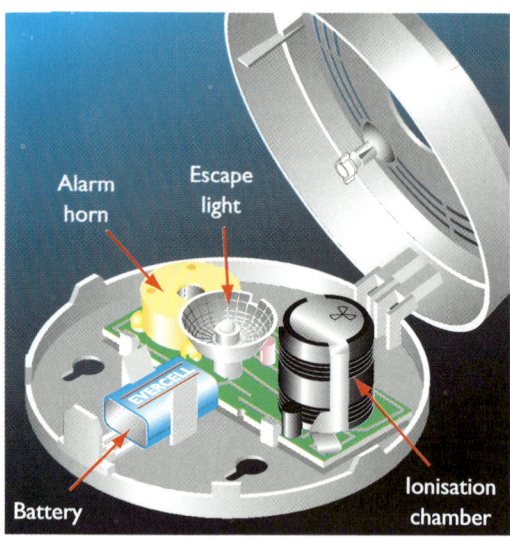

The ionisation smoke detector uses a radioactive source.

Some smoke detectors use radioactive sources. This type is called an ionisation smoke detector. Radiation from the source remains inside a special chamber and the detector is quite safe.

The radioactive source is used to ionise the air molecules inside a chamber. At each end of the chamber there is a metal plate joined to a battery. The charge on each plate attracts the ions in the chamber. The flow of ions across the chamber sends a continuous electric current through the electronic circuit.

If smoke particles enter the chamber, some of the ions stick to them. This reduces the number of ions crossing the chamber and consequently the current in the circuit also gets less. The circuit responds to a drop in current by switching on the alarm.

DETECTING RADIATION

Because radiation emitted by radioactive materials is invisible, it has to be detected by the effects it produces. Becquerel noticed the effect radiation has on photographic film when he made his accidental discover of radioactivity. However, the time needed to develop the film means that this is not useful for immediate identification. Here are some other ways that you can detect radiation.

Geiger counter

The Geiger counter relies on ionisation to detect radiation. The instrument uses a special tube, called a **Geiger-Müller tube** after its inventors. The tube detects radiation and produces a sudden pulse of electric current. This current causes a click in a loudspeaker and can be recorded on a counting device.

A Geiger-Müller tube has two electrodes. The tube itself is metal and is joined to the negative terminal of a high voltage supply. A thin wire running along the length of the tube is joined to the positive terminal. About 450 volts are needed to make the tube work properly.

One end of the tube is sealed with a mica window. Mica is a rock-forming mineral that is usually transparent. It is much thinner than glass and it will allow radiation to pass through it easily. The other end of the tube is used to make the electrical connections to the two electrodes. The space inside the tube contains an inert gas like argon at very low pressure.

Radiation may enter the tube through the mica window or, if it is very penetrating, through the metal wall. When radiation enters the tube it ionises the argon gas by removing electrons from the atoms. This produces positively charged argon ions and electrons. The electrons are accelerated very rapidly towards the thin wire in the centre of the tube. This causes the electrons to ionise more atoms and the process multiplies very quickly. A single ionisation

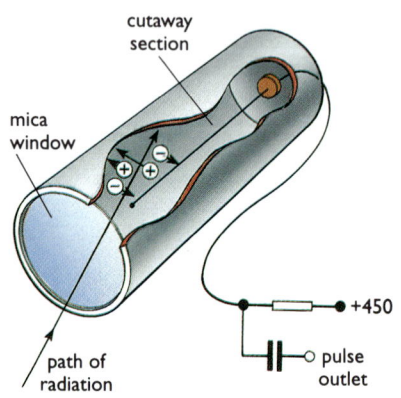

RADIOACTIVITY

1. Which type of radioactive source, alpha, beta or gamma, is most suitable to use in a smoke detector? Give reasons for your answer.
2. Draw a diagram of a Geiger-Müller tube, label the parts and describe how it works.
3. The Geiger-Müller tube operates with a voltage of about 450 volts.
   a Why would it not work properly if the voltage was only 6 volts?
   b What would happen if the voltage was increased too much?

by radiation can lead to an avalanche with millions of electrons reaching the anode. When the ions reach the electrodes a single pulse of electricity is produced and is identified by a click on a loudspeaker or a single count on a counter.

Cloud Chamber

A visual impression of radioactive events can be seen in a cloud chamber. Tracks are produced by tiny drops of liquid condensing on ions. The tracks show the path that the ions followed across the chamber.

To create the conditions necessary to produce vapour trails around moving ions, the diffusion cloud chamber is cooled by placing chunks of dry ice (solid carbon dioxide) beneath the metal base of the chamber. A mixture of water and alcohol soaked into a felt ring at the top of the chamber. As the alcohol vapour sinks in the chamber it is gradually cooled until it is ready to condense easily. When a charged ion passes through this vapour, tiny liquid drops are formed around the ion.

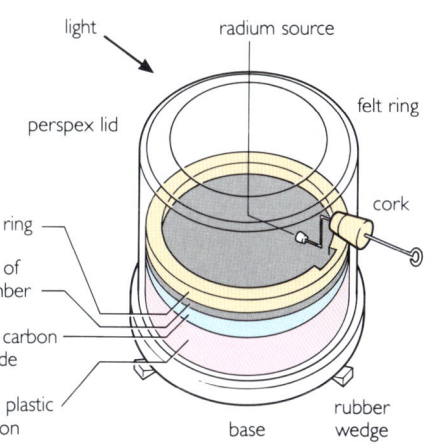

A diffusion cloud chamber

Cloud chamber pictures

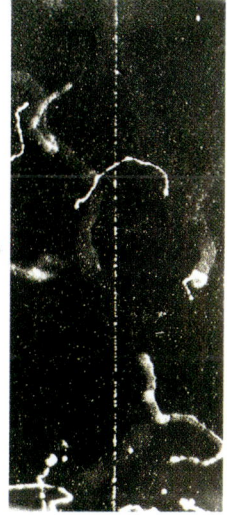

In a cloud chamber alpha particles will produce bright, straight tracks. Beta particles produce two types of tracks: thin straight lines are made by fast moving beta particles while slower ones produce thick wiggly tracks. When gamma rays or X-rays pass through a cloud chamber they cause slow moving electrons to be released from atoms in the air. You will see a line of thick wiggly tracks, moving in all directions, where the radiation went through the chamber.

4. Draw a labelled diagram of a diffusion cloud chamber and describe how it works.
5. Identify the type of radiation passing through the cloud chambers in each of the photographs above.
6. Use a Geiger-Müller tube joined to a scaler to check the background radiation in your school. Set the tube voltage to 450 volts and place the tube on a flat surface.
   a Record the number of pulses produced by the tube in two minutes.
   b Repeat this measurement five times.
   c Calculate the mean number of pulses per minute.
   d Why did you count different numbers of pulses each time?

USING ENERGY

ABSORBING ACTIVITIES

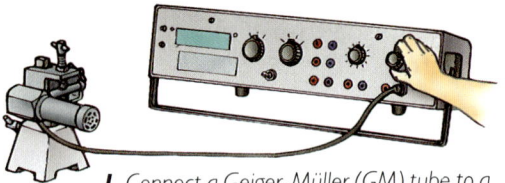

1 Connect a Geiger-Müller (GM) tube to a scaler and check the background radiation count.

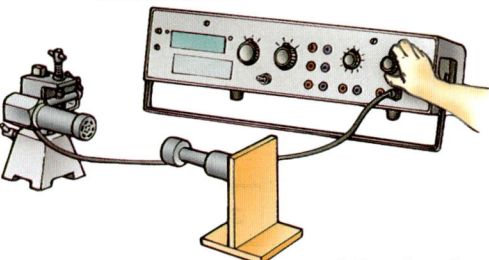

2 Arrange an americium-241 radioactive source close to the window of the GM tube. Check the number of pulses counted in a minute and repeat this five times. Insert a sheet of paper between the source and the tube. Check the number of pulses again.

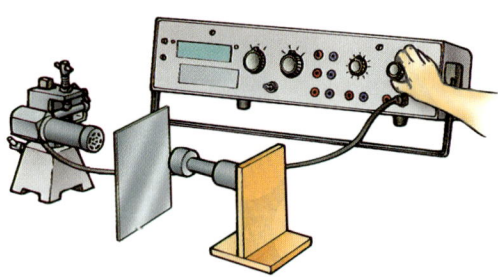

3 Fix a strontium-90 radioactive source about 10 cm from the window of a GM tube. Check the count rate five times. Insert a thin sheet of aluminium between the tube and the source and check the count rate again. Repeat this several times using thicker sheets of aluminium.

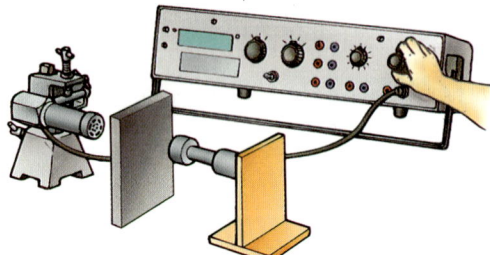

4 Arrange the GM tube and a cobalt-60 source so that the source is pointing at the wall fo the tube. Check the count rate five times. Place a thin sheet of lead between the tube and the source and check the count rate again. Repeat this using thicker sheets of lead.

PENETRATING POWER

This demonstration will show you the different penetrating powers of the three types of radiation: alpha, beta and gamma.

Three types of radiation emitted by radioactive sources

Radiation	Structure	Ionising power	Penetrating power
alpha (α)	2 protons + 2 neutrons	very strong	stopped by a few centimetres of air or a sheet of paper?
beta (β)	electron	medium	stopped by a few millimetres of aluminium
gamma (γ)	electro-magnetic wave	weak	stopped by a few centimetres of lead

You cannot predict when a particular atom in a sample of radioactive material will emit its radiation. Radioactive decay is a random process. You can measure how many atoms decay each second, but you don't know which atoms they will be. The number of atoms that decay each second is called the **activity** of a radioactive material. It is measured in **becquerels** (Bq). One becquerel is an activity of one radioactive decay per second.

The activity of a sample of radioactive material depends on how many radioactive atoms there are in a sample. Some of the atoms in the sample will have already decayed. The activity of the sample will gradually decrease as the number of radioactive atoms left gets less. When all the radioactive atoms have decayed and changed to stable atoms, the activity is zero.

HALF-LIFE

The time it takes for half the number of radioactive atoms in any sample to decay is called the **half-life**. It varies depending on the material. The most common isotope of uranium has a half-life of 4.5 billion years, while one of plutonium's isotopes has a half-life of a billionth of a second.

Suppose the half-life of a substance was 1 day. If there are 10 million radioactive atoms in a particular sample then by tomorrow 5 million atoms will have decayed. So, if 5 million atoms have decayed in 24 hours, you may calculate the mean activity over that length of time.

During the day after that, half the number of atoms will decay again. As there are only 5 million radioactive atoms left, then 2.5 million atoms will decay during the second day. Again, you can calculate the mean activity over the 24 hours as 2.5 million atoms decay. As you can see, the mean activity will be half what it was during the first day.

RADIOACTIVITY

Carbon-14 is a radioactive isotope of carbon and it is present in samples of the remains from all living things, including human remains. The half-life of carbon-14 is 5730 years. This long half-life means that scientists can date ancient remains by studying the amount of radioactive carbon that remains in any sample. So if the material contains half the amount of carbon-14 that it would have if it was still alive then it must be 5730 years old.

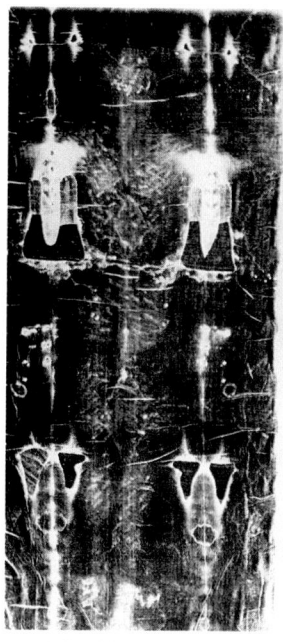
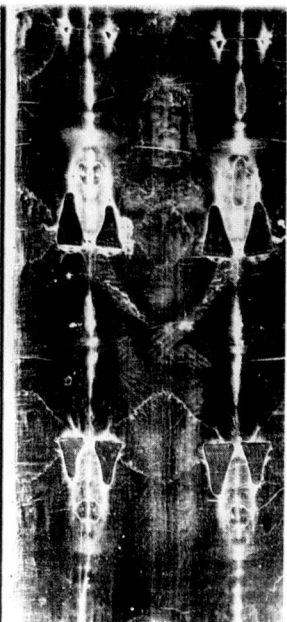

The Turin Shroud is a relic kept at Turin Cathedral in Italy. It has a faint imprint of bearded, long-haired man with injuries similar to those suffered by Jesus Christ when he was crucified. It was believed that the shroud was the cloth that was used to wrap Christ's body after the crucifixion. In 1988 three separate fragments were tested by scientists in Britain, USA and Switzerland using radiocarbon dating techniques. All three independent tests produced a date between 1260 and 1390 indicating that the shroud was a medieval forgery.

1 Vanessa and Nick investigated the radiation given out by a cobalt-60 source. Vanessa placed the source 20 cm from a GM tube and she noted the count rate five times and then worked out the mean. Nick then placed different materials between the source and the tube and Vanessa recorded the mean count rate each time. The distance between the source and the tube was not changed. These are their results:

Material between source and GM tube	Mean count rate in counts per second
air	129
sheet of paper	130
steel 1 mm	126
5 mm	128
lead 5 mm	95
10 mm	48
15 mm	11

a Why did Vanessa make five measurements of the count rate and then work out the mean count rate?
b Vanessa and Nick's results show that the mean count rate was higher when a 5 mm thick steel plate was used than a 1 mm thick steel plate. Does this suggest that they made a mistake? Give reasons for your answer.
c Which type of radiation does cobalt-60 give out?

2 Lisa was investigating a substance with a half-life of 1 minute. She measured the activity of the sample to be 256 Bq.
a How many radioactive atoms were decaying each second from Lisa's sample as she made her measurement?
b What would you expect the activity of Lisa's sample to be 1 minute after she made her measurement?
c What would you predict the activity to be 5 minutes after Lisa made the measurement of 256 Bq?

3 Jim measured the activity of a sample of sodium-24 over a period of time. These are the results he obtained.

Time (hr)	0	10	20	30	40	50	60
Activity (Bq)	319	202	128	79	53	31	19

a Plot a graph to show Jim's results.
b Use the graph to work out the half-life of the material that Jim used.
c Predict what the count rate will be after 90 hours.

USING ENERGY

HAZARDS AND BENEFITS

People working near radioactive sources wear a *dosimeter* which gives a visual record of the radioactive dose it, and the wearer, has received.

DOSES OF RADIATION

When ionising radiation penetrates your body it may cause chemical changes to atoms or molecules in your body tissues. This damage may not be important because the cells in your body are constantly being repaired. However, the more radiation you receive, the more likely it is that cells will be damaged. If a large number of cells are damaged by radiation the effects may be harmful and possibly fatal.

Ionising radiation transfers energy. With radioactive sources, the energy is transferred from the nucleus of an atom. When your body absorbs radiation, this energy is transferred to the tissue in your body cells. The **absorbed dose** of radiation is measured in units called **grays**. A dose of one gray, (symbol Gy), indicates that each kilogram of your body absorbs one joule of energy.

$$1 \text{ gray} = 1 \text{ joule per kilogram}$$

However, equal absorbed doses do not necessarily have the same biological effects on your body. Different forms of radiation have different ionising effects. Alpha particles carry most charge and travel slowly so they concentrate the energy transfer to a small amount of tissue. To be able to make better comparisons, a term called **dose equivalent** is used. Dose equivalent is measured in **sieverts**, (symbol Sv). The dose equivalent is found by multiplying the absorbed dose by an effectiveness factor. For beta and gamma radiation, the effectiveness factor is 1, so the dose equivalent in sieverts is the same as the absorbed dose in grays. For alpha particles the effectiveness factor is 20. This means that an absorbed dose of 1 Gy from alpha radiation has a dose equivalent of 20 Sv. It is reckoned that 1 Sv of alpha radiation to the lung will have the same risk of producing lung cancer as 1 Sv of beta radiation. Dose equivalent in sieverts is the basic quantity used in estimating the effects of radiation on humans.

Doses of radiation less than 10 millisieverts (1 millisievert = 1000 microsieverts) are thought to have little effect on humans although some people consider that any dose will increase your risk of getting cancer. A dose of radiation less than 1 Sv is unlikely to kill you immediately. However, damage will be done to cells in your body and there will be an increased chance that you may suffer from cancer some years later. A 10 Sv dose will kill you because it damages too many cells for your body to be able to work properly afterwards. You would have a 50% chance of surviving after a 5 Sv dose depending on how long you were exposed to the radiation.

Exposure to radiation	Dose equivalent in microsieverts
From nuclear power stations (per year)	10
From watching television (for a year)	10
From a four hour flight in an aircraft	20
From a single chest X-ray	200
From cosmic radiation (in a year)	250
From a brick house (in a year)	750
Typical dose received by a member of the public (per year)	1500
Maximum permitted dose for workers exposed to radiation (per year)	50 000

Average radiation doses received by humans from common sources of ionising radiation.

1 Why is alpha radiation potentially more dangerous than beta or gamma?
2 Explain what the units sieverts measure.
3 Why are you recommended not to have more than one chest X-ray every five years?

RADIOTHERAPY

Radiation is used in medicine to destroy cancer cells that have developed in a patient's body. High does of gamma rays are aimed with great precision at the malignant cells. It is regarded as a severe measure and is only used for conditions which are serious.

Radioactive 'tracers' are used for medical diagnosis and biological research. Artificial isotopes of elements are produced for these purposes. They are made by firing neutrons or charged particles at stable elements in a nuclear reactor or a particle accelerator. The radioactive isotope produced is chemically identical to the stable element and will take part in the same chemical reactions. The isotope is contained in a drug taken by the patient. The drug is chosen to be taken up by the particular body organ or tissue being investigated. The distribution of the radiation is recorded by special cameras.

In industry, leaks in underground pipes can be detected by adding a small quantity of a radioactive solution to the liquid in the pipe. Some manufacturing processes, such as paper production, use radioactive sources in automatic control systems. The thickness of the paper is controlled by a radioactive source on one side and a GM tube on the other side of the paper being produced.

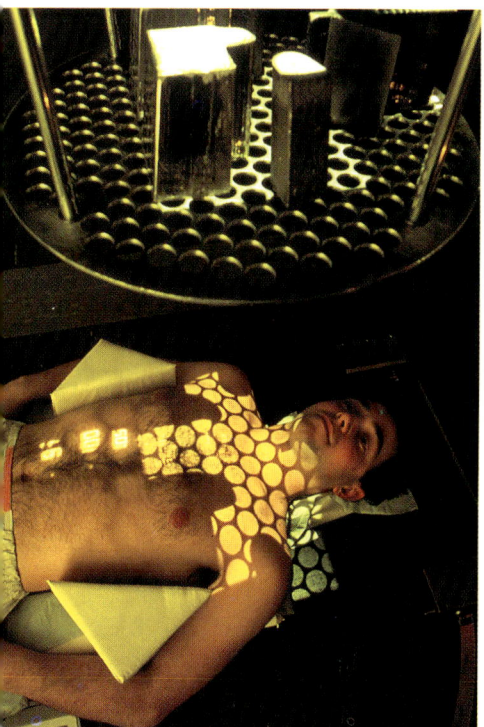

Person undergoing radiotherapy on a linear accelerator to treat Hodgkin's disease.

4 Ron was investigating the effects of different doses of radiation on the germination of seeds. He had six sets of seeds. One set had not been irradiated at all, but the other five sets were given different doses of radiation. The doses were 50, 100, 250, 500 and 1000 grays.

Ron put 20 seeds from each sample in different labelled plant pots. He used the same compost in each and gave them all the same amount of water. The pots were then placed in the same greenhouse so that they were all at the same temperature and received the same amount of sunlight. They were all watered the same amount over the next few weeks.

Ron counted how many seeds had germinated in each pot over a period of about four weeks. His observations are shown on the right.

b What conclusion would you make from Ron's results?

c Can you suggest a reason why more seeds germinated from the sample which had received a dose of 50 grays than those from the sample which had not been irradiated at all?

d Why did Ron make sure that all the seeds had the same amount of sunlight and water, and that they were all kept at the same temperature during the investigation?

Dose of radiation (Gy)	0	50	100	250	500	1000
seeds germinated after 4 days	5	4	3	1	0	0
after 1 week	15	16	12	4	0	1
after 4 weeks	15	18	11	5	0	1

USING ENERGY

QUESTIONS

1 a Many elements have naturally occurring isotopes. Isotopes can be made artificially by bombarding an element with neutrons. Some of these isotopes are radioactive and decay over a period of time. Isotopes are usually distinguished by their mass number. For example, radium-226 is the isotope of radium with a mass number of 226. Use this information and the information in the table below to help you to answer the questions which follow. The letters used to represent each atom in the table are not the symbols for the atoms.

Atom	Proton number (Atomic number)	Mass number
T	1	2
V	1	3
W	2	3
X	3	6
Y	4	9
Z	5	11

 i How many **electrons** are there in an atom of **Y**?
 ii How many **neutrons** are there in an atom of **Z**?
 iii Which **two** atoms are isotopes? Explain your answer.
b When radium-226 decays it forms radon-222 and positively charged parties.
 i What change in mass number occurs?
 ii What type of radiation is given out?

2 Some materials send out (emit) radiation all the time. These materials are radioactive.

The table shows how the level of the radiation from some radioactive material changes with time.

Time (minutes)	Level of radiation (counts per minute)
0	80
5	39
10	21
15	10

a Draw a graph to show this information in the most suitable way.
b i Describe, as fully as you can, the pattern shown by the graph.

 ii What will the level of radiation be at 20 minutes?
c The carbon in a grain of barley is slightly radioactive. It takes 6000 years for this radioactivity to fall to half of its original level.

An archaeologist finds some grains of barley at a site where she is digging. The carbon in the barley is only one quarter as radioactive as the carbon in some barley grown this year.

What does this tell you about the date of the site?

Explain your answer.

3 a Anna is worried that packets of food marked with the symbol shown will be radioactive. The symbol means that the food has been irradiated. (Fruit is sometimes treated in this way.)

 i Suggest how the food may have been irradiated.
 ii State and explain one reason why it may be useful to treat the food in this way.
 iii Describe how you would explain to Anna that the treated food could not be radioactive.
b Radioactive isotopes have many uses.
 i State one use other than to irradiate food.
 ii Explain why radioactive waste cannot be disposed of by burning.

10

ELECTRO-MAGNETISM

When an electric current flows, it forms a magnetic field. In this chapter you will learn about the different magnetic field patterns produced around wires of different shapes when they carry a current. Electric motors use the force between magnetic fields to spin around an axle. You will find out how the motor works. Electricity itself is generated by moving wires through magnetic fields. This is what happens in a power station generator. You will also study how electricity moves from the power station to your home and the part played by transformers.

Contents
Turning round
Shaking and making
Stepping up and down
Power to the people
Paying for power
Questions

The force of repulsion between electromagnets is strong enough to support the weight of this train and its passengers. This produces a smooth, almost frictionless ride.

USING ENERGY

TURNING ROUND

The French TGV is one of the fastest trains in the world. It uses an electric motor to transfer energy from an electric current.

ELECTRIC MOTORS

To understand how an electric motor works, you should make a working model motor like the one shown below. This page explains how it works.

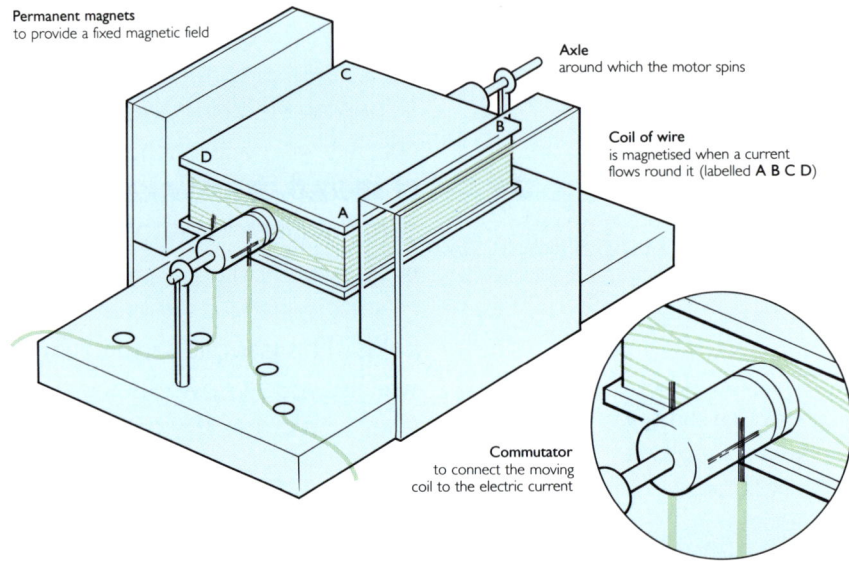

Permanent magnets to provide a fixed magnetic field

Axle around which the motor spins

Coil of wire is magnetised when a current flows round it (labelled **A B C D**)

Commutator to connect the moving coil to the electric current

THE CATAPULT FIELD

1 The permanent magnets provide a uniform magnetic field between the poles of the magnets.

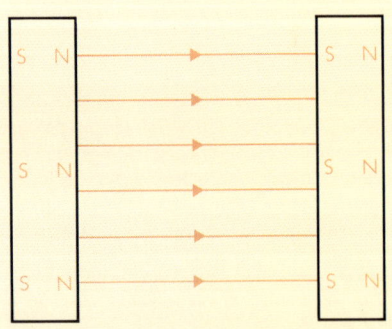

2 When an electric current flows through a wire, it creates a circular magnetic field around the wire. This diagram cuts through a wire that is perpendicular to the page. The electric current is flowing into the page.

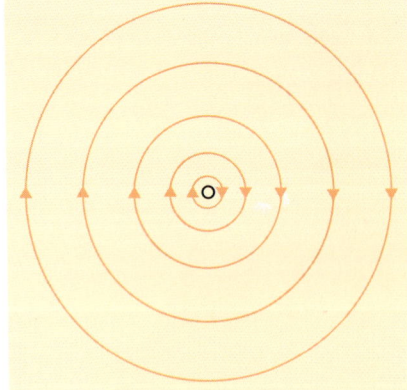

3 If a wire carrying an electric current cuts across the magnetic field formed by permanent magnets, the two magnetic fields combine together. As you can see in this diagram, both magnetic fields act in the same direction above the wire, so a stronger magnetic field is formed here. Below the wire the two magnetic fields oppose each other. This means that the effect of one field cancels the other.

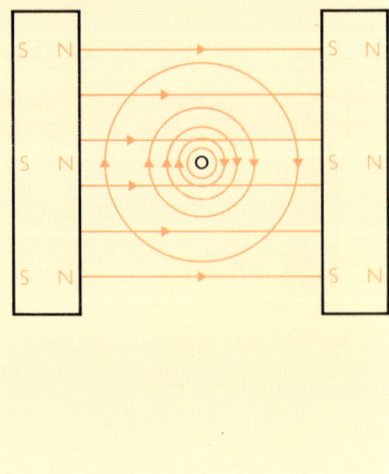

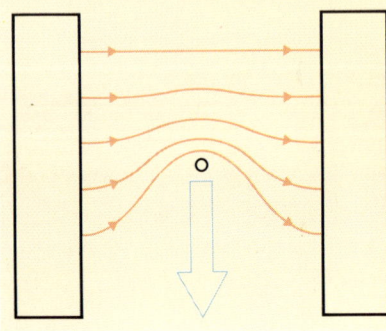

4 The result of this combination of magnetic fields is called the **catapult field**. It is so called because the field exerts a force on a wire. If the wire is able to, it will move in the direction shown by the red arrow.

ELECTROMAGNETISM

In an electric motor, energy is transferred from the electric current to the motion of the coil of wire as it spins around its axle. This kinetic energy may then be transferred for many useful purposes as illustrated by the electric train. This combination of electricity and permanent magnetic fields to produce motion can be summarised like this:

ELECTRICITY + MAGNETISM → MOTION

1 **a** What is meant by a uniform magnetic field?
   b How can you show that a magnetic field is uniform in a diagram?
   c Describe how the circular magnetic field around a straight wire carrying an electric current changes with distance from the wire.

2 Plan an investigation to see what effect each of the following will have on your model electric motor.
   a Changing the strength of the electric current in the wire.
   b Changing the strength of the permanent magnetic field.
   c Changing the number of turns of wire on the coil.
   When you have finished your plan, show it to your teacher before collecting the apparatus you need to carry it out.
   Write an account of your investigation showing how you carried it out and what conclusion you reached.

3 **a** Draw a circuit diagram to show how you could control the speed of your model electric motor. You may use other components in your circuit.
   b How do you think the speed of an electric train is controlled?

4 Copy these diagrams and add a red arrow to indicate the direction of the force on the wire in each case

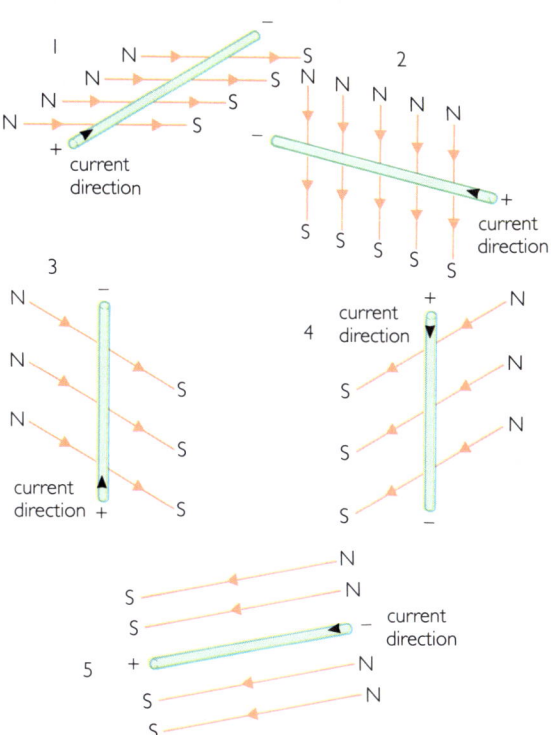

STARTING A CAR

A powerful electric motor is used to start a car engine. In order to turn the engine over, the starter motor needs a large current of about 300 A. Thick, short wires are needed to carry this large current to the motor from the battery. Because the ignition switch you use inside the car is a long way from the motor, it is necessary to use a **relay** to switch on the motor.

When you turn the ignition key a small electric current flows though the relay and magnetizes the coil inside it. When it is magnetized, the iron core is attracted by two iron contacts. Once these contacts are joined a large electric current flows through the starter motor. As soon as you release the ignition key it springs back and disconnects the relay. When it is no longer magnetized, the iron core joining the contacts is pulled back by a spring and the starter motor is switched off.

Using a relay to switch on the starter motor in a car.

USING ENERGY

SHAKING AND MAKING

Zhang Heng's earthquake detector which used a sensitive pendulum to detect tremors 700 km away.

DETECTING EARTHQUAKES

You will remember from Book 1 that the earliest known earthquake detector was invented in the year 132 AD by Zhang Heng in China. The device consisted of a huge and heavy bronze vase about two metres in diameter. Eight dragon's heads were fixed at equal intervals around the vase and an iron ball was delicately balanced in the mouth of each dragon. When the ground moved even slightly, the iron ball would drop from the dragon's mouth into a bronze toad on the base below. The noise would alert people to the fact that the ground had moved and the toad with the ball gave the direction from which the tremor had started.

Today scientists use seismographs to detect earthquakes. Modern seismographs use electromagnetic induction to indicate Earth tremors.

A seismograph contains a coil of wire in the magnetic field of a very heavy magnet. When the Earth shakes the coil of wire moves but the magnet remains still because it is so heavy. Whenever a wire moves in a magnetic field, electromagnetic induction causes an electric current to flow in the wire. The currents from the coil are amplified and fed into a computer which converts the currents into wave patterns on a VDU.

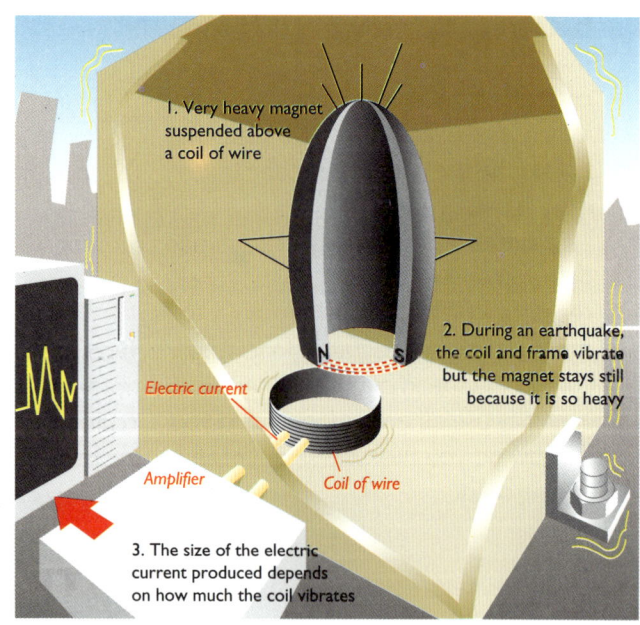

A modern seismograph uses the same principle as Zhang Heng's device. The inertia of the magnet holds it steady while the light coil of wire moves when the Earth shakes.

1. Very heavy magnet suspended above a coil of wire
2. During an earthquake, the coil and frame vibrate but the magnet stays still because it is so heavy
3. The size of the electric current produced depends on how much the coil vibrates

ELECTROMAGNETIC INDUCTION

Electric motors convert electrical energy into mechanical energy. But the process can be put in reverse. If you turn a small motor by hand you convert kinetic energy to electricity. This is known as electromagnetic induction. This can be summarised as:

MOTION + MAGNETISM → ELECTRICITY

MAKING ELECTRICITY FLOW

Generators make electricity by using magnets and coils of wire. When one is kept still and the other moves, electricity is induced in

ELECTROMAGNETISM

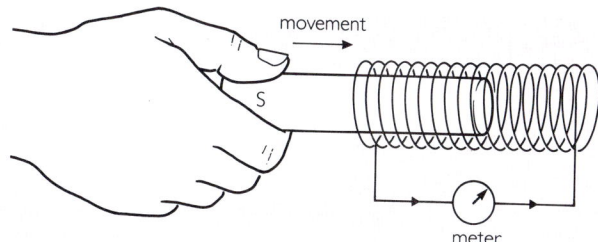

Moving magnet. Join a solenoid (a long coil of wire) to a sensitive meter. Push a magnet in and pull it out of one end of the solenoid. Repeat it with the other pole of the magnet.

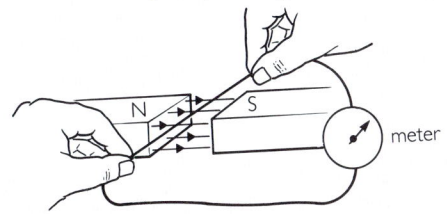

Moving wire. Join a straight wire to a sensitive meter. Move the wire up and down between the opposite poles of two magnets. Try moving the wire horizontally between the poles.

1 On the left two ways that you can demonstrate electromagnetic induction are shown. One involves moving the magnet whilst the other relies on the wire moving. Try them both out before you go on to investigate the strength of the induced voltage.

2 Predict how you think the following will affect the strength of the induced voltage in a wire.
   a The speed of movement of the magnet or wire.
   b The strength of the magnet
   c The length or number of coils of wire
   d The direction which the wire or the magnet moves relative to each other.
   Plan an investigation to test your predictions. Carry out your plan and write a report linking your results to your original predictions.

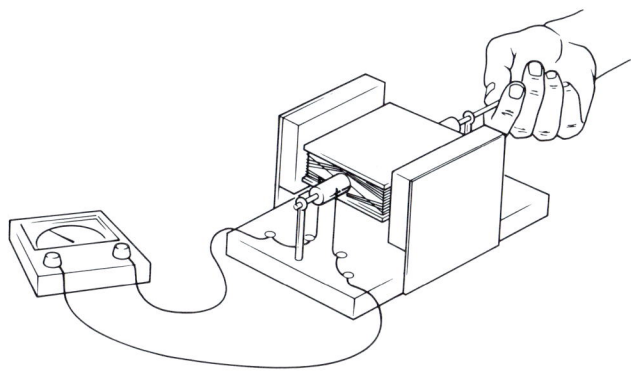

A generator can make electricity flow. This one is constructed in the same way as an electric motor. When the coil spins round, electricity is made. A d.c. generator like this is also called a **dynamo**.

the wire. Energy is transferred from kinetic energy of the moving part to the electric current.

You can make electricity with the same model used for an electric motor. This time, instead of supplying electricity to produce motion, you provide the motion to produce electricity. Because it has a commutator this type of generator will produce direct current (d.c.). This means that the electric current it produces always flows in the same direction.

3 The diagram below shows a coil of wire in four different positions as it rotates in a magnetic field.

The ends of the coil are joined to a commutator. When the coil is joined to an oscilloscope, the following trace is produced as the coil is turned.

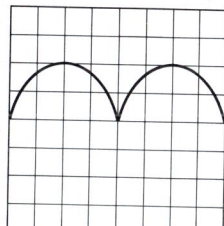

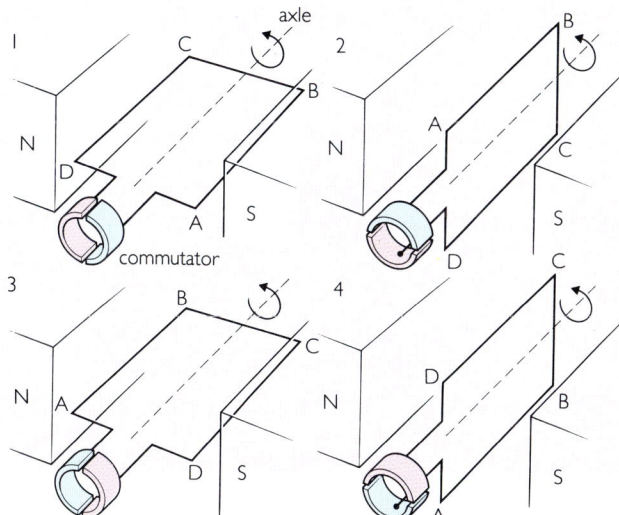

a Copy the oscilloscope trace and indicate on it the four positions of the coil showing where the coil was as it produced the fluctuating voltage.
b Explain why the commutator is essential for producing direct current.

143

USING ENERGY

STEPPING UP AND DOWN

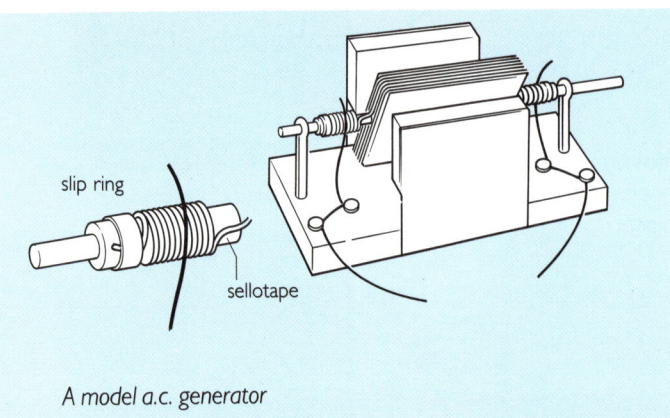

A model a.c. generator

ALTERNATING CURRENT

When an alternating current (a.c.) flows in a circuit the electrons flow round the circuit in one direction then in the opposite direction alternately. Alternating current changes direction rapidly. For example, the mains supply in your home is a.c. which changes direction 50 times each second. We say that its frequency is 50 cycles per second, or 50 **hertz** (Hz). For heating and lighting circuits a.c. and d.c. have the same effect.

1 a Make a model a.c. generator as shown in the illustration above.
b Connect your model to a sensitive meter and turn the coil slowly. Describe what happens to the meter.
c What do you think will happen if you rotate the coil quickly? Try it and see if your prediction is true.

2 The diagram on the right shows a coil of wire in four different positions as it rotates in a magnetic field. The ends of the coil are joined to slip rings. When the coil is joined to an oscilloscope, the following trace is produced as the coil is turned.
a Copy the oscilloscope trace and indicate on it the four positions of the coil showing where the coil was as it produced the alternating current.

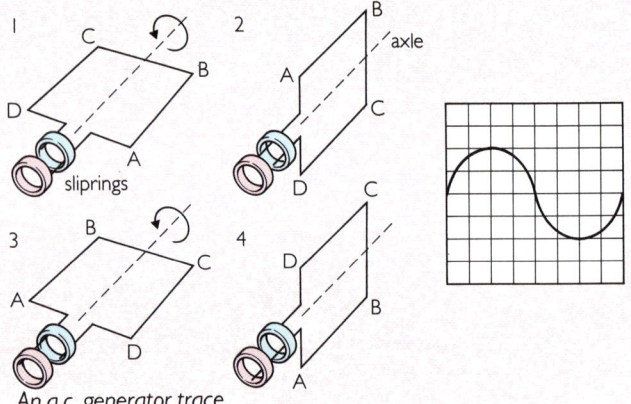

An a.c. generator trace.

b Explain why slip rings are used instead of simply joining the connecting leads to the ends of the coil.
c How long would it take the coil to make one complete revolution if this generator produced a.c. at 10 Hz?

TRANSFORMERS

Transformers are built into many electrical appliances you use at home. The principles of electromagnetic induction are used in transformers. However, by using alternating currents, there are no moving parts.
  Two coils are independently wound onto the same iron core. Alternating current is passed through one coil, the primary coil. This magnetizes the core which also passes through the other coil, the secondary coil. Because the magnetic field produced by the primary coil is always changing, it has the same effect as moving a magnet in and out of the secondary coil. This means that an alternating electric current is induced in the secondary coil. Transformers will only work if a.c. is supplied to the primary coil.

ELECTROMAGNETISM

A **step-up** transformer has more coils of wire on the secondary coil than those on the primary coil. The voltage induced in the secondary coil will be greater than that supplied to the primary coil. If the transformer was 100% efficient then the secondary coil would produce twice the voltage if it had twice as many turns of wire on its coil than the primary and five times the voltage if it had five times the number of turns etc.

Suppose you supplied 10 volts a.c. to the primary coil and induced 20 volts a.c. in the secondary coil of a transformer.

At first you might think that you have gained energy because each coulomb in the secondary coil is carrying 20 joules whilst each coulomb in the primary coil only carries 10 joules. However, if you were to measure the currents in each coil you would find that the current in the secondary coil was only half the current in the primary coil. This means that the same amount of energy is transferred in each.

A **step-down** transformer has fewer coils of wire on the secondary coil and produces a lower voltage but a bigger current.

The following activities are intended to help you to understand how transformers work. You will need to collect the equipment shown in the diagrams.

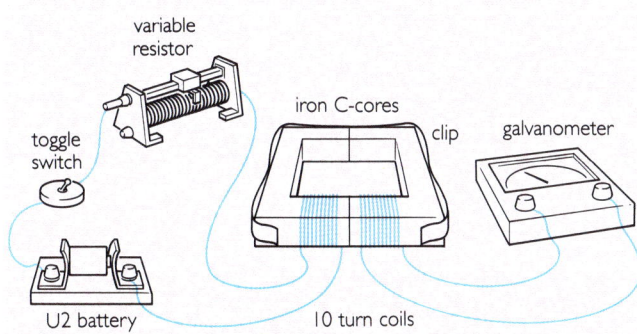

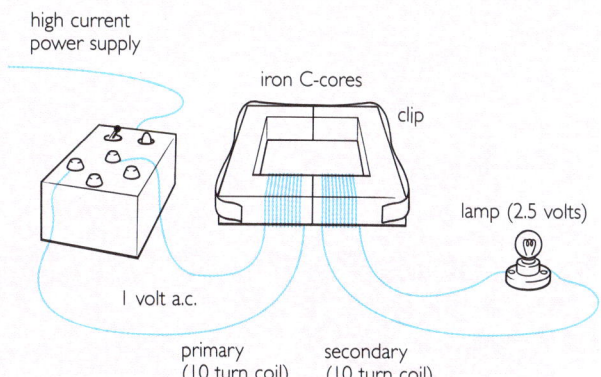

3 a Set up the apparatus as shown above and predict what will happen when you do each of the following:
  i Switch on a current through the primary coil from the battery.
  ii Send a steady current from the battery through the primary coil.
  iii Switch off the current from the battery.
  iv Switch on the current and then change it by moving the variable resistor very quickly.
  b Use the principles of electromagnetic induction to explain what happens in each case.

4 a Set up the apparatus as shown above (right) and predict what will happen when you supply 1 volt a.c. to the primary coil.
  b Suggest how you can make the bulb joined to the secondary coil glow brighter without supplying more than 1 volt a.c. to the primary coil.
  c Try out your suggestion and use the principles of electromagnetic induction to explain what happens.

5 Asha was investigating a transformer. She connected 12 V a.c. to the primary coil and used the secondary coil to light a 240 V, 60 W lamp. Asha measured the current and voltage for both coils. These are her results:

	Primary coil	Secondary coil
Number of turns	100	2000
Current (A)	5	0.22
Voltage (V)	12	230

a What type of transformer did Asha use?
b How much power did Asha supply to the primary coil?
(power = current × voltage)
c How much power did the secondary coil transfer to the lamp?
d What is the efficiency of Asha's transformer?
e What happens to the energy which is supplied to the primary coil, but is not transferred to the lamp joined to the secondary coil?
f Would Asha's transformer light a 240 V 100 W lamp? Give reasons for your answer.

USING ENERGY

POWER TO THE PEOPLE

POWER STATION GENERATORS

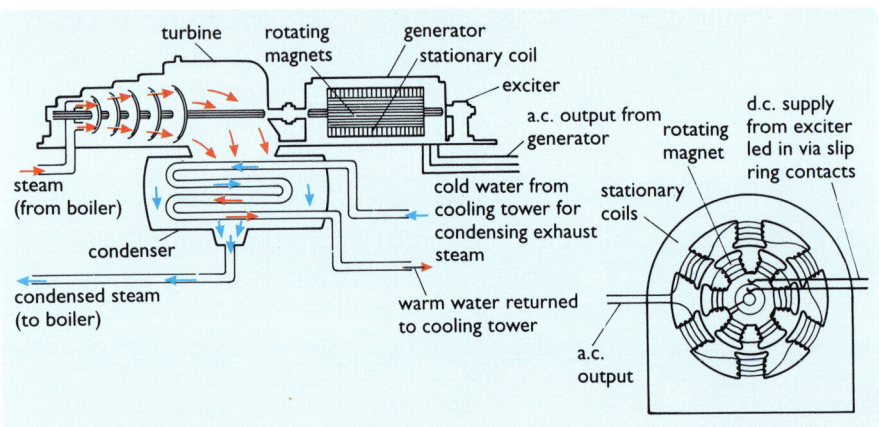

Most power station generators are driven by steam turbines. Power stations use different fuels to heat the water that produces steam.

There are over 36 000 electricity pylons in Britain, carrying more than 7000 kilometres of cable.

How electricity is distributed from a power station to the National Grid and from the National Grid to your home and industry.

Large generators in power stations have rotating magnets and stationary coils of wire. The magnets are electromagnets powered by a d.c. dynamo called an **exciter**. The advantage of this is that a small current passes through the slip rings to the electromagnet compared to the large currents that would pass through slip rings if the coil was moving.

Energy is transferred from steam, blasted at high pressure through the blades of the turbine, to the rotating shaft which turns the magnet in the generator. The moving magnet transfers energy by electromagnetic induction to moving charges in the coil of wire.

THE NATIONAL GRID

Electricity, generated at power stations, is distributed through a nationwide network of cables called the National Grid. In a power station electricity is generated at 25 000 volts. It is immediately stepped up by a transformer to 275 000 or 400 000 volts before it is transmitted by cables over long distances.

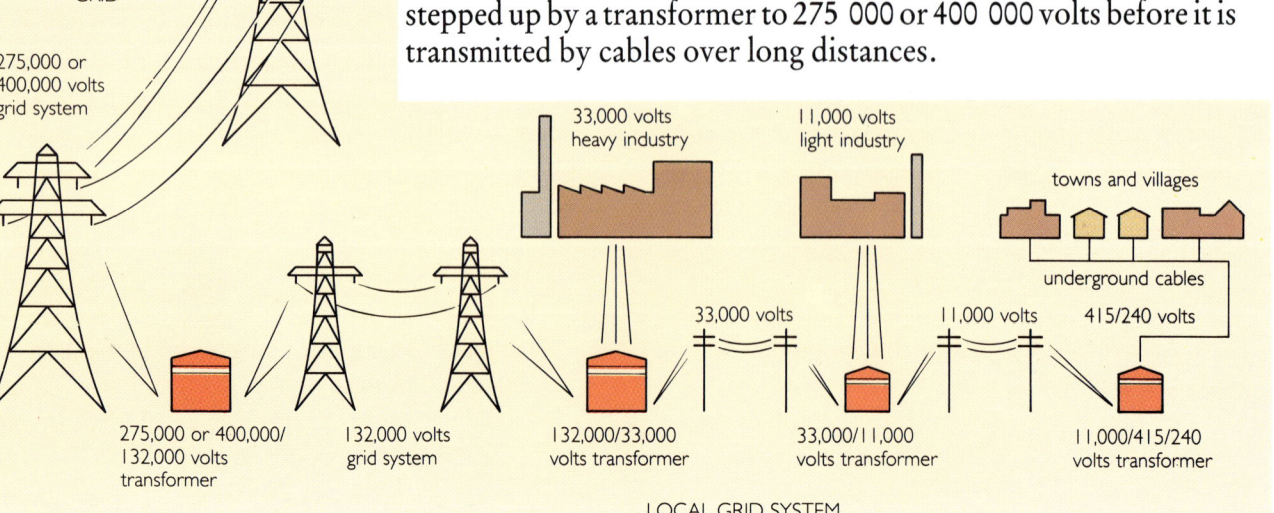

ELECTROMAGNETISM

The National Grid delivers electricity to large substations near towns and cities. Here it is stepped down by transformers and transmitted to smaller substations where it is stepped down again. By using more transformers it is stepped down further and eventually it reaches your home at 240 volts.

THE NEED FOR HIGH VOLTAGE POWER LINES

Even the best conductors still have some resistance. With short lengths of wire this resistance is negligible. However, the resistance of power cables is not negligible because they are miles long. This resistance transfers energy from the moving charges to heat the cable and the air around it.

This wasted energy depends on the strength of the electric current in the power cables. The power loss caused by the wasted energy is given by I^2R, where I is the current in the wire and R is the total resistance. When the transformer steps up the voltage at the power station, it consequently reduces the strength of the current. The power lines carry electricity at high voltages but small currents. This keep the power loss to a minimum.

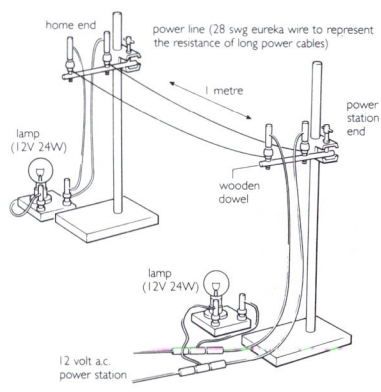

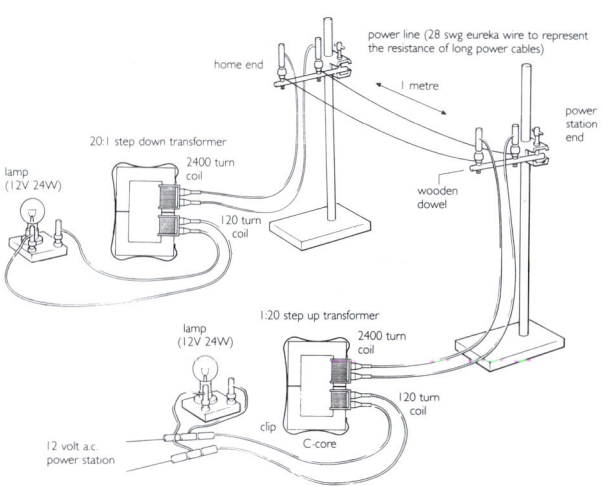

A model power line with transformers. This demonstration should only be carried out by a teacher.

1 Ask your teacher to set up the model power line as shown above.
   a How does the brightness of the 'home' lamp compare to the power station lamp?
   b Using a.c. meters, measure the voltage and the current at each end of the power line. Draw a circuit diagram to show how you connect the meters. Record your measurements.
   c Calculate the electrical power at each end of the power line. (Electric power in watts = current in amperes × voltage). How much power is 'lost' along the power line?
   d Calculate the resistance of the power line.

2 When your teacher has set up the power line with transformers, answer the following questions.
   a How does the brightness of the 'home' lamp compare to the power station lamp?
   b Ask your teacher to measure the voltage and the current at each end of the power line, between the power line and the 2,400 turn coils, using a.c. meters. Record the measurements.
   c Calculate the electrical power at each end of the power line. How much power is 'lost' along the power line now?
   d Ask your teacher to measure the current and voltage in the primary coil of the transformer at the power station end and in the secondary coil of the transformer at the home end. Record the results.
   e Calculate the power input to the transformer at the power station end. Compare this to the power output going onto the power line. What is the efficiency of the step-up transformer?
   f Calculate the power output of the step-down transformer at the home end. Compare this to the power input from the power line. What is the efficiency of the step-down transformer?
   g Remove the spring clip from one fo the transformers. What do you observe? Explain why it has this effect.

USING ENERGY

PAYING FOR POWER

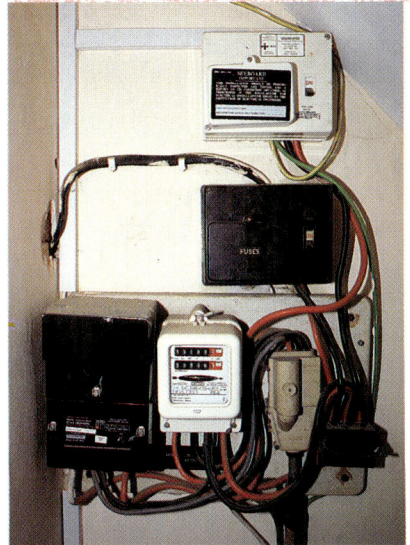

When electricity enters a home it passes through the electricity board's fuse, a meter and a consumer unit as shown here.

ELECTRICITY AT HOME

Mains electricity enters most homes through underground cables. If you live in the country, overhead wires may be used. Before you use it, the electricity passes through three important components: the electricity board's fuse, your electricity meter and your consumer unit.

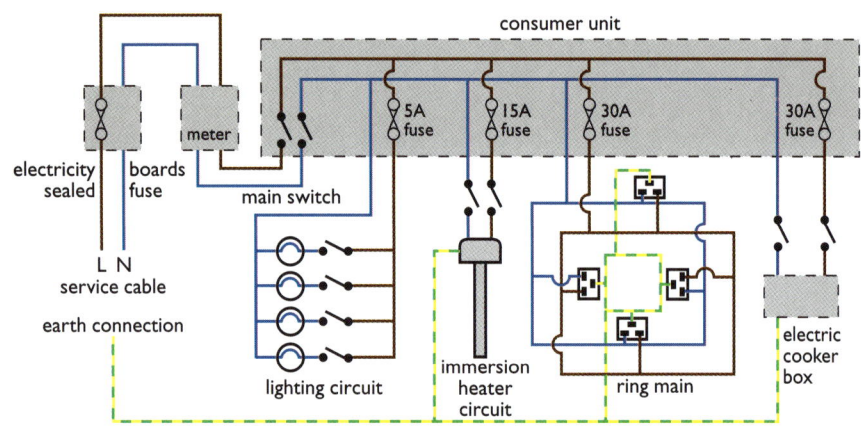

A simplified circuit diagram of a house wiring system.

A cartridge fuse from a consumer unit

EARTH WIRE

Alternating current is carried on two wires called **live** and **neutral**. Electric shocks can be received from the live wire. A third wire is also used in domestic circuits which is connected to earth for safety reasons. This protects you from receiving an electric shock if a fault develops in an appliance and joins the live wire to the case. The electricity would flow to earth along the earth wire and this would probably melt the fuse.

FUSES

You can see in the circuit diagram shown (above) that all switches and fuses are fitted to the live wire. This is a very important safety requirement. Each circuit in your home is protected by a fuse in the consumer unit. This fuse will melt if there is a fault in the circuit which draws a large current from the mains.

The ring main joins your socket outlets together. Appliances need a three pin plug before they can be used from the ring main. This plug also contains a fuse which melts if there is a fault in the appliance. The fuses most commonly used are 3, 5 and 13 amps.

A three pin fused plug. The fuse can be up to 13 amps.

ELECTROMAGNETISM

CHARGING FOR ELECTRICITY

Your electric meter records how much energy is transferred by the electric current when it flows round your home. This is measured in units which are shown on your meter display. Each of these units is a **kilowatt-hour** (kWh). You can work out how many joules of energy there are in a kilowatt-hour like this:

> power of 1 watt = transfer of 1 joule per second
>
> power of 1 kilowatt = transfer of 1000 joules per second
>
> 1 kilowatt-hour means using the power of a kilowatt for an hour
>
> 1 kilowatt-hour = 1000 × 60 × 60 joules
>
> 1 kWh = 3 600 000 J

Some electricity meters are pre-paid. That means you insert coins and pay for the units before using them. Other meters record how many units you have used and the electricity board will send you a bill every three months to charge you for the units you have used from one meter reading to the next one. The cost of a unit of electricity was 7.24 pence per unit in 1995.

1 Which fuse would be best for each of these appliances?
   a electric iron   750 W
   b hairdryer   360 W
   c kettle   2200 W

2 Suppose you went to America on holiday and you took your hairdryer with you. The mains voltage in America is 110 V. What do you think would happen if you tried to use your hairdryer in America?

3 Anna's Dad is always complaining because she leaves the hall light on all through the evening. Anna is fed up with her Dad's complaints, so she decides to calculate how much extra it costs if she leaves this light on. There is a 100 W lamp in the socket.
   Anna usually switches the lamp on as soon as it goes dark and leaves it on until bedtime, which is usually about 10.30pm.
a Estimate how many hours the lamp is used for each year.
b Calculate how much this costs if electricity is 7p per unit (check what the present price of electricity is).
c Do you think Anna's Dad is justified in trying to make her more energy efficient? Give reasons for your answer.

4 Calculate the cost of using the following appliance if electricity costs 7p per unit.

Appliance	Power	Hours used
a Electric fire	1 kW	5
b Refrigerator	200 W	24
c Kettle	2.2 kW	4
d Immersion heater	3 kW	0.5

5 **a** What is the maximum power of an appliance that can be used with a 13 amp plug in a ring main?
b What would happen if two 3 kW electric fires and a 2 kW kettle were all plugged into the same ring main at the same time?

USING ENERGY

QUESTIONS

1 a The diagram shows a step-up transformer being used to light a lamp.

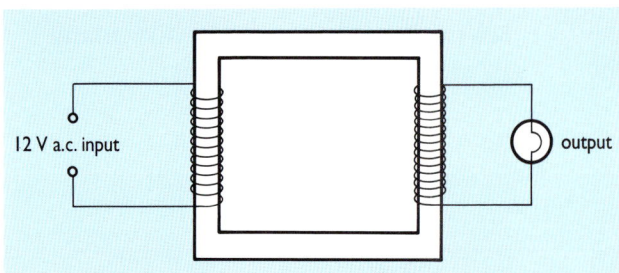

  i Which of the following is a possible output voltage?
  6 V a.c., 6 V d.c., 12 V a.c., 12 V d.c., 24 V a.c., 24 V d.c.
  ii Suggest two changes which could be made to increase the brightness of the lamp.
b The 12 V a.c. supply is replaced by a 12 V d.c. supply. What happens to the lamp? Explain your answer.

2 The diagram represents part of the National Grid. Electricity is generated at 20 000 V and is transmitted by the National Grid at much higher voltages.

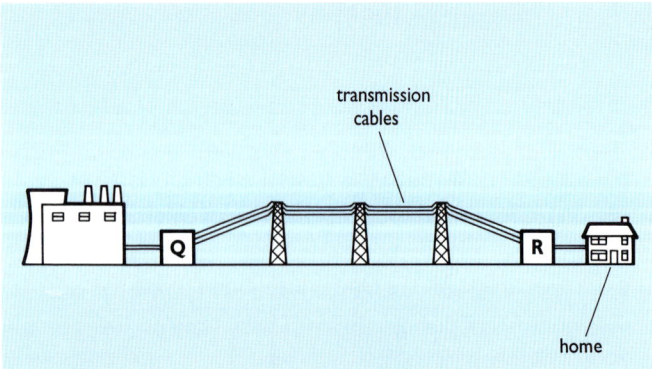

  a What is the purpose of transformer **Q**?
  b Suggest an advantage of using transformers in the distribution of electrical energy.
  c Why is transformer **R** necessary?
  d The overhead transmission cables are made from aluminium. State **two** reasons for aluminium being a suitable material.
  e What provides the electrical insulation between the aluminium cables and the earth?
  f When in use the cables become hot. Suggest how the excess heat energy is lost from the cables.
  g It is possible to use underground cables instead of overhead ones. Suggest two reasons why the cost of using underground cables is greater than that of overhead ones.

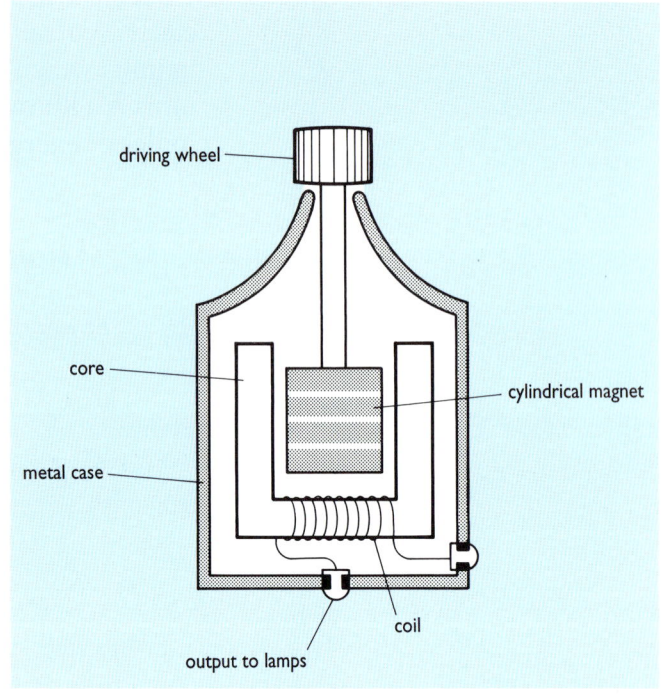

3 Some cyclists use a dynamo to power their lights.
  a Which of these materials
      copper, iron, plastic, steel, wood
  would be most suitable for
      i the magnet?
      ii the core?
  b State what has to happen for the dynamo to generate electricity.
  c Describe one disadvantage of using a dynamo instead of batteries to power cycle lights.

11 ELECTRONIC CONTROL

Contents
Switches and sensors
In control
Logically speaking
Flip-flop
Questions

Developments in microelectronics have produced a so called 'new technology'. This enables us to store and transmit large quantities of information very quickly. It also gives us ways of controlling things automatically. Before looking at some of this control, you will learn about the different switches and components used in electronic circuits. Digital electronics involves the use of 'logic gates' which are made from simple circuits. Combinations of these gates are produced on microchips that are so small you need a powerful microscope to see the circuits. In this chapter you will learn about the basic gates that are used in microchips.

A silicon chip enlarged 833 times showing some of the gold microwires which link the integrated circuit to pins which fix the chip into a computer.

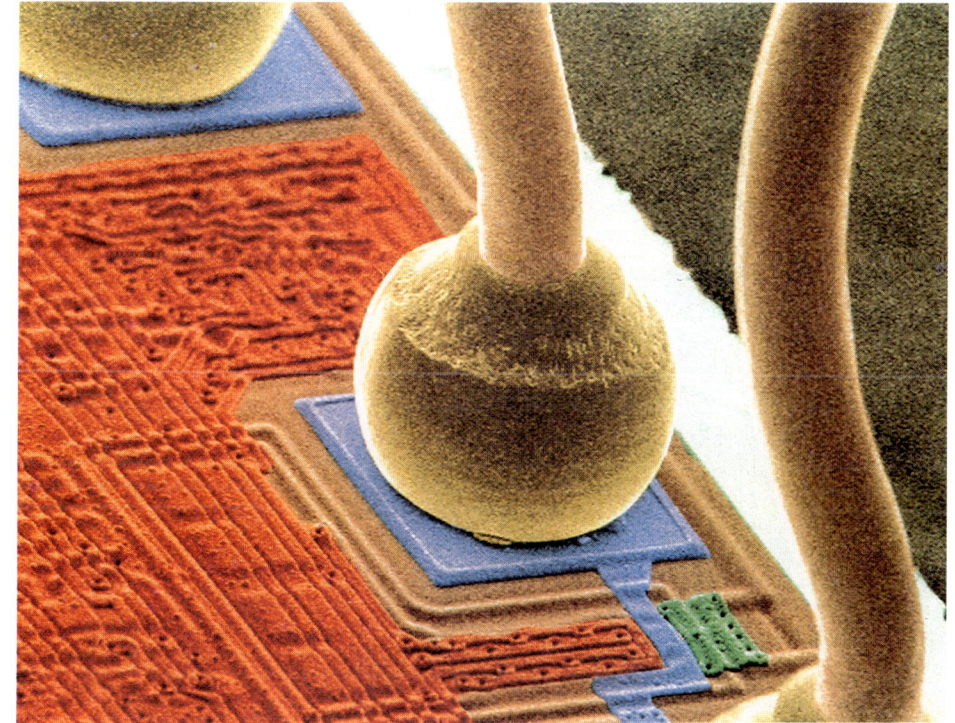

USING ENERGY

SWITCHES AND SENSORS

Electronic circuits used to control different appliances and devices contain a wide range of components. Here you can find out how some switches and sensors work so that you will be able to use them to design your own circuits and solve problems.

PUSH BUTTON SWITCH

A series of push-button switches are used on this calculator.

Circuit symbol for a push-button switch.

A push button switch is also called a 'press-to-make' switch, which describes what it does. The circuit symbol indicates how it works. The circuit is completed when a piece of conducting material is pressed onto a pair of contacts below. As soon as the button is released, a spring pushes the button back up and the circuit is broken once more. Computer keyboards use push button switches like these. Once a key has been pressed, information is stored in the computer's memory.

REED SWITCH

A reed switch operates by magnetism. It contains two pieces of springy steel, called reeds, inside a narrow glass tube. Normally the reeds are apart and the switch is 'off'. When the magnet is brought close to the glass, the reeds become magnetized and attract each other. The reeds are joined together and the switch is 'on'.

A reed switch is used to trigger a burglar alarm when this door is opened (and the alarm has been set!).

Circuit symbol for a reed switch.

In a burglar alarm a magnet is fixed into the door and a reed switch is set in the door jamb so that when the door is closed the magnet will turn the reed switch on. If the reed switch is joined to the burglar alarm, it will start the alarm when someone opens the door, moves the magnet away and turns the reed switch off.

VARIABLE RESISTOR

You have already used a variable resistor, or potentiometer, in electric circuits. When joined across a power supply it can be used to alter the voltage supply. When it is joined in series it alters the current flow in the circuit.

Dimmer switches allow you to change the brightness of a lamp. They contain a variable resistor.

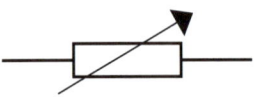

Circuit symbol for a variable resistor.

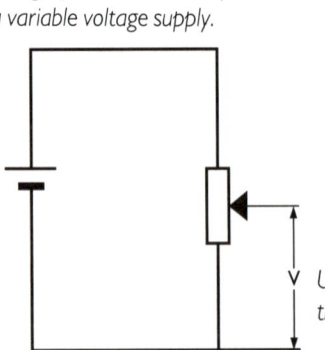

Using a potentiometer to provide a variable voltage supply.

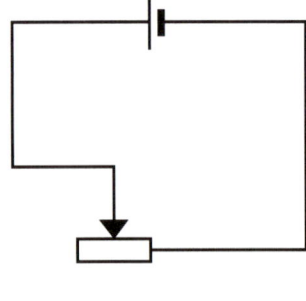

Using a potentiometer to control the current in a circuit.

LIGHT DEPENDENT RESISTOR (LDR)

Light dependent resistors contain cadmium sulphide. This material changes its resistance according to the amount of light falling on it. Light affects the movement of electrons in cadmium sulphide. In bright light the LDR has a

ELECTRONIC CONTROL

Some photographers use light meters to help them choose the correct exposure settings. Light dependent resistors control the reading on the light meter.

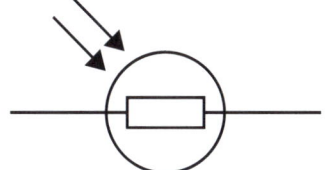

Circuit symbol for a light dependent resistor.

low resistance compared to its resistance in darkness, which is more than a million ohms. The LDR can be used as a switch which is controlled by light. In bright light, with a low resistance, it is switched on. In darkness, with such a high resistance, it works like an 'off' switch in a circuit.

THERMISTOR

The resistance of many conductors changes with temperature as this affects the movement of electrons in the conductor. Thermistors are useful because their resistance changes significantly at a particular range of temperatures. If its resistance increases as the temperature rises, the thermistor has a positive temperature coefficient. If its resistance decreases with temperature, the thermistor has a negative temperature coefficient. Thermistors can be made to respond to high or low temperatures. Using one in a circuit provides a temperature control.

REED RELAY

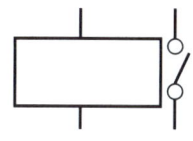

Circuit symbol for a relay.

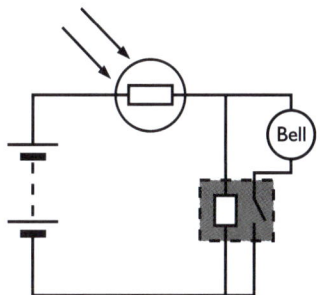

An automatic light switch which operates a bell.

The reed relay consists of a reed switch with a coil of wire wound over the glass tube. When a current flows through the coil it magnetizes the reeds and turns the switch 'on'. As soon as the current stops the reeds will no longer be magnetized and the switch is 'off'. This simple relay is frequently used in electronic circuits.

There are many uses for relays. For example, in the circuit above the LDR is joined to a circuit with the coil of the reed relay. When no light falls on the LDR its resistance is high and the coil will not be magnetized. When sufficient light falls on the LDR its resistance will decrease. This allows a current to flow through the coil on the relay, magnetize it and turn on the reed switch. As soon as the reed switch goes 'on' the bell will ring. This allows light to control a bell which could be used for some sort of alarm system.

This automatic fire alarm uses a thermistor.

1 Use the components mentioned on these pages, and others, to design circuits that will enable you to do the following.
  a Push a button in your room in a block of flats that will open the front door to the block.
  b Hear a buzzer at the back of a shop when somebody opens the shop door.
  c Supply any voltage between 0–6 volts from four 1.5 V cells.
  d Change the speed of an electric paint stirrer.
  e Automatically open your curtains in the morning.
  f Automatically switch on a greenhouse heater when the temperature falls lower than 4 °C.

2 a Use these components to design some circuits of your own which provide you with a useful control system. Describe what the circuit will do.
  b Collect the necessary components from your teacher and try your circuits out. Write a report about how successful your circuit was and describe any modifications you had to make.

USING ENERGY

IN CONTROL

In addition to the switches and sensors you have used so far in electric circuits, there are some other devices which you can use to control electric circuits. Here are four that are commonly used.

CAPACITOR

A capacitor will store electric charge. In its simplest form it consists of two parallel plates made from conducting materials, separated by a non-conductor. It could be two copper plates with an air gap between them.

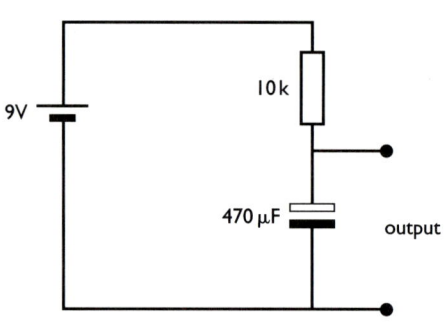

Using a capacitor to provide a time delay.

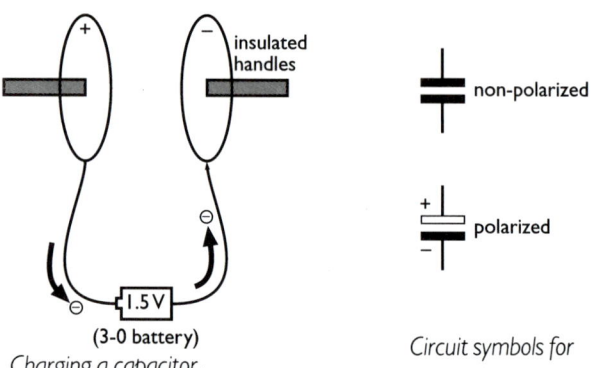

Charging a capacitor.

Circuit symbols for a capacitor.

When a capacitor is joined to a battery, electrons will flow onto one plate giving it a negative charge and electrons will leave the other plate and flow to the battery leaving the plate positively charged. The charge flows quickly at first but as the charge builds up on the plates it starts to repel any more charges reaching the plate.

The size of the capacitor is measured by the number of coulombs of charge it will store for each volt between the plates. The units of capacitance are **farads** and 1 farad = 1 coulomb per volt.

The farad is a very big unit and most capacitors you will use will have values in microfarads or picofarads.

1 000 000 picofarads = 1 microfarad
1 000 000 microfarads = 1 farad

A capacitor in series with a resistor will introduce a time delay into a circuit. The amount of time it takes for the charge to build up on the capacitor plates depends on the size of the capacitor and the resistor. It can be a fraction of a second or several hours. During this time the voltage across the resistor gradually decreases as the voltage across the capacitor increases. Either of these could be used as the voltage input, with an automatic time delay, to another circuit.

DIODE

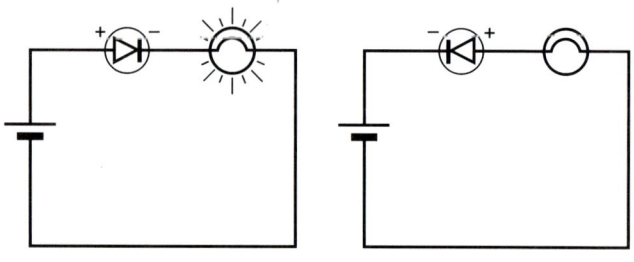

(a) forward-biased, current flows, (b) reverse-biased, no current. The circuit symbol for a diode showing how it may be connected.

A diode contains two specially treated types of a semiconductor. The junction of these two materials will only allow electricity to flow one way. When the potential difference is joined so that the charge flows across the junction, it is called **forward-biased**. If the diode does not conduct when a potential difference is applied, it is **reverse-biased**.

$$\text{CAPACITANCE}(C) = \text{CHARGE}(Q) \div \text{VOLTAGE}(V) \qquad C = \frac{Q}{V}$$
$$\text{(in farads, F)} \qquad \text{(in coulombs, C)} \qquad \text{(in volts, V)}$$

ELECTRONIC CONTROL

LIGHT-EMITTING DIODE (LED)

The circuit symbol for the LED.

Sets of seven LEDs can be arranged to form numbers when different combinations are lit.

The LED is a special type of diode that glows when it is forward-biased. The most common LEDs are red when they are lit. Green and yellow LEDs are also used. They may be joined in strips to form a seven segment numerical display.

1 This diagram shows the arrangement of LEDs in a seven segment numerical display. Each strip will glow when the LED in it is forward-biased. Both the common terminals are joined to the negative of a cell. Say which combination of the terminals a–g you would make positive in order to display each number from 0–9.

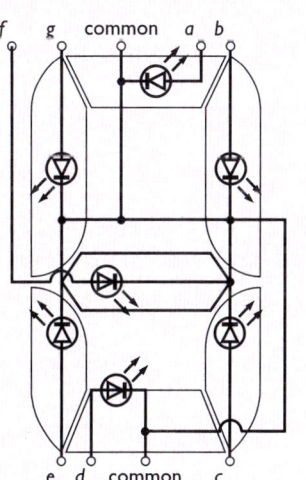

TRANSISTOR

The circuit symbol for a transistor.

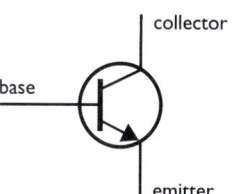

The transistor is made from a sandwich of three layers of semiconductor. Each layer has its own connection and these are called **collector, base** and **emitter.** The name transistor is short for 'transfer resistor' which describes how it works. The base connection controls the resistance between the collector and the emitter. With no current on the base, there is a high resistance between the collector and the emitter. When a very small current flows through the base connector, the resistance between the collector and the emitter is reduced significantly. When it is used, a resistor must be joined to the collector and the base to protect the transistor.

Using a transistor as a switch

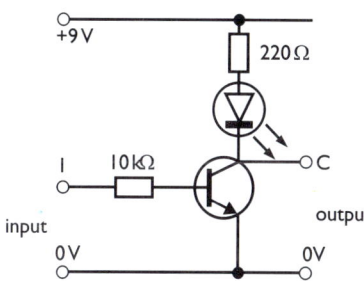

A transistor can be used as a switch in a circuit as shown above. An LED is joined to the collector to indicate what happens. I is the input to the base and C is the output from the collector. The switch works like this:

OFF – When there is no input to the base, the resistance between the collector and the emitter is large. This means that current cannot flow from the 9 V line to the 0 V line through the transistor. The LED does not light. The voltage across the output from C will be 9 V. This can be shown by joining I to the 0 V line.

ON – When a current flows through the input I to the base, the resistance between the collector and the emitter is small. This means that the current from the 9 V line flows through the 220 ohm resistor and the LED and then through the transistor to the 0 V line. The LED lights up. The voltage across the output from C will be 0 V because all the p.d. is across the 220 ohm resistor. This can be shown by joining I to the 9 V line.

If the LED was replaced by the coil of a relay, the transistor could be used to switch other circuits on and off.

USING ENERGY

LOGICALLY SPEAKING

Electronic logic gates are used to make decisions in many appliances. For example the lock on a washing machine door will not open while the drum is moving or the water level is high. The lock will only open when the drum stops and the water is pumped out of the machine. This decision is made by a simple gate. Electronic gates are made from semiconductor materials. They are very cheap to make and can be switched thousands of times a second without wearing out. Here you can learn how five simple gates operate.

ANALOGUE AND DIGITAL SIGNALS

Two types of electrical flow are used in electronic systems. These are called **analogue** and **digital** signals.

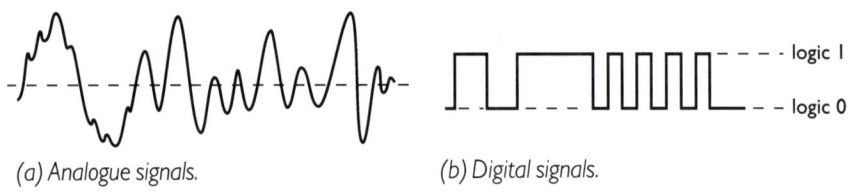

(a) Analogue signals.   *(b) Digital signals.*

With analogue signals the voltage and current may fluctuate with any value. For example the signal picked up by your radio receiver is an analogue signal. Digital signals only have two states they can be in. This may be 'on' and 'off', or 'high' and 'low' voltage. Digital signals are used in gates because they can make logical decisions which are totally reliable. Millions of logic gates are used in personal computers. To help you work out the logic, digital signals are described as 0 or 1. They cannot have any other value.

A microchip like this may contain thousands of electronic gates on an integrated circuit.

THE AND GATE

The AND gate has two inputs and one output. The output is 1 only when both the inputs are 1. The logic of the gate is shown in a circuit with two switches A and B joined in series with a lamp. The lamp will only light when both A **and** B are switched 'on'. A real AND gate works differently than the circuit with two switches, but the effect is the same.

You can summarise all the possible combinations of inputs to a gate in a table and work out what the output will be for each combination of inputs. This is called a **truth table**.

A	B	Q
0	0	0
0	1	0
1	0	0
1	1	1

Truth table for the AND gate.

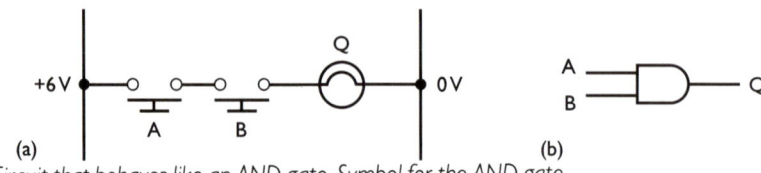

Circuit that behaves like an AND gate. Symbol for the AND gate.

ELECTRONIC CONTROL

THE OR GATE

The OR gate has two inputs and one output, like the AND gate. With the OR gate the output is 1 when either **or** both of the inputs is 1. Two parallel switches connected in a circuit to a lamp have the same effect as an OR gate. The truth table shows all the possible input combinations and what the output will be for each one.

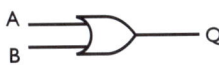

Symbol for the OR gate.

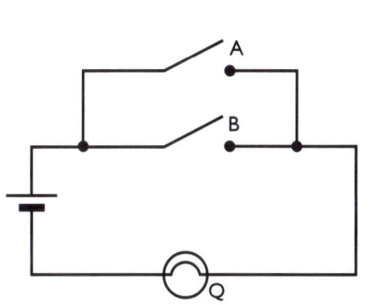

Circuit that behaves like an OR gate.

A	B	Q
0	0	0
0	1	1
1	0	1
1	1	1

Truth table for the OR gate.

THE NOT GATE

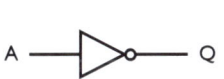

A	Q
0	1
1	0

Symbol and truth table for the NOT gate.

This is the simplest gate with one input and one output. With a NOT gate the output is always the *opposite* of the input.

THE NAND GATE

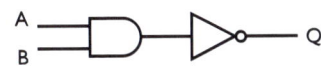

Inverting the output from an AND gate.

Symbol for the NAND gate.

A	B	Q
0	0	1
0	1	1
1	0	1
1	1	0

Truth table for the NAND gate.

If the output from the AND gate was used as the input to a NOT gate, the combination of gates produces a NAND gate. The NAND gate is a single gate which is easy to make. In fact, all the other gates can be made from different combinations of NAND gates or NOR gates.

THE NOR GATE

The NOR gate is made by adding a NOT gate to the output from the OR gate.

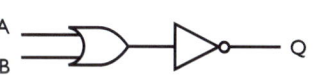

Inverting the output from an OR gate.

Symbol for the NOR gate.

A	B	Q
0	0	1
0	1	0
1	0	0
1	1	0

Truth table for the NOR gate.

1 A NOT gate is easily made from a NAND gate by joining the two inputs together like this:

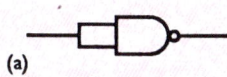
(a)

a Write out a truth table for this converted NAND gate.

Look at the following combinations of NAND gates. For each one write out a truth table and compare it with the truth tables of the other gates. Write down which single gate will produce the same truth table as each combination.

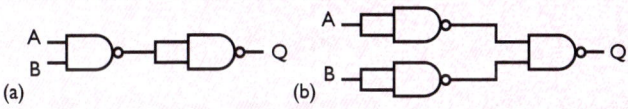

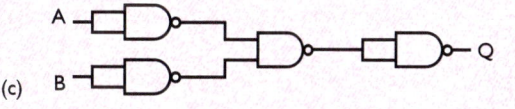
(c)

2 Write out a truth table for the following combination of gates. It will help if you make a table with six columns. The first three columns are labelled A, B and C for the inputs. The next two are labelled X and Y to show the outputs from the first gates and the last column is Q to show the final output from the combination. Begin by completing columns A, B and C for each of the eight possible inputs.

FLIP-FLOP

BURGLAR ALARMS

Modern burglar alarms use different sensors to trigger the alarm. They include magnetic switches, light beams, infra-red detectors, floor pressure pads and detectors which sense movement. These only switch the alarm on when the burglar passes the sensor. For example, if the alarm system had a magnetic reed switch attached to a door, the alarm would be switched on when the door was opened but it would switch off again as soon as the burglar closed the door. Obviously this would not be much use.

This problem can be solved by using a combination of logic gates called a **flip-flop** or **bistable.** By using this device in an alarm system, the alarm switches on when the sensor is activated and it remains on even when the sensor is returned to its original condition. This means that the alarm remains ringing. The only way to switch off the alarm is shown on the page opposite.

THE BISTABLE SWITCH

The bistable switch is so named because it has two stable states, or outputs, when both inputs are 0. You can see this in the truth table. The switch is quite simple to construct and uses feedback. The output from each of the NOR gates is fed back as one input to the other NOR gate. This means that there are still only two external inputs to the switch. These are called the Set and Reset inputs, or S and R. When the S input is made there is an output from Q. This is stable and remains there even after the S input goes down. The only way the switch can be changed is by making the R input. When that happens there is no output from Q and the switch flips over to its other stable state. It remains like this even if the input at R is removed and will stay like that until an input is made at S.

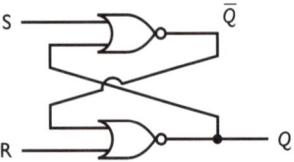

A flip-flop or bistable unit made from two NOR gates.

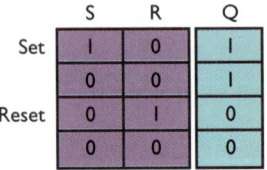

	S	R	Q
Set	1	0	1
	0	0	1
Reset	0	1	0
	0	0	0

Truth table for the SR bistable switch.

ELECTRONIC CONTROL

HOW THE BISTABLE WORKS IN A BURGLAR ALARM

You can see how the bistable operates the burglar alarm system by following it through each stage, starting on the left.

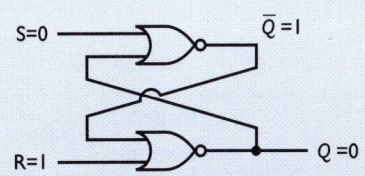

1 The alarm is reset by switching R on. When R = 1 the output Q will be 0 because it is a NOR gate. This means the alarm must be off. But Q feeds back as a 0 input to the upper NOR gate. Now the output from that gate $\bar{Q}$ = 1 because the other input from S is also 0. Even though $\bar{Q}$ makes a 1 input to the lowest NOR gate the output Q is still 0.

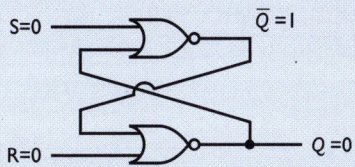

2 When R is switched off the switch remains in its stable state with no output at Q. This is because the lower NOR gate still has an input = 1 red back from the upper NOR gate.

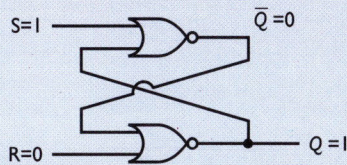

3 When a burglar triggers one of the sensors an input is made at S. This sets the alarm ringing. When S = 1 the output from the upper NOR gate will change so $\bar{Q}$ = 0. This now removes the input from the lower NOR gate and if R = 0 as well then the output Q = 1 and the alarm is switched on. Even though Q feeds back a 1 input to the upper NOR gate, the output from that gate, $\bar{Q}$, will still remain 0.

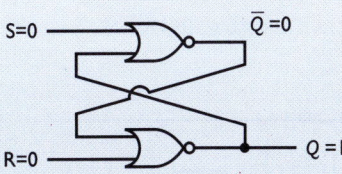

4 As the burglar passes through the sensor it will return to its original state. This means that the input at S goes back to 0. This will not have any effect on the output Q because the switch is in its other stable state. Despite the fact that S = 0, the upper NOR gate still has an input = 1 from the lower NOR gate. This means that $\bar{Q}$ will still be 0 and as long as R remains 0 the alarm will continue ringing.

MEMORY

The bistable has other important uses. It is the basic memory unit in a computer. Once it has been set it remains in that stable state until it is reset. All computer operations are carried out with binary digits so the memory can be 1 or 0. Once it has been set, a bistable will retain 1 in the computer's memory until it is reset or cleared. Each bistable in a computer memory can remember one 'bit' of information. The word 'bit' is short for binary digit. A personal computer may contain millions of bistables on a few small chips.

1 Draw a circuit diagram showing how a bistable switch can be joined to a magnetic sensor switch, a reset switch and a burglar alarm to form an alarm system.

2 a Draw a diagram to show how a single NOR gate may be replaced by a combination of NAND gates.
  b Now draw a diagram to show how a bistable can be made from NAND gates.

3 Using switches, sensors, semiconductors, logic gates or bistables, design circuits for the following devices.

a An automatic switch for a fan which turns it on when the temperature in a room reaches a certain value.
b An alarm that sounds when it is raining to alert you to bring your washing in.
c An automatic watering system which can be used to water your plants when you go on holiday.
d An automatic switch that will turn a light on when it goes dark and turn it off again in the morning.

USING ENERGY

QUESTIONS

1 The following system is used in a bathroom.

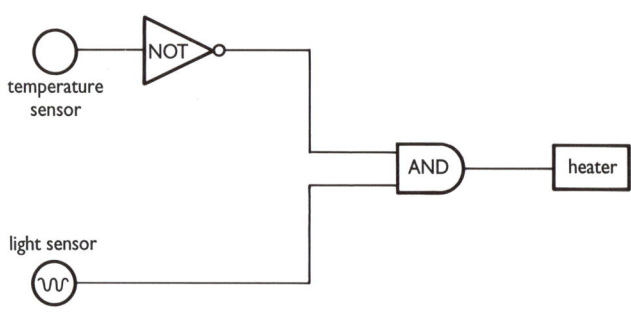

Would the heater be ON or OFF when it was?
a cold and dark?
b cold and light?
c warm and light?
d Explain what would happen if someone made a mistake and put an OR gate in the system instead of an AND gate.

2 The diagram below shows part of a signalling system designed for a model railway. **A**, **B** and **Y** are inputs to LEDS on the control panel for the railway. Two switches, **SW1** and **SW2**, control the LEDs.

SW1 is operated by a track-side signal which can show either red or green.

SW2 is operated by the person controlling the railway.

The outputs of SW1 and SW2, S and D, are '0' when the switches are open and '1' when they are closed.

The logic gates connecting SW1 and SW2 have been omitted from the diagram.

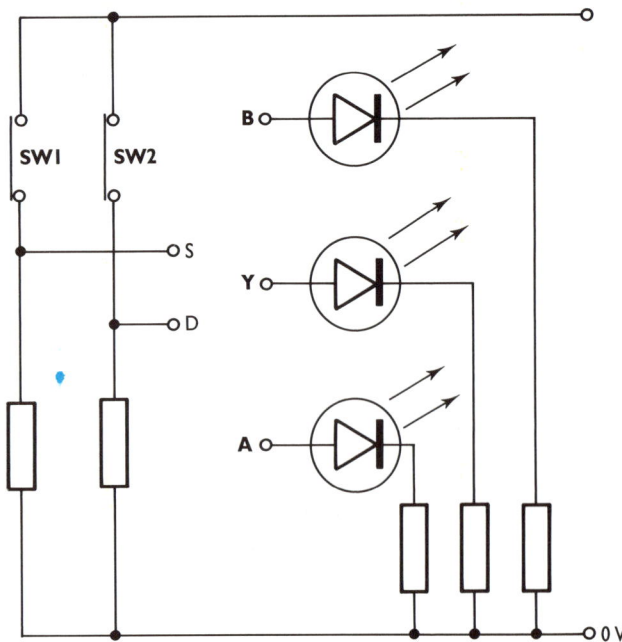

a Complete the truth table for the control system.

Signal colour	Switch inputs		LED states	Switch outputs		LED inputs		
	SW1	SW2		S	D	A	B	Y
Green	Open	Open	all OFF	0	0	0	0	0
Green	Open	Closed	only B ON					
Red	Closed	Open	only Y OFF					
Red	Closed	Closed	only A OFF					

b Draw a circuit showing the logic gate which connects S, D and B.
c Draw a circuit for the logic gate which connects S, D and Y.
d Draw a circuit showing the combination of TWO logic gates which connect S, D and A.

3 a The diagram shows a logic gate circuit.

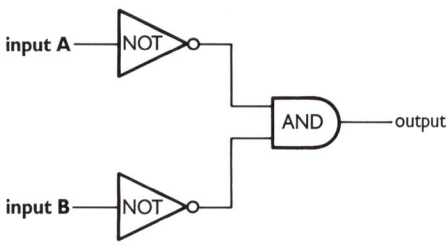

Draw a truth table for the circuit which shows the outputs for all the possible input combinations.

b A student is experimenting with a thermistor and a light-dependent resistor (LDR). The thermistor is in a circuit which gives a high output (logic 1) when it is warm and a low output (logic 0) when it is cold. The LDR circuit gives a high output when the LDR is illuminated and a low output when it is dark. The thermistor and LDR are connected to the logic circuit.

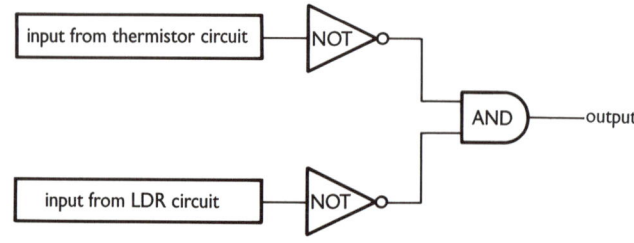

What conditions of light and temperature are necessary for the output to be at logic 1?

12 CHANGES

Contents
Spare parts for worn out limbs
All about Eve
Deserts on the march
Nature's polymer industry revealed
Spots of bother
Current pictures above the mantle
Mercury the mystery planet
Big Bang and the time detectives
Controlling changes
Getting the message
Cold storage
Climatic change

As science develops, our knowledge and understanding of nature and the world around us changes. These changes are taking place all the time.

In this chapter you will be able to put together what you have learnt throughout book 2. If you find you are unsure about something, look back to earlier in the book.

CHANGES

SPARE PARTS FOR WORN OUT LIMBS

NEW LIMBS FOR OLD

Human spare part technology has certainly moved a long way since the time of Long John Silver. Artificial legs aren't exactly like the 'real thing' but they do bend, and people can use them without the need of crutches. In recent years much progress has been made in making artificial limbs which do what their owners want. Moving an arm needs the interaction of nerves, muscles and bones. The best artificial arm at the moment is a **myoelectric limb** which operates by picking up signals from muscle fibres remaining in the arm of the wearer. The signals are relayed to small motors which can move the arm in 6 different ways. This does not provide the range of movements of a real arm but it's a big improvement on earlier artificial arms. A far more sophisticated set of movements would be possible if the artificial arm could detect nerve signals. Research currently in progress suggests that this may be possible. Electrodes might be used to pick up nerve impulses and radio signals could transmit these messages to the motors of the artificial limb.

1 Investigate and record with diagrams the different movements of which the human arm is capable.

2 Using ideas developed from work on co-ordination and movement (Pages 32–3) produce an information sheet for someone who is about to be fitted with a modern artificial limb. Explain how the movement of the limb occurs normally and what they can expect to do with their artificial limb.

CHANGES

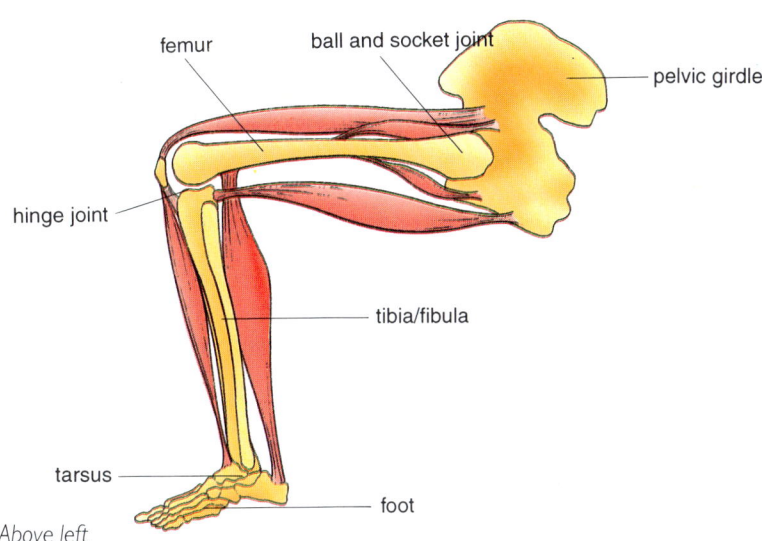
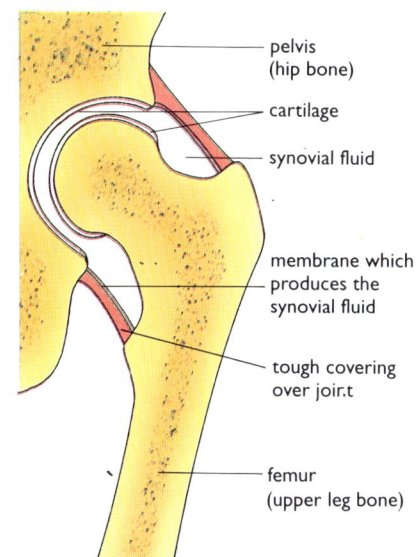

Above left
Diagram to show the arrangement of muscle and bones in a human leg.

Above right
Diagram to show, in detail, the tissues in a human joint.

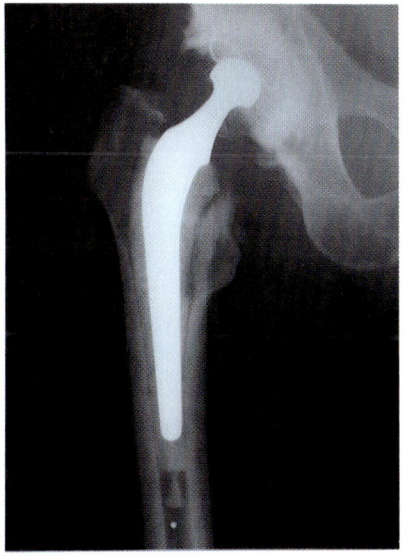

X-ray showing hip replacement materials in position.

REPLACING JOINTS

One of the most successful operations ever to be developed is that of hip replacement. Each year around half a million people throughout the world benefit from the new artificial hips. The loading on the hip joint is about twice the body weight (strenuous activity can increase this by ten times). If you consider the average person will put pressure on their hip and knee joints about two million times a year, its not surprising that the joints do wear out. The cartilage, which reduces friction between bones, wears away resulting in misshapen bones and much pain. As a result of this, diseases like osteo- and rheumatoid arthritis affect the joints. In Britain alone, five million people suffer from arthritis. Most hip operations in Britain are done on these arthritis sufferers.

In the early days of hip replacement surgery, the new joint was covered with a material called PTFR: the material used in non-stick pans. This led to a number of problems. The tiny particles of PTFE wore away and reacted with the joints. These days the ball of the hip joint is replaced by a ball of metal alloy which is driven into the marrow of the femur bone. The new socket is made of very dense plastic. These new joints can last a lifetime.

3 Organise yourselves into a research team of 3–5 people. Your task is to devise tests to be used on new materials for hip replacement surgery. The following hints may help you in planning.
  a You need to find
    i the best materials to coat the surfaces
    ii the best materials for the replacement of the ball part of the hip joints.
  b Brainstorm a list of ideal characteristics for **i** and **ii**
  c Decide on the characteristics you will devise tests for and divide the work among members of your research team.
  d Each subgroup of the team should plan their tests and give a presentation to the whole group which gives details of apparatus and procedures they would use.

CHANGES

THE DEBATE ABOUT EVE

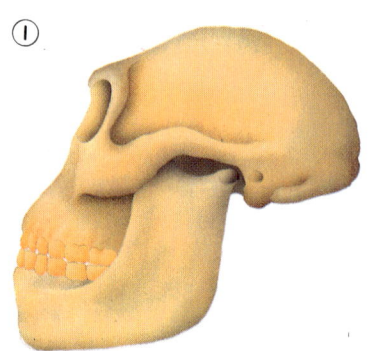

Skull of *Australopithecus robustus*

Reconstructed skull of *Homoerectus*

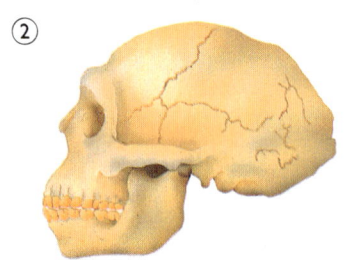

Homo sapiens neanderthalensis,

Homo sapiens sapiens

Human evolution has always been a controversial topic. When he first suggested the theory of evolution, Darwin was made fun of by the most famous scientists of the day. For example, he was asked in one debate at the Royal Society whether he traced his inheritance from the apes from his grandfather or grandmother. Today, scientists are still debating the origins of the human species. Research groups opposed to each other use different research techniques to support their ideas. Look at the arguments used by the opposing sides.

THE FOSSIL SCIENTISTS

Much of the evidence for human evolution since Darwin's time has come from the study of fossils from all the continents of the world. Modern man is known as *Homo sapiens*. Palaeo-scientists believe that fossils found on different continents are related to the present *Homo sapiens* as shown in the diagram.

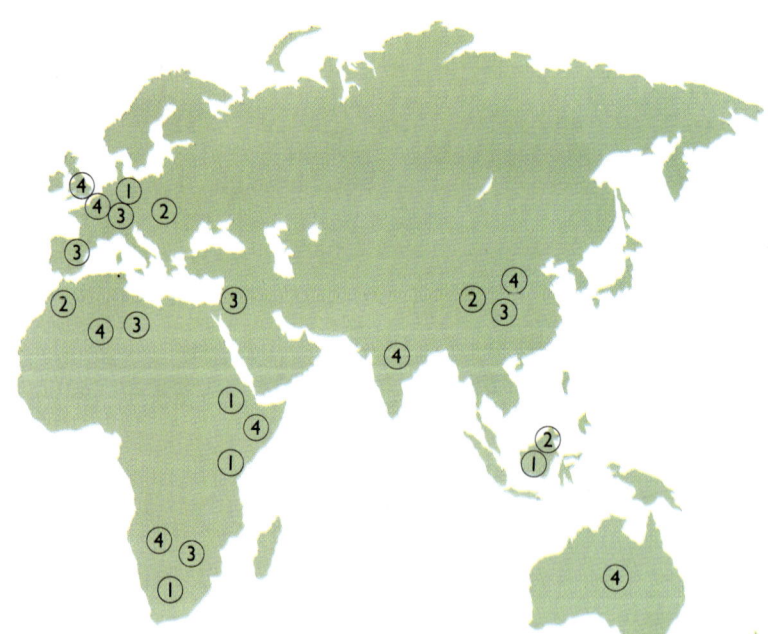

At the beginning of the 1980s there were two hypotheses about human origins based on fossil data.

Hypothesis 1: Modern humans evolved in different parts of the world at different times. For example, the fossil of Peking man was an ancestor of the modern Chinese people.

Hypothesis 2: Modern Man, *Home sapiens sapiens* evolved in one place and then spread out by mating with individuals from the ancient species in different parts of the world. Therefore there is a gradual mixing of genes between ancient species and *Homo sapiens sapiens*. There was no agreement among this group about the continent of origin. Africa, Asia and even Europe were suggested.

CHANGES

THE GENETICISTS

Improvement in genetic techniques in the 1970s and 1980s provided a new tool for the study of evolution. One of the first developments was the use of **DNA hybridisation.** This technique can identify common sequences of DNA between different species. The more DNA there is in common, the nearer the two species are in terms of evolution.

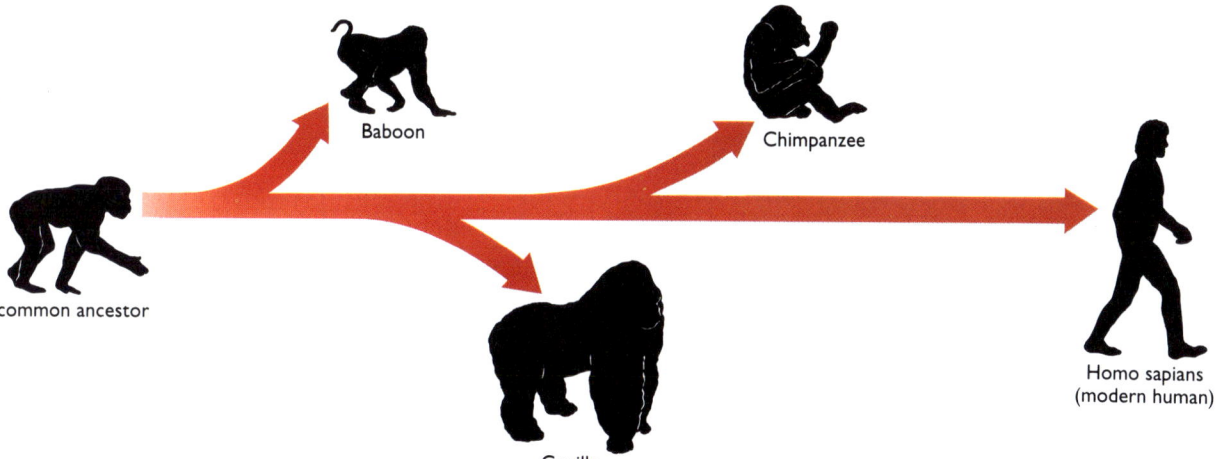

Recent work has used mitochondrial DNA (mDNA). This is the DNA found in mitochondria of cells. We know that the mDNA can only be inherited from the mother, it is easier to plot the mutations than for chromosomal DNA. Work by Allan Wilson and Anna DiRienzo at the University of California studied the variation in mDNA from the blood and hair of people from different parts of the world. They therefore would act as a good evolutionary clock. They found that the variation in mDNA between the different populations around the world was very small indeed. Their research suggests that modern humans originated in Africa about 100 000 to 200 000 years ago. (Previous estimates had been for *Home sapiens sapiens* being around for nearly a million years.) To explain the short time taken for *Homo sapiens* to populate the globe, they hypothesised that they moved to other continents in search of food and 'replaced' the ancient species. This is in stark contrast to the slow evolution by inter-breeding suggested by paleo-scientists. Wilson and DiRienzo published their conclusions in 1987 and rocked the scientific community. Their ideas have been dubbed the **Eve hypothesis**.

The hypothesis has gained support among some scientists but there is still considerable debate. The paleo-scientists argue that the fossil skulls in different parts of the world resemble the modern day populations so must be their ancestors. The geneticists feel their evidence is more dependable than the random way in which very rare fossils are unearthed and dated. The political implications have been considered by some. The Eve Hypothesis strong suggests that racial differences are very recent, and therefore slight and unimportant.

1 Compare the three hypotheses presented here with the use of the following headings:
 • research techniques
 • proposed origin of *Homo sapiens*
 • time scale of human evolution
 • method of colonisation by *H. sapiens sapiens*
 • supporting arguments
2 Explain how fossils are formed and dated.
3 Why is it easier to plot mutations in mitochondrial DNA than in chromosomal DNA?
4 What effects might a scientist's political ideas have on their scientific ideas?

CHANGES

DESERTS ON THE MARCH?

The effects of drought in Africa are familiar to all of us. One of the reasons put forward for the African droughts of the 1970s and 1980s has been the misuse of land by local inhabitants. New research into weather patterns and archaeology challenge this assumption. So what is the cause of droughts?

HOW ARE DESERTS FORMED?

A desert is defined as an area which receives less than 25 cm of rain in a year. This is caused by the pattern of air circulation around the globe.

The amount of energy from the Sun varies considerably depending upon where you are on the Earth. Surprisingly enough, increased energy results in desert shrinkage. This is because the air gets warmer, absorbs more moisture and the cloud belt over the equator expands. Interestingly, French geologists have demonstrated the link between climate changes in Africa and the Earth's orbit around the Sun.

Sahel crisis: No rain for five years

FAMINE PREDICTED IN AFRICA

Drought brings misery to millions

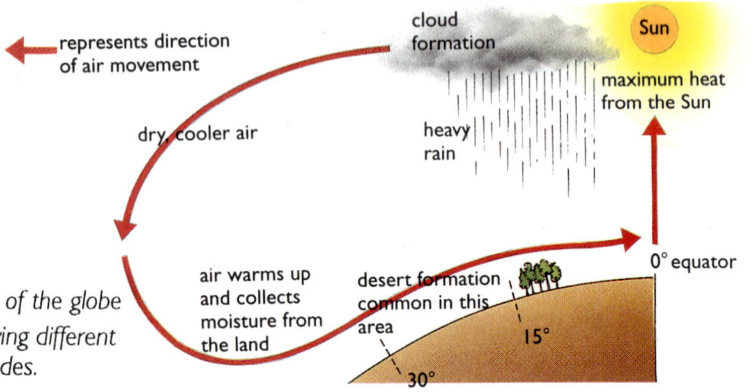

Part of the globe showing different latitudes.

CHANGES

The Sahel desert can be shown to have expanded north between 18 000–8000 years ago and contracted in the last 6000 years. These changes link with major changes in atmospheric patterns.

SOME ANCIENT SOLUTIONS TO SURVIVAL IN DRYLANDS

Archaeological finds in the Sahara and other desert lands give clues to how ancient civilisations survived by 'harvesting' rainwater. For example, the Negev desert has the remains of much ancient engineering designed to capture and store water. There are stone walls everywhere which divert water into huge cisterns carved into the hillside. These ensured drinking water all the year round for flocks of sheep and goats kept by the local Bedouins. Similar structures in the Thar desert of India allow 60 people per square kilometre to survive in the most densely populated desert on Earth. In Peru the Incas built hundreds of kilometres of canals which supplied water for desert areas. They also created massive terraced fields which enabled irrigation in this hostile environment.

SOME MODERN SOLUTIONS FOR TACKLING DESERTIFICATION

This plastic tree (left) is claimed to be one answer to the problem of drought. The tree creates cooler air by absorbing moisture that condenses onto its surface at night and releasing it through evaporation during the day. Its roots are long hollow tubes which are injected with liquid polyurethane when the tree is planted. The polyurethane sets to provide a firm anchorage. The plastic tree imitates many of the physical features of a real desert tree but requires no water to maintain it. The idea is that when warm air meets the cool air around the trees, the drop in temperature will be sufficient to cause rain. Several Africa countries are experimenting with plantations of plastic trees.

Another development to assist irrigation of the desert is being tested in Egypt. Radar pictures from satellites are being used to pinpoint ancient rivers 5 m and more below the sand. Wells have been dug and the water from these rivers is irrigating a 2024 hectare experimental farm.

1 Use an atlas to identify existing deserts on Earth and use the information on this page to suggest the reason for their formation.
2 The settling of nomadic tribes by governments can assist development of deserts.
   a How did the nomadic way of life assist survival?
   b How do settled communities assist desertification?
3 a Draw a diagram to explain how plastic trees might cause rain.
   b Explain which living processes in a real tree in a desert can help cause rain.

CHANGES

NATURE'S POLYMER INDUSTRY REVEALED

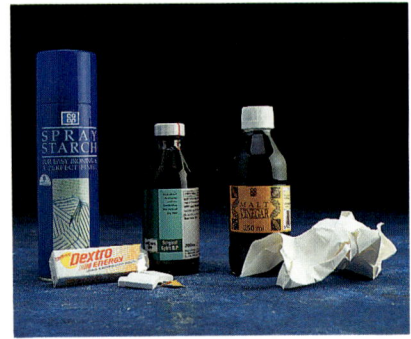

The substances in the photograph all look and behave quite differently. What do they have in common? A closer look at the molecules which make up each substance gives a clue. The molecules may be different shapes and sizes but they consist only of the atoms carbon, hydrogen and oxygen. The differences between the substances is caused by the fact that each molecule has:

- a different number of these atoms
- a different arrangement of these atoms

Let's take a look at alcohol and vinegar. Ethanol is an alcohol which has the chemical formula C_2H_5OH. It is sometimes written as shown in the diagram (top left) to show where the chemical bonds are. Vinegar (or ethanoic acid) has the chemical formula CH_3COOH and can be shown as in the diagram (below left). Anyone tasting either would easily tell the difference between the two substances and yet they are very similar chemically. In fact alcohol is very easily converted to vinegar as many amateur wine makers have found to their cost!

Alcohol (ethanol molecule)

Vinegar (ethanoic acid molecule)

BUILDING BIG MOLECULES FROM SMALLER ONES

Sometimes molecules are closely related because one acts as a building block for the other. Do you remember from Book 1 how glucose was used by plants as a building block for so many other plant molecules? One of them is starch, made by joining lots of glucose units together. Starch is a polymer and is made of glucose, the monomer.

a glucose molecule — a starch molecule

ethene

poly (ethene) polymer

Making polymers from monomers is big business and earns the chemical industry millions of pounds every year. The plastics we use daily are polymers made by the **polymerisation** process. Polythene is one of many plastics produced by polymerisation. The gas ethene is the monomer. When polymerised it becomes polythene.

1 How many atoms are there in:
   a one molecule of vinegar?
   b one molecule of ethanol?
2 What is the difference between an atom and a molecule?
2 How do you think winemakers sometimes end up with vinegar? (Give chemical equations for the reactions involved.)

CHANGES

4 a Produce a table to compare the properties of starch and glucose as follows:

	Glucose	Starch
Size		
Appearance		
Solubility		
Taste		

5 Cellulose is built up from chains of glucose molecules too, but it has quite different properties to starch. Find out more about cellulose and the ways in which it is different to starch.

6 Polymers are grouped as thermoplastics or thermosets. Find out the difference between the two groups.

USING SPIDERS IN INDUSTRY

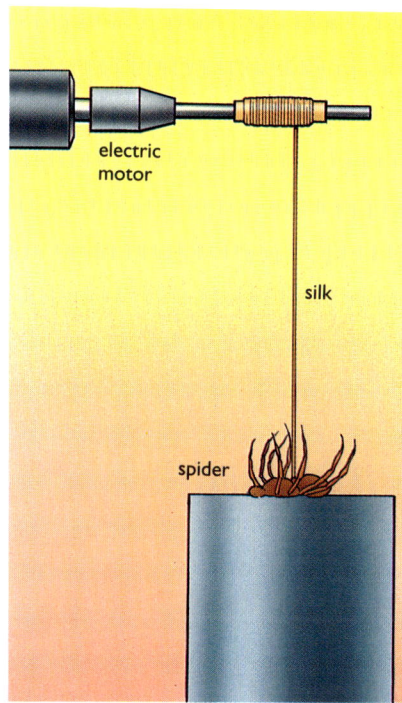

An animal polymer which is in great demand is the silk from a spider's web. Silk is used to make bullet-proof vests. It is at least twice as strong as steel and it can stretch as much as 15 per cent before braking. The threads of a web are able to dissipate the energy which ensures the captured creatures are not catapulted away once they have made contact. These properties mean that vests made of spider-silk can absorb much of the kinetic energy of a bullet, thus reducing injuries.

Synthetic polymers produced to do the same job aren't half as good as the real silk which is why scientists are paying so much attention to spiders. In fact they have found that some spiders can produce seven different kinds of silk. Each type has different properties. Some remain sticky after being produced, some form strong fibres immediately, while others contract in the presence of water.

The commercial extraction of the silk is itself interesting. Each spider can produce up to 320 m of fibre per day. Initially this was used for chemical analysis. The fibres were found to be polymers of amino acids, in other words, proteins. The reason for the different types of silk remains a mystery. Are the amino acids different or are they simply arranged in different combinations? The research is continuing.

7 Describe the energy transfers which take place when:
a a fly lands on a spider's web.
b a bullet hits a bullet-proof vest made using spider's silk.

8 a Explain the advantages and disadvantages of using spider-silk on a large scale.
b Suggest some other uses of spider's silk and explain your reasons.

9 Spider-silk is 20 times stronger than human tendon tissue and is more elastic. Scientists think that it could be used to replace tendons and ligaments.

a Explain what tendons and ligaments do and why they may need replacing.
b Many people would need to be convinced that spider-silk provides a safe and effective replacement for damaged tendons and ligaments. Make a list of some of the tests and experiments which would need to be carried out before spider-silk could become an accepted treatment.

10 Scientists are interested in mass production of spider-silk. They believe that genetic engineering techniques might one day produce a solution. Describe in detail how this may be possible.

CHANGES

SPOTS OF BOTHER?

In 1611 Galileo was the first to observe sunspots. Nearly 400 years later scientists are still observing the spots which appear on the Sun's surface.

WHAT DO WE KNOW?

The Sun is an active ball of hot gas (mainly hydrogen). Scientists estimate that the Sun's weight is 300 000 times that of the Earth, and that the pressure at the centre of the Sun is about 300 million times the pressure we feel on the surface of the Earth. Within the Sun temperatures are around 15×10^6 °C. Nuclear reactions convert hydrogen to helium, and release large amounts of energy. About 4 million tonnes of the Sun's matter 'disappears' every second through these reactions. The visible surface of the Sun's surface has dark spots, which appear and disappear. When the Sun is most active, there are more sunspots, and there are more gigantic eruptions of hot gases (solar flares). The charged particles from solar flares disrupt the Earth's magnetic field. This disruption is linked to intense displays like the aurora borealis, and is known to interrupt telephone and radio communication and make compasses unreliable.

Explosions on the surface of the Sun fires electrically charged particles far into space. These solar flares can disrupt the Earth's magnetic field.

CHANGES

SPOT THE PATTERN

The number of sunspots varies in a cycle of about 11 years. Links have been made between this cycle and certain events on Earth. For instance, there were few sunspots during the years 1640-1700. During this time there was a very cold period on Earth: in southern England, the River Thames froze over. The box shows just some of the Earth happenings which have been linked to the sunspot cycle.

> declarations of war
> number of driving licences issued
> occurrence of earthquakes
> speed of chemical reactions in water
> suicide rates
> thickness of layers in sedimentary rocks
> thickness of tree rings
> time taken for samples of blood to clot
> variance in stock market prices

SUPPORTING THE SOLAR CONNECTION

In the early 1990s Danish scientists published results which support the link between variations in the Sun's activity and the temperature on Earth. The cycle of sunspot activity varies from 8–14 years. According to the Danish scientists, when the cycle is longest the Earth's temperature falls. They suggest that the changing length of sunspot cycle follows a cycle of about 80–90 years. This is supported by evidence from cores drilled in the deep Greenland ice.

Solar prominence.

Aurora borealis, seen in Alaska, USA.

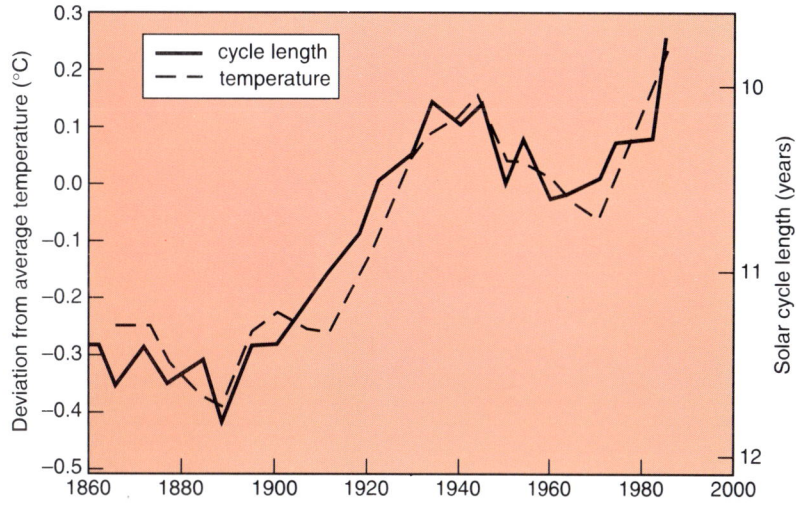

1. Explain how nuclear reactions in the Sun could produce
   a. new atoms
   b. energy
2. Tree rings are thicker when more rain falls.
   a. Explain how rings in tree trunks are formed.
   b. Suggest why these rings are thicker when there is more rainfall.
   c. How might the link between Earth temperature and solar activity help to explain the thickness of tree rings.
3. Study the Earth happenings in the box which have been linked to the sunspot cycle. You might like to do this in a group. For each one, develop an explanation of how the link might happen. Decide how likely you think it is, and suggest any further evidence you would want before you felt the link was strong.

CHANGES

CURRENT PICTURES OVER THE MANTLE

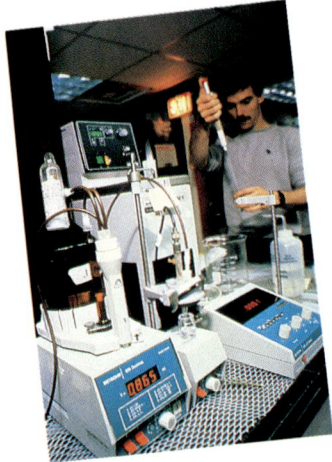

Scientists are in little doubt that the Earth's mantle is fluid. Plate tectonics is now used to explain much of what we see on the surface: there is much evidence that continents and the ocean crust have shifted by thousands of kilometres in the past 200 million years. This movement is an outward sign of convection as the hot mantle cools, but we don't know whether this happens in stages or through the whole mantle.

It's important to discover the pattern of mantle flow because it helps us understand the forces that drive earthquakes, volcanoes and the whole of plate tectonics. Currents of hot rock transfers energy from deep in the earth, so the flow pattern also tells us something of the way the Earth is cooling. Scientists 'view' the interior of the planet by studying wave patterns generated by earthquakes and explosions.

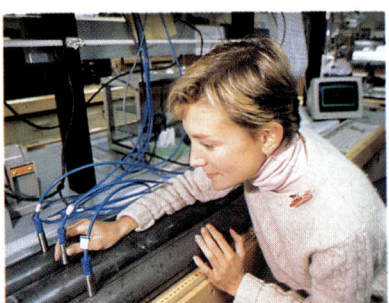

Scientists taking part in the Ocean Drilling Project.

I use powerful computers to model the way materials flow inside the Earth.

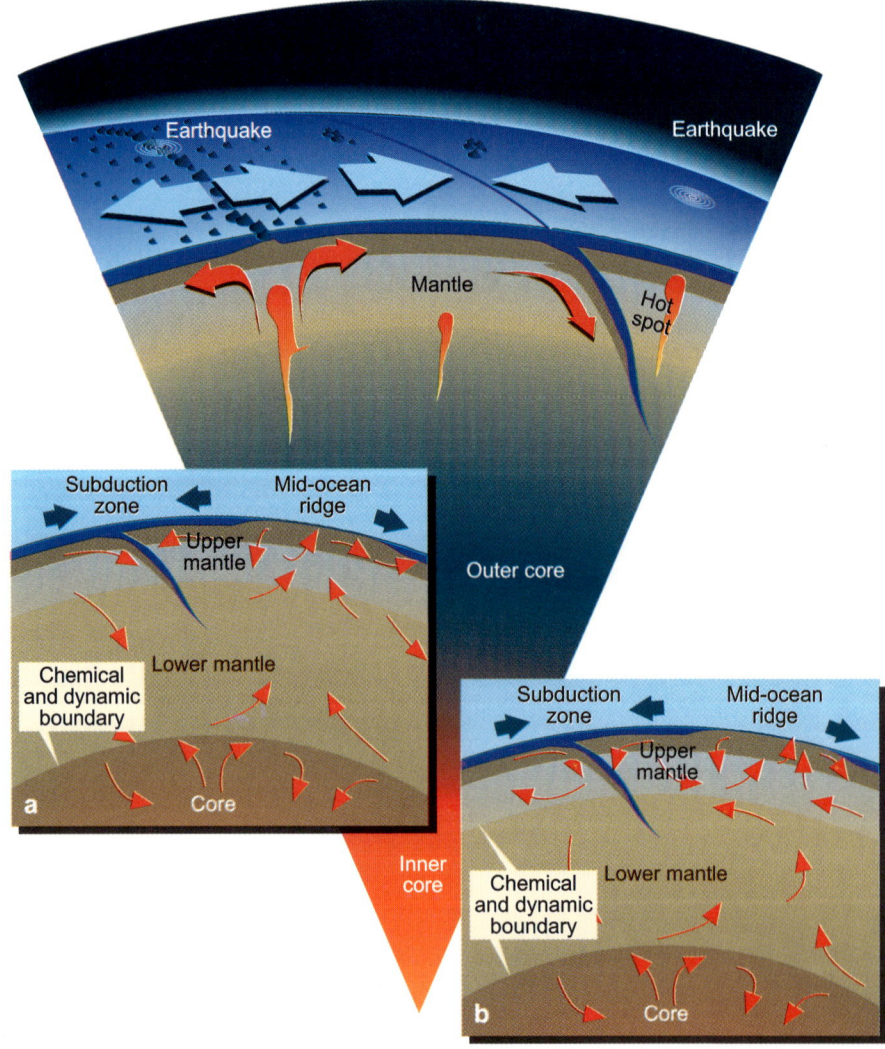

CHANGES

I analyse thousands of readings from earthquake waves to build up an internal picture of the Earth.

Such seismic waves are refracted and reflected by the internal structure of the mantle. Seismic studies indicate there are three layers in the mantle: upper, lower and a transition zone. There are boundaries between them where the rock density changes and changes the velocity of waves passing through them.

Scientists think that changes in rock density in the mantle are linked to the mineral composition of the layers. They have tested this out by using upper mantle minerals like olivine and putting them under high pressures. Olivine transforms into a denser form, perovskite ($CaTiO_3$), under high pressure. Properties of such dense, high pressure minerals match the densities and wave velocities observed for the transition zone and the lower mantle.

Computer simulations made using temperature and density data show that small differences in density could make the upper and lower mantle behave as two different fluids (like oil and water). A number of scientists have examined the movements of two different fluids, and have used computer models of the currents in the different layers. They find that the pattern gets complicated after a while and produces 'leaky layering' where there is mixing between two layers. This would explain the formation of the plumes of magma which gave rise to the Deccan Traps in India and Yellowstone in the USA.

An upper mantle mineral, Olivine.

I use high temperatures and pressures to change minerals and compare their properties to those materials in the mantle.

1 Draw a diagram to show the structure of the Earth as we think it is. Label your diagram with the names gives to the different regions within the Earth and give an indication of the distances and temperatures.

2 What is *plate tectonics*? Explain **three** pieces of evidence which support the idea of plate tectonics.

3 Study the examples of data gathering shown in the pictures. For each one explain how scientists get data, and explain it can provide evidence about Earth's structure.

4 Use the diagrams on these pages to explain the different theories for the convection currents in the mantle.

5 **a** Explain how the changing density of rocks could affect seismic waves passing through them.
  b Describe how scientists have tested out their findings using samples of different minerals.

173

CHANGES

MERCURY THE MYSTERY PLANET

The surface of Mercury.

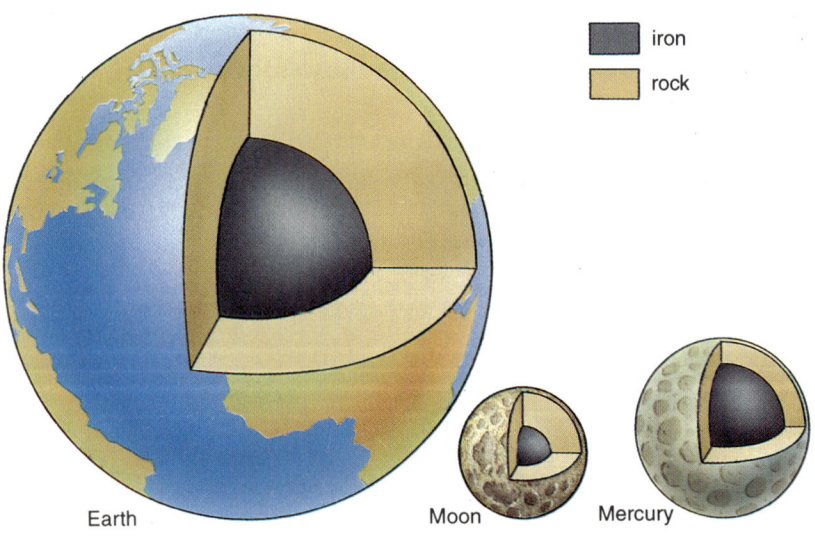

Mercury is the closest planet to the Sun. It travels fastest round the Sun and is both very hot and very cold. Very few space missions have included Mercury. Scientists have used data from such missions and their own observations to work out something of Mercury's structure.

The planets in the Solar System formed from dust and gas that surrounded the Sun at its birth. We think that this dust and gas spun around the Sun in a disc shape. Particles collided and formed clumps which grew in size until there were nine planets spinning around the Sun. In 1972 John Lewis put forward a theory to explain how this process produced planets with different compositions. According to his theory the inner planets should be iron and rock, and the outer worlds should also contain substances like ice and ammonia.

CHANGES

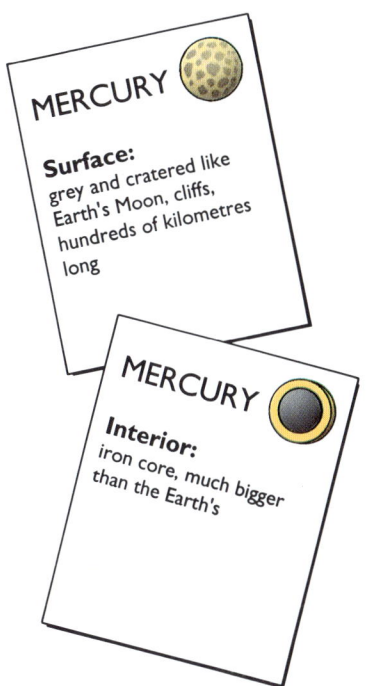

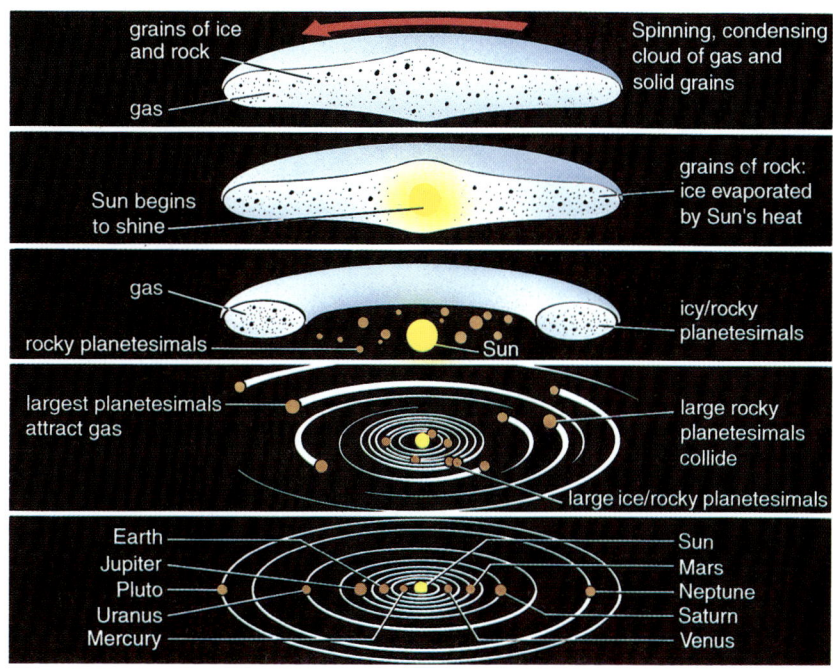

Lewis' Theory: as the cloud around the Sun condenses, substances with high melting points (iron, alloys and silicates) condensed close to the Sun. Substances with lower melting points (ice and ammonia) could only condense far from the Sun where it was cold.

Mercury, Venus, Earth and its moon and Mars are made of iron and rock. By working out the densities of these, scientists have worked out that Mercury's structure is more like that of Earth than the Moon's, and contains more iron than they expected.

Many planets have magnetic fields. Scientists think that these are caused by electric currents stirred up in the liquid core of a planet if it spins fast enough. Earth is one planet where this explanation fits. Mercury spins slowly and scientists think it has a solid core. It shouldn't have a magnetic field, but the spacecraft Mariner 10 found that Mercury has a magnetic field equivalent to 1% of the Earth's. Some scientists feel that this is evidence that part of Mercury's core may be molten. A substance dissolved in the iron could lower its melting point: just like salt on the roads makes water turn into solid ice at a lower than normal temperature. A likely substance would be sulphur because it dissolves in iron. However, according to Lewis' Theory sulphur shouldn't be there because its melting point is too low.

1 Some scientists think that Mercury was once a bigger planet, with the same iron core it now has, but with a larger mantle of rock on the outside. This would make it fit predictions. They say that the rocky surface could have been blasted away by heat from the Sun, or by the impact of a large asteroid.

Explain how these suggestions could explain the proportions of iron and rock Mercury seems to have now.

2 Use your understanding of kinetic theory to explain the Lewis Theory of the composition of the plants. Give another example of where the same ideas can explain what we see happening.

3 Scientists think Mercury core is solid. Though Earth and Mercury started hot and molten Mercury cooled faster: "just as a freshly baked roll cools faster than a large loaf of bread," said one scientist. Explain how this comparison might account for Mercury's solid core.

4 What is your view of the theories for the structure of Mercury? Support your view by picking out the evidence that you feel is strongest and explain why. If you can, carry out some research of your own to find out some additional evidence. You could compare your views with someone else.

CHANGES

BIG BANG AND THE TIME DETECTIVES

In 1992 the US space agency, NASA, announced that it had found traces of the radiation produced at the beginning of the Universe. The story covered in the press and on radio and TV.

The radiation from the Big Bang was first detected in 1964. It came from all over the sky and appeared to come from a gas at a temperature of 3 Kelvin. This cosmic background radiation must be coming from the hot gas that filled the Universe soon after the Big Bang. As the Universe expands, the wavelength of the radiation is increased. This makes it appear as if it came from a cooler source. The temperature of radiation found in 1964 fitted this explanation.

The 1964 discovery posed a problem. It suggested that gas 300 000 years after the Big Bang was very smooth: any lumps or holes in the gas would show up as hot and cold spots in the radiation. We know that the Universe today is lumpy. It is made up of galaxies bunched together with empty voids in between. These must have grown from lumps in the original gas like milk curdling into cheese.

Scientists felt that if they looked hard enough at the cosmic background radiation they should find some temperature variations. This is hard to do on Earth, because radiation from our own galaxy and water vapour in our atmosphere cause problems. Scientists designed a Cosmic Background Explorer satellite (COBE). COBE was launched in 1989, carrying instruments which took millions of measurements. Careful computer analysis allowed scientists to pick out the temperature variations (or ripples). Nancy Boggess of the Goddard Space Flight Center says they spent four months 'working like dogs' to complete the analysis. The hottest ripples are about 30 millionths of a degree warmer than the average with an error of 5 millionth of a degree.

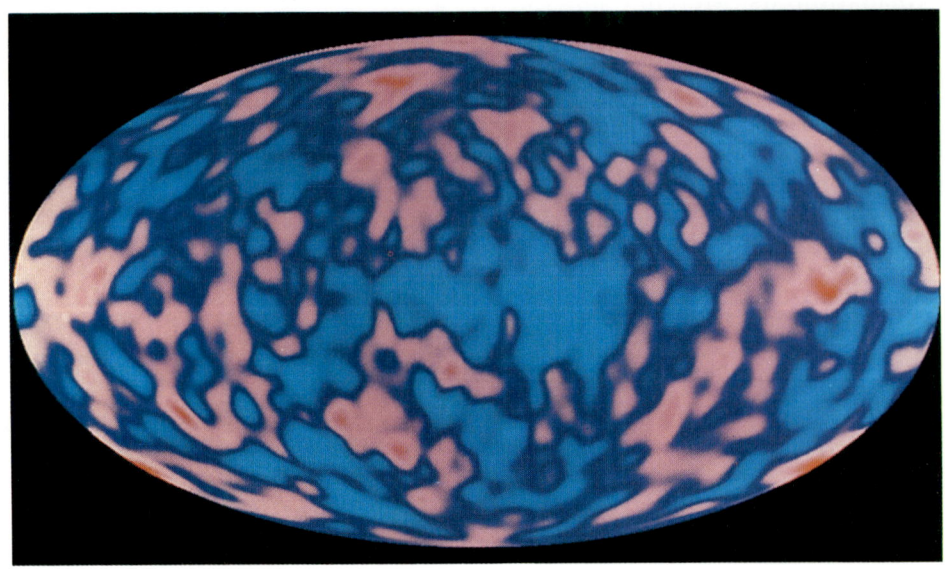

Pink hotspots reveal background radiation.

CHANGES

'If COBE hadn't found the fluctuations, we would have to re-think a lot of our basic theories,' said Jasper Wall of the Royal Greenwich Observatory.

Writing in a British newspaper at around the same time, scientists Stephen Hawking said:

> The results from the COBE satellite show the kind of fluctuations that were predicted. This is tremendously important. It confirms our theories of how galaxies, stars and planets and even human beings came into existence, in a Universe that began in a smooth way.
>
> It is an observation of equal importance to the discovery that the Universe is expanding, or the original discovery of the background radiation.

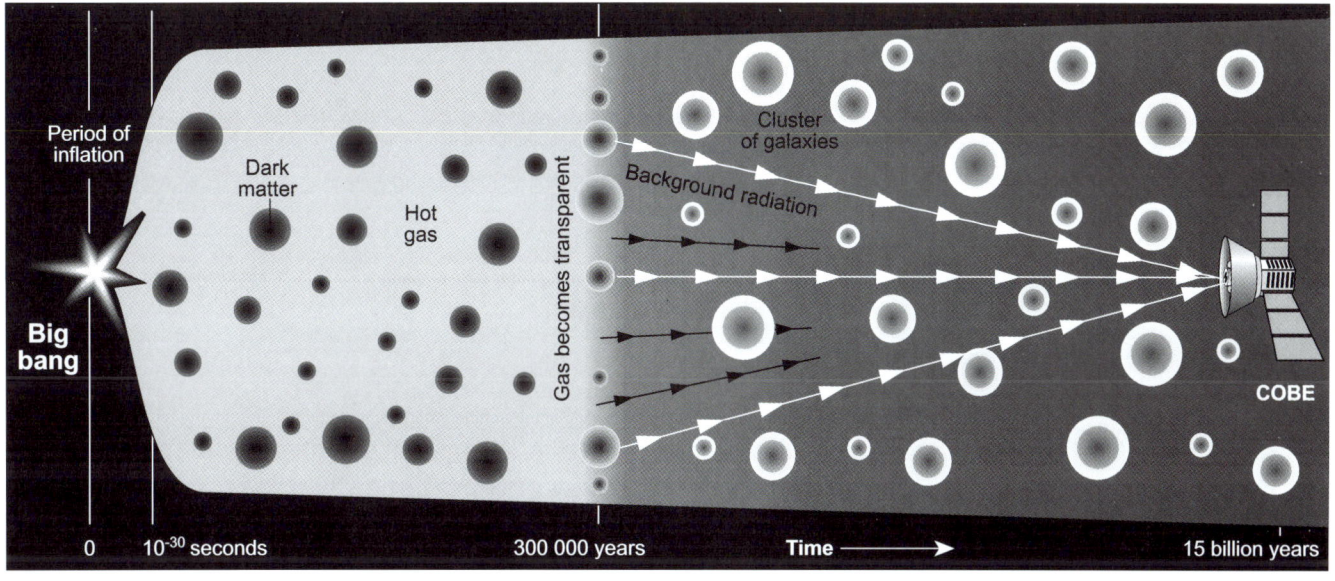

1. Explain what scientists mean whey they talk about the Big Bang. How is it linked to the way in which galaxies are thought to form?
2. When the COBE results were published, reports on the news often talked about the findings as showing ripples at the edge of time. Explain what this means.
3. Suggest how the Milky Way and Earth's atmosphere might have made it difficult to make the measurements which were made by COBE.
4. Explain why scientists like Jasper Wall were pleased to have the COBE results.
5. Explain what Stephen Hawking means when he talks about the way in which galaxies, stars and planets and even human beings came into being. Do you agree with his view that the theories are confirmed by COBE?

CHANGES

CONTROLLING CHANGES

We use many electrical and electronic devices to control appliances and machines. A control system is useful because it automatically carries out what would be a tedious job. For example, the thermostat in an oven controls the energy supply so that the oven keeps to a set temperature. Without the thermostat, you would need to adjust the energy supply yourself according to the oven temperature. As well as electrical systems, there are other types of control systems that work mechanically, biologically or chemically. While each control system is quite different, there is a common pattern that we can identify. Here are some examples of control systems that automatically control changes.

HOMEOSTASIS

The iris

A car thermostat

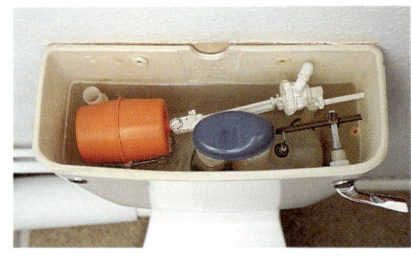
A ballcock

Each picture shows an example of a control system which relies on **feedback**. This way of controlling changes is called homeostasis. Automatic control can only happen if there is a message fed back when the situation changes from the level required. Whatever is being controlled is called the *controlled variable*. There needs to be a *sensor* to detect the variable and a *comparator* to register any difference between the level of the variable and the desired level. Finally, something has to change the variable; this is called the *actuator*.

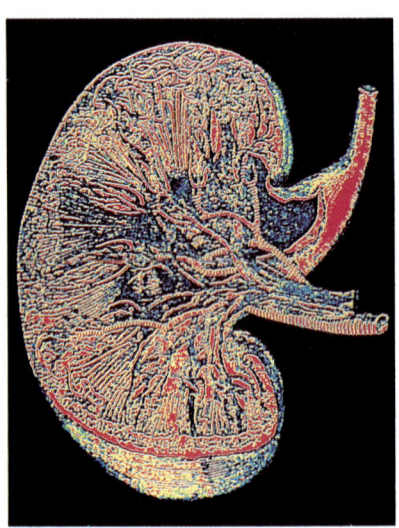
A human kidney

A tight rope walker controls his balance.

CHANGES

1 For each example of homeostasis shown in the photographs, find out and describe how they work.
2 Think about each of these examples of homeostasis and, for each one, write down
   a the controlled variable,
   b the sensor,
   c the comparator,
   d the actuator.

Think about how you manage to walk in a straight line. This is an example of homeostasis. The level that is set is to walk along a straight line. Here are the parts of the control system:

- controlled variable – direction of walking
- sensor – eye
- comparator – brain
- actuator – muscles in body

The control system can be represented by this diagram.

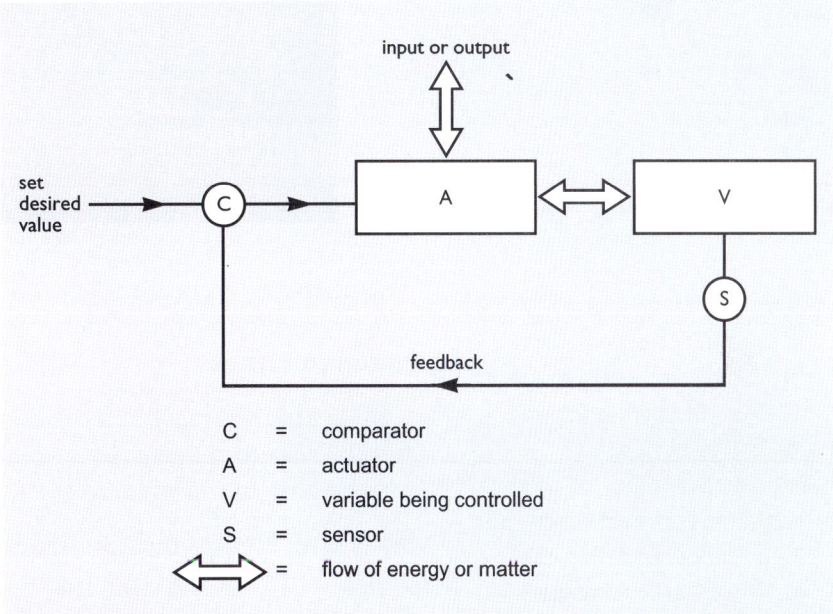

How homeostasis is achieved.

BUFFER SOLUTIONS

You will remember that the pH of an alkali such as ammonia solution is greater than 7 and the pH of an acid such as hydrochloric acid is less than 7. Adding hydrochloric acid to ammonia solution decreases the pH and *vice-versa*. However, it is possible to make a buffer solution is one in which the pH will remain constant whether acid or alkali is added. The buffer solution automatically controls the pH of the liquid because chemical reactions take place to neutralise the acid or alkali which has been added.

3 Look back at the electronic control systems you studied in Chapter 11.
   a Choose one which is an example of homeostasis and describe what it does and how it works.
   b Identify the following: the controlled variable, the senor, the comparator and the actuator.
4 Electronic control systems have replaced many jobs that were previously carried out by people. Think about the following and describe which is, or may be, controlled partly or entirely by an automatically controlled system.
   a Nursing.
   b Car manufacture.
   c Banking.
   d Hair dressing.
   e Composing music.

CHANGES

GETTING THE MESSAGE

During an opera a story is told within a music form.

The purpose of communication is to transfer information from one person to another. There are three essentials for communication:

- to be able to transmit a message,
- to be able to receive the message,
- to be able to understand the message.

Successful communication takes place when the receiver understands the message that was intended. Transmitting it efficiently is only one stage of the process.

TELEGRAPH

> **1** Think about an opera as a means of communication.
> **a** What special requirements are needed by the singers?
> **b** Microphones and loudspeakers may be used to assist the communication. Explain how each works.
> **c** The design of an opera theatre is important because of its acoustics. Would the building have a long or short reverberation time? How would it be achieved?
> (Book 1, p. 273)
> **d** Explain how the human ear works in receiving the sounds.

The telegraph used the magnetic effect of an electric current to send signals over long distances.

One of the earliest systems used to communicate quickly over long distances was the telegraph. It was simply a buzzer connected by wires to a switch some miles away. The operator would press the switch and send the message using morse code. This is a special code of short and long buzzes used to represent dots and dashes for each letter of the alphabet.

CHANGES

2 Design a circuit that could be used to enable two people to send telegraph signals to each other and also receive them.
3 What do you think are the disadvantages of the telegraph?
4 The earliest telegraph systems used batteries known as galvanic cells. Today we use dry cell batteries in torches and other portable electrical appliances.
  a Draw a diagram of a carbon zinc dry cell.
  b Explain how it produces electricity.
  c Show the chemical reaction taking place at each electrode.

Guglielmo Marconi (1874–1937) who invented wireless communication at the age of 20.

RADIO

The first 'wireless' telegraphy was invented by Guglielmo Marconi in 1894. This was only six years after the discovery of electromagnetic waves by Heinrich Hertz. At first the radio signals were only in morse code but later developments enable us to send sound and pictures by electromagnetic waves. Today the television is an important global communication system. By bouncing the electromagnetic waves off satellites, we are able to watch live events in our homes from all over the world and even the Moon.

5 Draw a diagram of the electromagnetic spectrum showing the relative positions of: cosmic rays, gamma rays, infra-red, microwaves, radar, radio, television, ultra-violet, visible and x-rays.
6 In 1980 the Voyager spacecraft sent pictures from the planet Saturn to Earth using radio waves. Saturn is about 1 280 million kilometres from Earth. All electromagnetic waves travel at 300 000 km/s. Calculate how long it takes for a radio signal to travel from Saturn to Earth.
7 The Moon is the Earth's largest satellite. There are hundreds of other satellites that now orbit our planet.
  a What is meant by a 'geostationary' satellite?
  b What force acts on a satellite to keep it in orbit?
8 What are the survival advantages of communication in the following cases:
  a Sonic communications between dolphins.
  b The invention of the printing press in the sixteenth century.
  c Non-verbal communication between humans.

CHANGES

COLD STORAGE

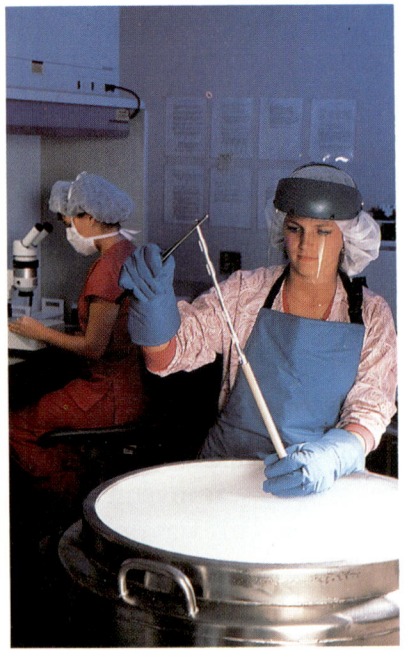

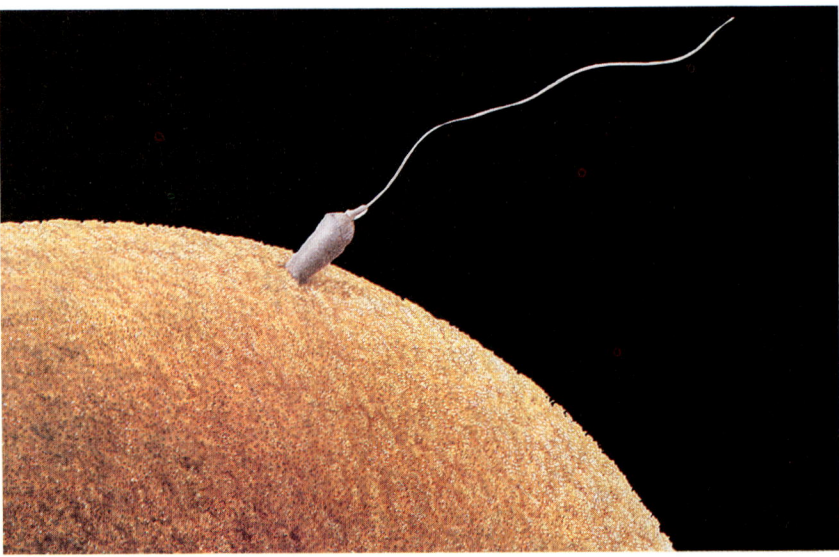

Frozen sperm for artificial insemination is stored in "banks".

Frozen spermatozoa are available to women desiring artificial insemination. Eight-cell fertilsed embryos can be frozen in liquid nitrogen (−196 °C) for later thawing and transfer into the womb. An antifreeze solution, called a **cryoprotectant**, is needed to prevent the formation of lethal ice crystals. Red blood cells can be successfully preserved by freezing with a cryoprotectant. They are useful for blood transfusions. Bone marrow cells can survive freezing at −79 °C. This provides bone marrow cells for the treatment of radiation damage. Corneas can be preserved in liquid nitrogen for later transplants and, subject to certain conditions, skin may be revitalised for use as skin grafts in burn victims.

Less success has been achieved with other whole tissues. Hamster hearts and rat hearts survive for 20 minutes when frozen at −20 °C, but none survive at −79 °C. Dog liver stored for two weeks at −60 °C has poor transplant success. Failure to freeze organs would seem to suggest that freezing whole animals is unlikely to succeed. Hamsters have been kept at −5.5 °C for up to four hours with 100 per cent recovery rate. However, rabbits subjected to similar conditions have low survival rates. At lower temperatures even the hamster recovery rate drops. When 55 per cent of the hamster's body-water froze, none survived.

Hamsters have been frozen alive and revived later.

CHANGES

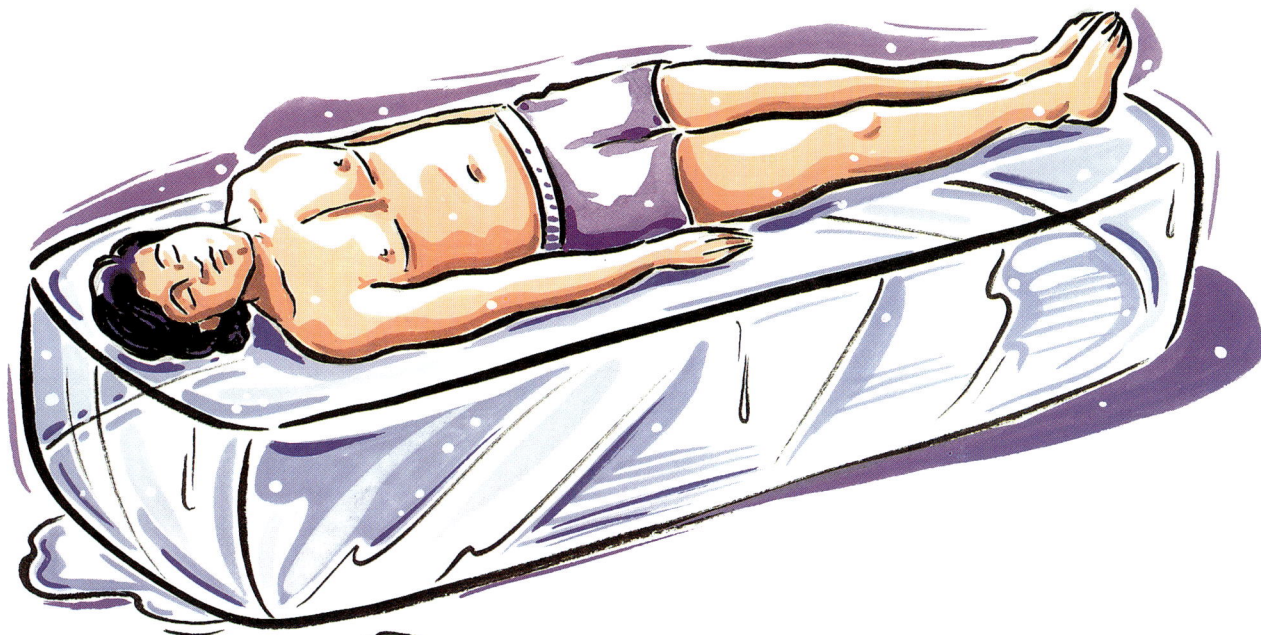

Cryonics technology is already being applied to humans. At present a number of people are known to be frozen in liquid nitrogen. Such people hope that they can be revived sometime in the future when the ageing process is under scientific control, or, if they were ill when they were frozen, when there is a cure for the diseases that were killing them.

1 How long would spermatozoa, blood cells and bone marrow survive if they were not frozen?

2 What is a cryoprotectant? What does it do?

3 Why would the formation of ice crystals be lethal to cells?

4 According to the evidence on these pages, how likely is it that humans can survive being frozen in liquid nitrogen? Give the evidence to support your view.

5 In what form is nitrogen at normal room temperatures?

6 Describe the difference in molecular activity between solids, liquids and gases.

7 For each of the following groups of people explain the advantages of using freeze preservation:
   a terminally ill people who hope the future will bring a cure for their illnesses,
   b depressed people who choose freezing instead of suicide,
   c dangerous criminals for whom there are now no methods of rehabilitation,
   d astronauts on space flights requiring many years of travel time.

8 What might be some of the problems facing a society that has the technology to freeze and later revive humans?

CHANGES

CLIMATIC CHANGE

In Book 1 you studied some of the evidence that supports ideas about the 'Greenhouse Effect' (page 244). It would be helpful to revise that work before continuing with this activity.

Let us suppose that the Earth's average global temperature rises by 2 °C as a result of the 'Greenhouse Effect'. Here are some suggestions about what effects this might have on the Earth's biosphere.

ICE CAPS AND GLACIERS

- Global warming would melt glaciers and ice caps
- Sea levels would rise
- Less reflection of Sun's energy.

OCEANS

- Water expands as it warms over 4 °C
- Sea levels will rise
- Fresh water supplies may be contaminated by seawater.

PLANT GROWTH

- Certain species will grow faster with increased carbon dioxide
- Weeds and insects will thrive
- Agricultural patterns will be affected, for example, northern European countries could grow crops now grown in Mediterranean regions.

CLOUDS

- Increased evaporation will produce more clouds
- This may reflect more solar energy and reduce global warming
- Water vapour is a 'greenhouse gas' and consequently more energy may be trapped in the Earth's atmosphere.

WATER RESOURCES

- More clouds will produce more rainfall
- Patterns of rainfall will change causing abundance in some places and drought in others
- Soil evaporation will increase.

FORESTS

- Trees that grow better with increased carbon dioxide will replace those that do not
- More forest fires are likely

BIOLOGICAL DIVERSITY

- Some species will not be able to find new niches or adapt to the rapidly changing habitat
- More species will become extinct
- Further evolutionary development may be stimulated in some species.

HUMAN HEALTH

- Hot days increase stress for the elderly and people with respiratory diseases
- Changing air circulation patterns may exacerbate problems due to pollution
- Insect pests and their transmitted diseases will increase
- Demand for air conditioning will increase.

1. Half fill a beaker or glass with warm water and float some ice cubes in the water. Mark the water level on the side of the beaker. Predict what will happen to the water level when the ice melts. Observe what happens and explain why.
2. The melting of the north polar ice cap will not raise sea levels. Why not?
3. Explain why more cloud could reduce global warming and also increase the greenhouse effect.
4. What effects will drought have on
   a agriculture?
   b river transport?
   c hydroelectric power?
5. Plants and animal species that now live on Earth have evolved in response to changing environmental conditions over millions of years. Why should global warming as a result of the greenhouse effect threaten some of them?
6. More air conditioning requires more energy to make it work. If this energy is transferred from fossil fuels, what further effect is this likely to have?
7. Draw a diagram of the Carbon Cycle and explain the following parts
   a photosynthesis,
   b respiration,
   c decay and decomposition,
   d effects of burning fossil fuels.

INDEX

absorbed dose 136
accomodation of the eye 28
acid 101
actin 33
activity 134
alkanes 106
alkenes 106
alkynes 106
alpha particles 133, 134
alternating currents 144
ammonia – manufacture 108
analogue signals 156
AND gate 156
animal testing 48, 49
arthritis 163
artificial selection 22
atom 52
atomic mass unit (amu) 52
atomic number 52
auxin 31

background radiation 131
ballcock 178
base 101
Becquerel, Henri 130
becquerels 134
behaviour 6, 26, 27, 34, 35
beta particles 133, 134
Big Bang 176
bio-engineering 19, 22, 45
bistable switch 158
body clocks 34
boiling 53
buffer solution 179
burglar alarms 158

calcium carbonate – reaction speed 95
camera 118
cancer 13
capacitor 154
carbon cycle 185
carbon cycle 74
carbon dating 135
carcinogens 13
catalyst 97
Chernobyl 12, 13
chromosomes 9, 10, 13, 14
circadian rhythm 34

CITES 40
classification 2
climate 72
climatic change 184
cloning 23
cloud chamber 133
colour vision 16, 28
compound 52
computer memory 159
consumer unit 148
control systems 178
core 65, 172
correcting eyesight 29
cracking 106
crude oil 106
crust 65, 172
cryonics 182
Curie, Marie 127, 131
cystic fibrosis 14
cytokinins 31

Darwin, Charles 20, 30
desert formation 165
desertification 166-167
digital signals 156
diode 154
DNA 8, 9, 11, 18, 19, 21, 46
DNA hybridisation 165
DNA replication 11
dominant gene 15
dose equivalent 136
dosimeter 136
Down's syndrome 13, 17
dynamo 143

Earth 59
Earth structure 61
earth wire 148
earthquakes 64
earthworm – movement of 33
El Niño 57
electric motor 140
electrolysis 102
electrolysis of brine 104
electromagnetic induction 142
electromagnetic spectrum 122

electrons 52, 100
element 52
endothermic 96
environment 42, 43, 40, 166, 167
environmental factors and variation 4, 6, 38, 39
enzymes 97
equilibrium 108
erosion 82
evolution 2, 3, 20, 21, 38
exoskeleton 33
exothermic 96
eye 118
eye 28, 29

farads 154
farming 43, 44, 45
feedback 178
flip-flop 158
flood plain 78
focal length 124
forming images 118
fossils 165, 166
friction 163
fuses 148

gamma rays 123
gamma rays 133, 134
Geiger-Müller tube 132
gene transfer 22, 45
generators 146
genes 4, 9, 12
genetic disorders 12, 13, 14
genetic engineering 18, 19, 45
genetic screening 17
geostationary 60
geosynchronous 60
giant ionic structure 93
giant structure 92
gibberelins 31
grays 136
greenhouse effect 184

Haber process 108
haemophilia 17
half-life 135
heart pacemaker 47
heart valve 47

Hertz Heinrich 181
hertz 144
homeostasis 178
Homo sapiens 164, 165
hormones 45, 30, 31
human evolution 165-166
Human Genome Project 12
human selection 22
hydrocarbons 106

in-breeding 22
inert gases 89
infra-red 122
infra-red 26
inheritance 9, 10-17
inherited diseases 15, 16, 17
ionic equation 101
ionisation 131
ions 100
iris 118
irrigation 167
isotopes 137

joints 162-63
Jupiter 59

keys 3
kidney 178
kilowatt-hour 149
kinetic theory 53

LDR 152
LED 155
lenses 119
life-expectancy 46
Linnaean system 3, 4
logic gates 156
long sight 119

magma 82
magnetic fields 140
magnetic radiation 12, 26, 35
mantle 65, 172
Marconi, Guglielmo 181
matter – structure 92
meiosis 11
melting 53
Mercury 59, 174
metal 84, 87

metals – reactivity 86, 94
microscope 124
microwaves 122
mineral 83
mitosis 10, 11, 13
molecular structure 93
molecule 52
movement in animals 32, 33
muscles 32
mutation 12
myosin 33

NAND gate 157
National Grid 146
natural selection 20-21
Nauru 70
near point 118
Neptune 59
neutralisation 101
neutrons 52
nitrogen-fixing bacteria 45
noble gases 89
non-metal 85, 87
NOR gate 157

ocean currents 57
OR gate 157
orbit 60
ores 83

P and S waves 65
Pangea 66
paramaecium movement of 33
periodic patterns 90

Periodic Table 52, 87, 88
   group 52
   period 52
pesticides 45
phosphate mining 70
phosphors 120
planets 59
plant hormones 30, 31
plate tectonics 67, 172
Pluto 59
pollution of the sea 42, 43
polymers 107
polymers 168-69
populations and changes 40-41
potentiometer 152
power lines 147
prevailing wind 56
primary colours 147
prism 121
protons 52
pupil 118

radar 122
radiation 12
radio 181
radio waves 122
radioactive decay 128
radioactivity 130
radiotherapy 137
radon 130
rain 56
rain forests 76
reaction speed 94, 96
reactivity series 86

receptor 27
recessive gene 15
reed relay 153
reflection 116
refraction 117
relay 141
retina 118
rhodopsin 28
ring main 148
rocket 61
rod and cone cells 28

satellites 60
saturated hydrocarbons 107
Saturn 59
secondary colours 120
seismographs 142
senses 26, 27
sex chromosomes 10, 16, 17
sex-linked inheritance 16, 17
short sight 119
sieverts 136
silicon chip 151
smoke detector 132
sodium carbonate 105
sodium hydroxide – manufacture 104
soil degradation 78
soil erosion 78
solar flares 170
solar navigation 34
Solar system 59
spectacles 119

speed of reaction 94, 96
stimulus 27
structure of matter 92
sun spots 170
switches 152

technology 39
telegraph 180
telescope 124
thermistor 153
thermostat 178
three pin plug 148
transformers 144
transistor 155
transplants 46
troposphere 56
truth tables 157

ultra-violet 122
unsaturated hydrocarbons 107
Uranus 59

variety 2, 4
Venus 59
visible spectrum 121
vivisection 48, 49

Wallace, Alfred 20
water waves 117
weather patterns 72
weathering 82

X-rays 123, 130